An Agenda for Peace

Boutros Boutros-Ghali
Secretary-General of the United Nations

An Agenda
for Peace
1995

Second Edition

With the new supplement
and related UN documents

United Nations • New York, 1995

Department of Public Information

Office of Conference and Support Services
Department of Administration and Management

Editor's note:
Section One of this publication contains the *Supplement to An Agenda for Peace*
by the Secretary-General, as well as *An Agenda for Peace*, the report prepared by
the Secretary-General in response to a request by the Security Council at its
Summit Meeting of 31 January 1992. Section Two contains additional United
Nations documents reflecting the ongoing debate on this subject. In the symbols
used for documents referred to or reproduced in this publication, the letter "A"
(e.g. A/50/60) indicates a document of the General Assembly and the letter "S"
(e.g. S/23500) indicates a document of the Security Council. Some documents
employ both designations.

United Nations Publication
Sales No.E.95.I.15
ISBN 92-1-100555-8

Published by the Department of Public Information
New York, NY 10017

CONTENTS

Preface

1   FOR almost three centuries, a set of principles of international cooperation has been in the making. Considerable progress has been achieved since the end of the Second World War and the creation of the United Nations. In almost every area, from securing international peace to promoting human rights and democracy to ensuring global cooperation for development, nations working together, through the United Nations, are setting the global agenda.

2   The general acceptance of the idea that peace and development, understood in their wider sense, are complementary rather than competitive owes much to the efforts of the United Nations. Just as there can be no lasting peace without development, so development efforts cannot succeed without a stable, peaceful environment.

3   In presenting this edition of *An Agenda for Peace*, together with the *Position Paper* I wrote on the basis of the experience of the United Nations in implementing *An Agenda for Peace*, I should like to direct the attention of readers to the companion volume, *An Agenda for Development*. These companion volumes represent two approaches to the same search for the realization of the goals of the United Nations. In both, I stress the complementarity between the search for peace and cooperation for development. Indeed, this complementarity has been noted by representatives of members of the Security Council who commented on the *Position Paper* soon after its publication in January 1995.

4   I have chosen to present the *Position Paper* before the original *Agenda for Peace* of 1992, in order to highlight current experience with peace operations. The set of general principles of the 1992 *Agenda for Peace* remains valid. Their reinterpretation in the light of the experience of two and a half years is necessary.

Section One
AN AGENDA FOR PEACE

Supplement to An Agenda for Peace

Position paper of the Secretary-General
on the occasion of the Fiftieth Anniversary
of the United Nations
A/50/60-S/1995/1, 3 January 1995

I. Introduction

1   ON 31 JANUARY 1992, the Security Council met for the first time at the level of heads of State or Government. The cold war had ended. It was a time of hope and change and of rising expectations for – and of – the United Nations. The members of the Council asked me to prepare an "analysis and recommendations on ways of strengthening and making more efficient within the framework and provisions of the Charter the capacity of the United Nations for preventive diplomacy, for peacemaking and for peace-keeping" (UN document S/23500: see page 115). Five months later, in June 1992, I submitted my report entitled *An Agenda for Peace* (UN document A/47/277-S/24111: see page 39). It dealt with the three problems the Council had requested me to consider, to which I added the related concept of post-conflict peace-building. It also touched on peace enforcement.

2   In submitting my recommendations on how to improve the Organization's capacity to maintain peace and security, I said that the search for improved mechanisms and techniques would be of little significance unless the new spirit of commonality that had emerged, of which the Summit was such a clear manifestation, was "propelled by the will to take the hard decisions demanded by this time of opportunity" (*An Agenda for Peace*, para. 6).

3   Subsequent discussion of *An Agenda for Peace* in the General Assembly, in the Security Council and in Member States' parliaments established that there was general support for the recommendations I had put forward. That discussion, and the new process initiated in 1994 for the elaboration of an Agenda for Development, have also served to advance international consensus on the crucial importance of economic and social development as the most secure basis for lasting peace.

4   Since the Security Council Summit the pace has accelerated. There have been dramatic changes in both the volume and the nature of the United Nations activities in the field of peace and security. New and more comprehensive concepts to guide those activities, and their links with development work, are emerging. Old concepts are being modified. There have been successes and there have been failures. The Organization has attracted intense media interest, often laudatory, more often critical, and all too often focused on only one or two of the many peace-keeping operations in which it is engaged, overshadowing other major operations and its vast effort in the economic, social and other fields.

5   All this confirms that we are still in a time of transition. The end of the cold war was a major movement of tectonic plates and the after-shocks continue to be felt. But even if the ground beneath our feet has not yet settled, we still live in a new age that holds great promise for both peace and development.

6   Our ability to fulfil that promise depends on how well we can learn the lessons of the Organization's successes and failures in these first years of the post-cold-war age. Most of the ideas in *An Agenda for Peace* have proved themselves. A few have not been taken up. The purpose of the present position paper, however, is not to revise *An Agenda for Peace* nor to call into question structures and procedures that have been tested by time. Even less is it intended to be a comprehensive treatise on the matters it discusses. Its purpose is, rather, to highlight selectively certain areas where unforeseen, or only partly foreseen, difficulties have arisen and where there is a need for the Member States to take the "hard decisions" I referred to two and a half years ago.

7   The Organization's half-century year will provide the international community an opportunity to address these issues, and the related, major challenge of elaborating an Agenda for Development,

and to indicate in a comprehensive way the direction the Member States want the Organization to take. The present position paper is offered as a contribution to the many debates I hope will take place during 1995 and perhaps beyond, inside and outside the intergovernmental bodies, about the current performance and future role of our Organization.

II. Quantitative and qualitative changes

8　It is indisputable that since the end of the cold war there has been a dramatic increase in the United Nations activities related to the maintenance of peace and security. The figures speak for themselves. The table on page 8 gives them for three dates: 31 January 1988 (when the cold war was already coming to an end); 31 January 1992 (the date of the first Security Council Summit); and today, on the eve of the Fiftieth Anniversary of the United Nations.

9　This increased volume of activity would have strained the Organization even if the nature of the activity had remained unchanged. It has not remained unchanged, however: there have been qualitative changes even more significant than the quantitative ones.

10　One is the fact that so many of today's conflicts are within States rather than between States. The end of the cold war removed constraints that had inhibited conflict in the former Soviet Union and elsewhere. As a result there has been a rash of wars within newly independent States, often of a religious or ethnic character and often involving unusual violence and cruelty. The end of the cold war seems also to have contributed to an outbreak of such wars in Africa. in addition, some of the proxy wars fuelled by the cold war within States remain unresolved. Inter-State wars, by contrast, have become infrequent.

11　Of the five peace-keeping operations that existed in early 1988, four related to inter-State wars and only one (20 per cent of the total) to an intra-State conflict. Of the 21 operations established since then, only 8 have related to inter-State wars, whereas 13 (62 per cent) have related to intra-State conflicts, though some of them, especially those in the former Yugoslavia, have some inter-State dimensions also. Of the 11 operations established since January 1992, all but 2 (82 per cent) relate to intra-State conflicts.

12 The new breed of intra-State conflicts have certain character-istics that present United Nations peace-keepers with challenges not encountered since the Congo operation of the early 1960s. They are usually fought not only by regular armies but also by militias and armed civilians with little discipline and with ill-defined chains of command. They are often guerrilla wars without clear front lines.

Some statistics on United Nations activities related to peace and security, 1988 to 1994

	As at 31 January 1988	*As at 31 January 1992*	*As at 16 December 1994*
Security Council resolutions adopted in the preceding 12 months	15	53	78
Disputes and conflicts in which the United Nations was actively involved in preventive diplomacy or peacemaking in the preceding 12 months	11	13	28
Peace-keeping operations deployed			
Total	5	11	17
Classical	5	7	9
Multifunctional	–	4	8
Military personnel deployed	9,570	11,495	73,393
Civilian police deployed	35	155	2,130
International civilian personnel deployed	1,516	2,206	2,260
Countries contributing military and police personnel	26	56	76
United Nations budget for peace-keeping operations (on an annual basis) (millions of US dollars)	230.4	1,689.6	3,610.0 [a/]
Countries in which the United Nations had undertaken electoral activities in the preceding 12 months	–	6	21
Sanctions regimes imposed by the Security Council	1	2	7

a/ Projected

Civilians are the main victims and often the main targets. Humanitarian emergencies are commonplace and the combatant authorities, in so far as they can be called authorities, lack the capacity to cope with them. The number of refugees registered with the Office of the United Nations High Commissioner for Refugees (UNHCR) has increased from 13 million at the end of 1987 to 26 million at the end of 1994. The number of internally displaced persons has increased even more dramatically.

13   Another feature of such conflicts is the collapse of State institutions, especially the police and judiciary, with resulting paralysis of governance, a breakdown of law and order, and general banditry and chaos. Not only are the functions of government suspended, its assets are destroyed or looted and experienced officials are killed or flee the country. This is rarely the case in inter-State wars. It means that international intervention must extend beyond military and humanitarian tasks and must include the promotion of national reconciliation and the re-establishment of effective government.

14   The latter are tasks that demand time and sensitivity. The United Nations is, for good reasons, reluctant to assume responsibility for maintaining law and order, nor can it impose a new political structure or new State institutions. It can only help the hostile factions to help themselves and begin to live together again. All too often it turns out that they do not yet want to be helped or to resolve their problems quickly.

15   Peace-keeping in such contexts is far more complex and more expensive than when its tasks were mainly to monitor cease-fires and control buffer zones with the consent of the States involved in the conflict. Peace-keeping today can involve constant danger.

16   I cannot praise too highly or adequately express my gratitude and admiration for the courage and sacrifice of United Nations personnel, military and civil, in this new era of challenge to peace and security. The conditions under which they serve are often extremely harsh. Many have given their lives. Many must persevere despite the loss of family members and friends.

17   It must also be recognized that the vast increase in field deployment has to be supported by an overburdened Headquarters staff that resource constraints have held at levels appropriate to an earlier, far less demanding, time.

18   A second qualitative change is the use of United Nations forces to protect humanitarian operations. Humanitarian agencies endeavour to provide succour to civilian victims of war wherever they may be. Too often the warring parties make it difficult or impossible for them to do so. This is sometimes because of the exigencies of war but more often because the relief of a particular population is contrary to the war aims of one or other of the parties. There is also a growing tendency for the combatants to divert relief supplies for their own purposes. Because the wars are intra-State conflicts, the humanitarian agencies often have to undertake their tasks in the chaotic and lawless conditions described above. In some, but not all, such cases the resulting horrors explode on to the world's television screens and create political pressure for the United Nations to deploy troops to facilitate and protect the humanitarian operations. While such images can help build support for humanitarian action, such scenes also may create an emotional environment in which effective decision-making can be far more difficult.

19   This has led, in Bosnia and Herzegovina and in Somalia, to a new kind of United Nations operation. Even though the use of force is authorized under Chapter VII of the Charter, the United Nations remains neutral and impartial between the warring parties, without a mandate to stop the aggressor (if one can be identified) or impose a cessation of hostilities. Nor is this peace-keeping as practised hitherto, because the hostilities continue and there is often no agreement between the warring parties on which a peace-keeping mandate can be based. The "safe areas" concept in Bosnia and Herzegovina is a similar case. It too gives the United Nations a humanitarian mandate under which the use of force is authorized, but for limited and local purposes and not to bring the war to an end.

20   A third change has been in the nature of United Nations operations in the field. During the cold war United Nations peace-keeping operations were largely military in character and were usually deployed after a cease-fire but before a settlement of the conflict in question had been negotiated. Indeed one of their main purposes was to create conditions in which negotiations for a settlement could take place. In the late 1980s a new kind of peace-keeping operation evolved. It was established after negotiations had succeeded, with the mandate of helping the parties implement the comprehensive settlement they had negotiated. Such operations have been deployed in Namibia, Angola, El Salvador, Cambodia and Mozambique. In most cases they have been conspicuously successful.

21   The negotiated settlements involved not only military arrangements but also a wide range of civilian matters. As a result, the United Nations found itself asked to undertake an unprecedented variety of functions: the supervision of cease-fires, the regroupment and demobilization of forces, their reintegration into civilian life and the destruction of their weapons; the design and implementation of de-mining programmes; the return of refugees and displaced persons; the provision of humanitarian assistance; the supervision of existing administrative structures; the establishment of new police forces; the verification of respect for human rights; the design and supervision of constitutional, judicial and electoral reforms; the observation, supervision and even organization and conduct of elections; and the coordination of support for economic rehabilitation and reconstruction.

22   Fourthly, these multifunctional peace-keeping operations have highlighted the role the United Nations can play after a negotiated settlement has been implemented. It is now recognized that implementation of the settlement in the time prescribed may not be enough to guarantee that the conflict will not revive. Coordinated programmes are required, over a number of years and in various fields, to ensure that the original causes of war are eradicated. This involves the building up of national institutions, the promotion of human rights, the creation of civilian police forces and other actions in the political field. As I pointed out in *An Agenda for Development,*[1/] only sustained efforts to resolve underlying socio-economic, cultural and humanitarian problems can place an achieved peace on a durable foundation.

III. Instruments for peace and security

23   The United Nations has developed a range of instruments for controlling and resolving conflicts between and within States. The most important of them are preventive diplomacy and peacemaking; peace-keeping; peace-building; disarmament; sanctions; and peace enforcement. The first three can be employed only with the consent of the parties to the conflict. Sanctions and enforcement, on the other hand, are coercive measures and thus, by definition, do not require the consent of the party concerned. Disarmament can take place on an agreed basis or in the context of coercive action under Chapter VII.

24   The United Nations does not have or claim a monopoly of any of these instruments. All can be, and most of them have been, employed by regional organizations, by ad hoc groups of States or by individual States, but the United Nations has unparalleled experience of them and it is to the United Nations that the international community has turned increasingly since the end of the cold war. The United Nations system is also better equipped than regional organizations or individual Member States to develop and apply the comprehensive, long-term approach needed to ensure the lasting resolution of conflicts.

25   Perceived shortcomings in the United Nations performance of the tasks entrusted to it have recently, however, seemed to incline Member States to look for other means, especially, but not exclusively, where the rapid deployment of large forces is required. It is thus necessary to find ways of enabling the United Nations to perform better the roles envisaged for it in the Charter.

A. Preventive diplomacy and peacemaking
   26   It is evidently better to prevent conflicts through early warning,

quiet diplomacy and, in some cases, preventive deployment than to have to undertake major politico-military efforts to resolve them after they have broken out. The Security Council's declaration of 31 January 1992 (UN document S/23500) mandated me to give priority to preventive and peacemaking activities. I accordingly created a Department of Political Affairs to handle a range of political functions that had previously been performed in various parts of the Secretariat. That Department has since passed through successive phases of restructuring and is now organized to follow political developments worldwide, so that it can provide early warning of impending conflicts and analyse possibilities for preventive action by the United Nations, as well as for action to help resolve existing conflicts.

27   Experience has shown that the greatest obstacle to success in these endeavours is not, as is widely supposed, lack of information, analytical capacity or ideas for United Nations initiatives. Success is often blocked at the outset by the reluctance of one or other of the parties to accept United Nations help. This is as true of inter-State conflicts as it is of internal ones, even though United Nations action on the former is fully within the Charter, whereas in the latter case it must be reconciled with Article 2, paragraph 7.

28   Collectively Member States encourage the Secretary-General to play an active role in this field; individually they are often reluctant that he should do so when they are a party to the conflict. It is difficult to know how to overcome this reluctance. Clearly the United Nations cannot impose its preventive and peacemaking services on Member States who do not want them. Legally and politically their request for, or at least acquiescence in, United Nations action is a *sine qua non*. The solution can only be long-term. It may lie in creating a climate of opinion, or ethos, within the international community in which the norm would be for Member States to accept an offer of United Nations good offices.

29   There are also two practical problems that have emerged in this field. Given Member States' frequently expressed support for preventive diplomacy and peacemaking, I take this opportunity to recommend that early action be taken to resolve them.

30   The first is the difficulty of finding senior persons who have the diplomatic skills and who are willing to serve for a while as special representative or special envoy of the Secretary-General. As a result of the streamlining of the senior levels of the Secretariat, the extra capacity that was there in earlier years no longer exists.

31   The second problem relates to the establishment and financing of small field missions for preventive diplomacy and peacemaking. Accepted and well-tried procedures exist for such action in the case of peace-keeping operations. The same is required in the preventive and peacemaking field. Although special envoys can achieve much on a visiting basis, their capacity is greatly enhanced if continuity can be assured by the presence on the ground of a small support mission on a full-time basis. There is no clear view amongst Member States about whether legislative authority for such matters rests with the Security Council or the General Assembly, nor are existing budgetary procedures well-geared to meet this need.

32   Two solutions are possible. The first is to include in the regular budget a contingency provision, which might be in the range of $25 million per biennium, for such activities. The second would be to enlarge the existing provision for unforeseen and extraordinary activities and to make it available for all preventive and peacemaking activities, not just those related to international peace and security strictly defined.

B. Peace-keeping

33   The United Nations can be proud of the speed with which peace-keeping has evolved in response to the new political environment resulting from the end of the cold war, but the last few years have confirmed that respect for certain basic principles of peace-keeping are essential to its success. Three particularly important principles are the consent of the parties, impartiality and the non-use of force except in self-defence. Analysis of recent successes and failures shows that in all the successes those principles were respected and in most of the less successful operations one or other of them was not.

34   There are three aspects of recent mandates that, in particular, have led peace-keeping operations to forfeit the consent of the parties, to behave in a way that was perceived to be partial and/or to use force other than in self-defence. These have been the tasks of protecting humanitarian operations during continuing warfare, protecting civilian populations in designated safe areas and pressing the parties to achieve national reconciliation at a pace faster than they were ready to accept. The cases of Somalia and of Bosnia and Herzegovina are instructive in this respect.

35   In both cases, existing peace-keeping operations were given additional mandates that required the use of force and therefore could not be combined with existing mandates requiring the consent of the parties, impartiality and the non-use of force. It was also not possible for them to be executed without much stronger military capabilities than had been made available, as is the case in the former Yugoslavia. In reality, nothing is more dangerous for a peace-keeping operation than to ask it to use force when its existing composition, armament, logistic support and deployment deny it the capacity to do so. The logic of peace-keeping flows from political and military premises that are quite distinct from those of enforcement; and the dynamics of the latter are incompatible with the political process that peace-keeping is intended to facilitate. To blur the distinction between the two can undermine the viability of the peace-keeping operation and endanger its personnel.

36   International problems cannot be solved quickly or within a limited time. Conflicts the United Nations is asked to resolve usually have deep roots and have defied the peacemaking efforts of others. Their resolution requires patient diplomacy and the establishment of a political process that permits, over a period of time, the building of confidence and negotiated solutions to long-standing differences. Such processes often encounter frustrations and set-backs and almost invariably take longer than hoped. It is necessary to resist the temptation to use military power to speed them up. Peace-keeping and the use of force (other than in self-defence) should be seen as alternative techniques and not as adjacent points on a continuum, permitting easy transition from one to the other.

37   In peace-keeping, too, a number of practical difficulties have
arisen during the last three years, especially relating to command and
control, to the availability of troops and equipment and to the information capacity of peace-keeping operations.

38   As regards command and control, it is useful to distinguish
three levels of authority:

(a) Overall political direction, which belongs to the
    Security Council;

(b) Executive direction and command, for which the
    Secretary-General is responsible;

(c) Command in the field, which is entrusted by the
    Secretary-General to the chief of mission (special repre-
    sentative or force commander/chief military observer).

The distinctions between these three levels must be kept constantly
in mind in order to avoid any confusion of functions and responsibilities. It is as inappropriate for a chief of mission to take upon himself
the formulation of his/her mission's overall political objectives as it is
for the Security Council or the Secretary-General in New York to
decide on matters that require a detailed understanding of operational
conditions in the field.

39   There has been an increasing tendency in recent years for the
Security Council to micro-manage peace-keeping operations. Given
the importance of the issues at stake and the volume of resources provided for peace-keeping operations, it is right and proper that the
Council should wish to be closely consulted and informed.
Procedures for ensuring this have been greatly improved. To assist
the Security Council in being informed about the latest developments
I have appointed one of my Special Advisers as my personal representative to the Council. As regards information, however, it has to be
recognized that, in the inevitable fog and confusion of the near-war
conditions in which peace-keepers often find themselves, as for
example in Angola, Cambodia, Somalia and the former Yugoslavia,
time is required to verify the accuracy of initial reports.
Understandably, chiefs of mission have to be more restrained than the

media in broadcasting facts that have not been fully substantiated.

40   Troop-contributing Governments, who are responsible to their parliaments and electorates for the safety of their troops, are also understandably anxious to be kept fully informed, especially when the operation concerned is in difficulty. I have endeavoured to meet their concerns by providing them with regular briefings and by engaging them in dialogue about the conduct of the operation in question. Members of the Security Council have been included in such meetings and the Council has recently decided to formalize them. It is important that this should not lead to any blurring of the distinct levels of authority referred to above.

41   Another important principle is unity of command. The experience in Somalia has underlined again the necessity for a peace-keeping operation to function as an integrated whole. That necessity is all the more imperative when the mission is operating in dangerous conditions. There must be no opening for the parties to undermine its cohesion by singling out some contingents for favourable and others for unfavourable treatment. Nor must there be any attempt by troop-contributing Governments to provide guidance, let alone give orders, to their contingents on operational matters. To do so creates division within the force, adds to the difficulties already inherent in a multinational operation and increases the risk of casualties. It can also create the impression amongst the parties that the operation is serving the policy objectives of the contributing Governments rather than the collective will of the United Nations as formulated by the Security Council. Such impressions inevitably undermine an operation's legitimacy and effectiveness.

42   That said, commanders in the field are, as a matter of course, instructed to consult the commanders of national contingents and make sure that they understand the Security Council's overall approach, as well as the role assigned to their contingents. However, such consultations cannot be allowed to develop into negotiations between the commander in the field and the troop-contributing Governments, whose negotiating partner must always be the Secretariat in New York.

43   As regards the availability of troops and equipment, problems have become steadily more serious. Availability has palpably declined as measured against the Organization's requirements. A considerable effort has been made to expand and refine stand-by arrangements, but these provide no guarantee that troops will be provided for a specific operation. For example, when in May 1994 the Security Council decided to expand the United Nations Assistance Mission for Rwanda (UNAMIR), not one of the 19 Governments that at that time had undertaken to have troops on stand-by agreed to contribute.

44   In these circumstances, I have come to the conclusion that the United Nations does need to give serious thought to the idea of a rapid reaction force. Such a force would be the Security Council's strategic reserve for deployment when there was an emergency need for peace-keeping troops. It might comprise battalion-sized units from a number of countries. These units would be trained to the same standards, use the same operating procedures, be equipped with integrated communications equipment and take part in joint exercises at regular intervals. They would be stationed in their home countries but maintained at a high state of readiness. The value of this arrangement would of course depend on how far the Security Council could be sure that the force would actually be available in an emergency. This will be a complicated and expensive arrangement, but I believe that the time has come to undertake it.

45   Equipment and adequate training is another area of growing concern. The principle is that contributing Governments are to ensure that their troops arrive with all the equipment needed to be fully operational. Increasingly, however, Member States offer troops without the necessary equipment and training. In the absence of alternatives, the United Nations, under pressure, has to procure equipment on the market or through voluntary contributions from other Member States. Further time is required for the troops concerned to learn to operate the equipment, which they are often encountering for the first time. A number of measures can be envisaged to address this problem, for example, the establishment by the United Nations of a reserve stock of standard peace-keeping equipment, as has been frequently proposed, and partnerships between Governments that need equipment and those ready to provide it.

46 An additional lesson from recent experience is that peace-keeping operations, especially those operating in difficult circumstances, need an effective information capacity. This is to enable them to explain their mandate to the population and, by providing a credible and impartial source of information, to counter misinformation disseminated about them, even by the parties themselves. Radio is the most effective medium for this purpose. In all operations where an information capacity, including radio, has been provided, even if late in the day, it has been recognized to have made an invaluable contribution to the operation's success. I have instructed that in the planning of future operations the possible need for an information capacity should be examined at an early stage and the necessary resources included in the proposed budget.

C. Post-conflict peace-building

47 The validity of the concept of post-conflict peace-building has received wide recognition. The measures it can use – and they are many – can also support preventive diplomacy. Demilitarization, the control of small arms, institutional reform, improved police and judicial systems, the monitoring of human rights, electoral reform and social and economic development can be as valuable in preventing conflict as in healing the wounds after conflict has occurred.

48. The implementation of post-conflict peace-building can, however, be complicated. It requires integrated action and delicate dealings between the United Nations and the parties to the conflict in respect of which peace-building activities are to be undertaken.

49 Two kinds of situation deserve examination. The first is when a comprehensive settlement has been negotiated, with long-term political, economic and social provisions to address the root causes of the conflict, and verification of its implementation is entrusted to a multifunctional peace-keeping operation. The second is when peace-building, whether preventive or post-conflict, is undertaken in relation to a potential or past conflict without any peace-keeping operation being deployed. In both situations the essential goal is the creation of structures for the institutionalization of peace.

50   The first situation is the easier to manage. The United Nations already has an entrée. The parties have accepted its peace-making and peace-keeping role. The peace-keeping operation will already be mandated to launch various peace-building activities, especially the all-important reintegration of former combatants into productive civilian activities.

51   Even so, political elements who dislike the peace agreement concluded by their Government (and the United Nations verification provided for therein) may resent the United Nations presence and be waiting impatiently for it to leave. Their concerns may find an echo among Member States who fear that the United Nations is in danger of slipping into a role prejudicial to the sovereignty of the country in question and among others who may be uneasy about the resource implications of a long-term peace-building commitment.

52   The timing and modalities of the departure of the peace-keeping operation and the transfer of its peace-building functions to others must therefore be carefully managed in the fullest possible consultation with the Government concerned. The latter's wishes must be paramount; but the United Nations, having invested much effort in helping to end the conflict, can legitimately express views and offer advice about actions the Government could take to reduce the danger of losing what has been achieved. The timing and modalities also need to take into account any residual verification for which the United Nations remains responsible.

53   Most of the activities that together constitute peace-building fall within the mandates of the various programmes, funds, offices and agencies of the United Nations system with responsibilities in the economic, social, humanitarian and human rights fields. In a country ruined by war, resumption of such activities may initially have to be entrusted to, or at least coordinated by, a multifunctional peace-keeping operation, but as that operation succeeds in restoring normal conditions, the programmes, funds, offices and agencies can

re-establish themselves and gradually take over responsibility from the peace-keepers, with the resident coordinator in due course assuming the coordination functions temporarily entrusted to the special representative of the Secretary-General.

54   It may also be necessary in such cases to arrange the transfer of decision-making responsibility from the Security Council, which will have authorized the mandate and deployment of the peace-keeping operation, to the General Assembly or other inter-governmental bodies with responsibility for the civilian peace-building activities that will continue. The timing of this transfer will be of special interest to certain Member States because of its financial implications. Each case has to be decided on its merits, the guiding principle being that institutional or budgetary considerations should not be allowed to imperil the continuity of the United Nations efforts in the field.

55   The more difficult situation is when post-conflict (or preventive) peace-building activities are seen to be necessary in a country where the United Nations does not already have a peacemaking or peace-keeping mandate. Who then will identify the need for such measures and propose them to the Government? If the measures are exclusively in the economic, social and humanitarian fields, they are likely to fall within the purview of the resident coordinator. He or she could recommmend them to the Government. Even if the resident coordinator has the capacity to monitor and analyse all the indicators of an impending political and security crisis, however, which is rarely the case, can he or she act without inviting the charge of exceeding his or her mandate by assuming political functions, especially if the proposed measures relate to areas such as security, the police or human rights?

56   In those circumstances, the early warning responsibility has to lie with United Nations Headquarters, using all the information available to it, including reports of the United Nations Development Programme (UNDP) resident coordinator and other United Nations personnel in the country concerned. When analysis of that information gives warning of impending crisis, the Secretary-General, acting on the basis of his general mandate for preventive diplomacy, peace-

making and peace-building, can take the initiative of sending a mission, with the Government's agreement, to discuss with it measures it could usefully take.

D. Disarmament

57 At their Summit on 31 January 1992, the members of the Security Council underscored their interest in and concern for disarmament, arms control and non-proliferation, with special reference to weapons of mass destruction. They committed themselves to taking concrete steps to enhance the effectiveness of the United Nations in those areas.

58 Considerable progress has been made since January 1992. The moratorium on nuclear testing continues to be largely observed. The Conference on Disarmament has finally decided to begin negotiations on a comprehensive test-ban treaty. The General Assembly has recommended the negotiation of a treaty to ban the production of fissile material. Efforts are under way to strengthen the Convention on the Prohibition of the Development, Production and Stockpiling of Bacteriological (Biological) and Toxin Weapons and on Their Destruction (resolution 2826 (XXVI), annex), ratified by 131 countries, through development of verification mechanisms. The Convention on the Prohibition of the Development, Production, Stockpiling and Use of Chemical Weapons and on Their Destruction[2/] has been signed by 159 countries, but has not yet entered into force, pending ratification by the required 65 signatories. There have been some important accessions to the Treaty on the Non-Proliferation of Nuclear Weapons (resolution 2373 (XXII), annex).

59 I attach special importance to a successful conclusion of the forthcoming conference of the parties to the Non-Proliferation Treaty. It is also of great importance that the Chemical Weapons Convention enter into force as soon as possible. The momentum in all these areas needs to be maintained. Ways have to be found for reconciling transfer of technology with measures necessary to prevent its misuse for military purposes.

60   These issues are of paramount importance both to the security of humankind and to the release of economic, scientific and technological resources for peace and human progress. In the present paper, however, devoted as it is to the Organization's recent experience in handling specific conflicts, I wish to concentrate on what might be called "micro-disarmament". By this I mean practical disarmament in the context of the conflicts the United Nations is actually dealing with and of the weapons, most of them light weapons, that are actually killing people in the hundreds of thousands.

61   The contemporary significance of micro-disarmament is demonstrated by the enormous proliferation of automatic assault weapons, anti-personnel mines and the like. Competent authorities have estimated that billions of dollars are being spent yearly on light weapons, representing nearly one third of the world's total arms trade. Many of those weapons are being bought, from developed countries, by developing countries that can least afford to dissipate their precious and finite assets for such purposes, and the volume of the trade in light weapons is far more alarming than the monetary cost might lead one to suspect.

62   Micro-disarmament plays an important part in conjunction with all the other techniques discussed in the present paper. The assembly, control and disposal of weapons has been a central feature of most of the comprehensive peace settlements in which the United Nations has played a peace-keeping role. As a result, the Organization has an unrivalled experience in this field. Micro-disarmament is equally relevant to post-conflict peace-building: Nicaragua has shown what can be achieved through imaginative programmes to mop up large numbers of small arms circulating in a country emerging from a long civil war. Disarmament can also follow enforcement action, as has been demonstrated in Iraq, where the United Nations Special Commission has played a pioneering role in practical disarmament, in this case involving weapons of mass destruction. All the sanctions regimes include an arms embargo and experience has confirmed the difficulty of monitoring cross-border arms flows into countries at war with their neighbours or within their own borders.

63   There are two categories of light weapons that merit special attention. The first is small arms, which are probably responsible for most of the deaths in current conflicts. The world is awash with them and traffic in them is very difficult to monitor, let alone intercept. The causes are many: the earlier supply of weapons to client States by the parties to the cold war, internal conflicts, competition for commercial markets, criminal activity and the collapse of governmental law and order functions (which both gives free rein to the criminals and creates a legitimate reason for ordinary citizens to acquire weapons for their own defence). A pilot advisory mission I dispatched to Mali in August 1994 at the request of that country's Government has confirmed the exceptional difficulty of controlling the illicit flow of small arms, a problem that can be effectively tackled only on a regional basis. It will take a long time to find effective solutions. I believe strongly that the search should begin now.

64   Secondly, there is the proliferation of anti-personnel mines. One of the positive developments in recent years has been the attention this problem has attracted. The international community has begun to address it. Current efforts in the context of the Convention on Prohibitions or Restrictions on the Use of Certain Conventional Weapons Which May Be Deemed to Be Excessively Injurious or to Have Indiscriminate Effects[3/] are giving priority to anti-personnel mines, and the General Assembly's call for a moratorium on their export has won much support from manufacturing countries. In addition, the International Committee of the Red Cross (ICRC) is developing new protocols to the Convention. Meanwhile work continues to try to deal with the approximately 110 million land-mines that have already been laid. This is an issue that must continue to receive priority attention. I agree with the view that the Register of Conventional Arms is important in these endeavours. In the wider context, it is essential that the Register be developed into a universal and non-discriminatory mechanism.

65   Progress since 1992 in the area of weapons of mass destruction and major weapons systems must be followed by parallel progress in conventional arms, particularly with respect to light weapons. It will take a long time to find effective solutions. I believe strongly that the search should begin now, and I intend to play my full part in this effort.

E. Sanctions

66   Under Article 41 of the Charter, the Security Council may call upon Member States to apply measures not involving the use of armed force in order to maintain or restore international peace and security. Such measures are commonly referred to as sanctions. This legal basis is recalled in order to underline that the purpose of sanctions is to modify the behaviour of a party that is threatening international peace and security and not to punish or otherwise exact retribution.

67   The Security Council's greatly increased use of this instrument has brought to light a number of difficulties, relating especially to the objectives of sanctions, the monitoring of their application and impact, and their unintended effects.

68   The objectives for which specific sanctions regimes were imposed have not always been clearly defined. Indeed they sometimes seem to change over time. This combination of imprecision and mutability makes it difficult for the Security Council to agree on when the objectives can be considered to have been achieved and sanctions can be lifted. While recognizing that the Council is a political body rather than a judicial organ, it is of great importance that when it decides to impose sanctions it should at the same time define objective criteria for determining that their purpose has been achieved. If general support for the use of sanctions as an effective instrument is to be maintained, care should be taken to avoid giving the impression that the purpose of imposing sanctions is punishment rather than the modification of political behaviour or that criteria are being changed in order to serve purposes other than those which motivated the original decision to impose sanctions.

69   Experience has been gained by the United Nations of how to monitor the application of sanctions and of the part regional organizations can in some cases play in this respect. However, the task is

complicated by the reluctance of Governments, for reasons of sovereignty or economic self-interest, to accept the deployment of international monitors or the international investigation of alleged violations by themselves or their nationals. Measuring the impact of sanctions is even more difficult because of the inherent complexity of such measurement and because of restrictions on access to the target country.

70   Sanctions, as is generally recognized, are a blunt instrument. They raise the ethical question of whether suffering inflicted on vulnerable groups in the target country is a legitimate means of exerting pressure on political leaders whose behaviour is unlikely to be affected by the plight of their subjects. Sanctions also always have unintended or unwanted effects. They can complicate the work of humanitarian agencies by denying them certain categories of supplies and by obliging them to go through arduous procedures to obtain the necessary exemptions. They can conflict with the development objectives of the Organization and do long-term damage to the productive capacity of the target country. They can have a severe effect on other countries that are neighbours or major economic partners of the target country. They can also defeat their own purpose by provoking a patriotic response against the international community, symbolized by the United Nations, and by rallying the population behind the leaders whose behaviour the sanctions are intended to modify.

71   To state these ethical and practical considerations is not to call in question the need for sanctions in certain cases, but it illustrates the need to consider ways of alleviating the effects described. Two possibilities are proposed for Member States' consideration.

72   The first is to ensure that, whenever sanctions are imposed, provision is made to facilitate the work of humanitarian agencies, work that will be all the more needed as a result of the impact of sanctions on vulnerable groups. It is necessary, for instance, to avoid banning imports that are required by local health industries and to devise a fast track for the processing of applications for exemptions for humanitarian activities.

73   Secondly, there is an urgent need for action to respond to the expectations raised by Article 50 of the Charter. Sanctions are a mea-

sure taken collectively by the United Nations to maintain or restore international peace and security. The costs involved in their application, like other such costs (e.g. for peacemaking and peace-keeping activities), should be borne equitably by all Member States and not exclusively by the few who have the misfortune to be neighbours or major economic partners of the target country.

74   In *An Agenda for Peace* I proposed that States suffering collateral damage from the sanctions regimes should be entitled not only to consult the Security Council but also to have a realistic possibility of having their difficulties addressed. For that purpose I recommended that the Security Council devise a set of measures involving the international financial institutions and other components of the United Nations system that could be put in place to address the problem. In response, the Council asked me to seek the views of the heads of the international financial institutions. In their replies, the latter acknowledged the collateral effects of sanctions and expressed the desire to help countries in such situations, but they proposed that this should be done under existing mandates for the support of countries facing negative external shocks and consequent balance-of-payment difficulties. They did not agree that special provisions should be made.

75   In order to address all the above problems, I should like to go beyond the recommendation I made in 1992 and suggest the establishment of a mechanism to carry out the following five functions:

(a) To assess, at the request of the Security Council, and before sanctions are imposed, their potential impact on the target country and on third countries;

(b) To monitor application of the sanctions;

(c) To measure their effects in order to enable the Security Council to fine-tune them with a view to maximizing their political impact and minimizing collateral damage;

(d) To ensure the delivery of humanitarian assistance to vulnerable groups;

(e) To explore ways of assisting Member States that are suffering collateral damage and to evaluate claims submitted by such States under Article 50.

76   Since the purpose of this mechanism would be to assist the Security Council, it would have to be located in the United Nations Secretariat. However, it should be empowered to utilize the expertise available throughout the United Nations system, in particular that of the Bretton Woods institutions. Member States will have to give the proposal their political support both at the United Nations and in the intergovernmental bodies of the agencies concerned if it is to be implemented effectively.

F. Enforcement action

77   One of the achievements of the Charter of the United Nations was to empower the Organization to take enforcement action against those responsible for threats to the peace, breaches of the peace or acts of aggression. However, neither the Security Council nor the Secretary-General at present has the capacity to deploy, direct, command and control operations for this purpose, except perhaps on a very limited scale. I believe that it is desirable in the long term that the United Nations develop such a capacity, but it would be folly to attempt to do so at the present time when the Organization is resource-starved and hard pressed to handle the less demanding peacemaking and peace-keeping responsibilities entrusted to it.

78   In 1950, the Security Council authorized a group of willing Member States to undertake enforcement action in the Korean peninsula. It did so again in 1990 in response to aggression against Kuwait. More recently, the Council has authorized groups of Member States to undertake enforcement action, if necessary, to create conditions for humanitarian relief operations in Somalia and Rwanda and to facilitate the restoration of democracy in Haiti.

79   In Bosnia and Herzegovina, the Security Council has authorized Member States, acting nationally or through regional arrangements, to use force to ensure compliance with its ban on military flights in that country's air space, to support the United Nations forces in the former Yugoslavia in the performance of their mandate, including defence of personnel who may be under attack, and to

deter attacks against the safe areas. The Member States concerned decided to entrust those tasks to the North Atlantic Treaty Organization (NATO). Much effort has been required between the Secretariat and NATO to work out procedures for the coordination of this unprecedented collaboration. This is not surprising given the two organizations' very different mandates and approaches to the maintenance of peace and security. Of greater concern, as already mentioned, are the consequences of using force, other than for self-defence, in a peace-keeping context.

80   The experience of the last few years has demonstrated both the value that can be gained and the difficulties that can arise when the Security Council entrusts enforcement tasks to groups of Member States. On the positive side, this arrangement provides the Organization with an enforcement capacity it would not otherwise have and is greatly preferable to the unilateral use of force by Member States without reference to the United Nations. On the other hand, the arrangement can have a negative impact on the Organization's stature and credibility. There is also the danger that the States concerned may claim international legitimacy and approval for forceful actions that were not in fact envisaged by the Security Council when it gave its authorization to them. Member States so authorized have in recent operations reported more fully and more regularly to the Security Council about their activities.

IV. Coordination

81   Just as the United Nations does not claim a monopoly of the instruments discussed above, neither can it alone apply them. All the efforts of the Security Council, the General Assembly and the Secretary-General to control and resolve conflicts need the cooperation and support of other players on the international stage: the Governments that constitute the United Nations membership, regional and non-governmental organizations, and the various funds, programmes, offices and agencies of the United Nations system itself. If

United Nations efforts are to succeed, the roles of the various players need to be carefully coordinated in an integrated approach to human security.

82   Governments are central to all the activities discussed in the present position paper. It is they who authorize the activities and finance them. It is they who provide directly the vast majority of the personnel required, as well as most of the equipment. It is they who set the policies of the specialized agencies of the United Nations system and of the regional organizations. It is they whose continuing support, and, as necessary, intervention with the parties, is essential if the Secretary-General is to succeed in carrying out the mandates entrusted to him. It is they who are parties, or at least one of the parties, to each conflict the United Nations is trying to control and resolve.

83   A new trend in recent years has been the establishment of informal groups of Member States, created on an ad hoc basis to support the Secretary-General in the discharge of peacemaking and peace-keeping mandates entrusted to him. They are normally referred to as "Friends of the Secretary-General for ...". They have no formal mandate from the General Assembly or the Security Council and comprise States with a particular interest in the conflict in question. They have material and diplomatic resources that can be used to support the Secretary-General's efforts. Their value to him is as a sounding-board, as a source of ideas and comment and as a diplomatic instrument for bringing influence to bear on the parties.

84   This arrangement has been of value in a number of instances. It is nevertheless necessary to maintain a clear understanding of who is responsible for what. The Secretary-General has the mandate from the relevant intergovernmental body and must remain in the lead. The members of the "Friends" group have agreed to support the Secretary-General at his request. If they take initiatives not requested by the Secretary-General, there is a risk of duplication or overlapping of efforts, which can be exploited by recalcitrant parties. Such initiatives can also raise questions in the intergovernmental body that expects the Secretary-General to retain responsibility for the mandate entrusted to him and to report to that body on his implementation of it.

85 As for regional organizations, Chapter VIII of the Charter defines the role they can play in the maintenance of peace and security. They have much to contribute. Since the Security Council Summit, the United Nations has extended considerably its experience of working with regional organizations in this field. On 1 August 1994, I convened a meeting in New York of the heads of a number of such organizations with which the United Nations had recently cooperated on the ground in peacemaking and peace-keeping. The meeting permitted a useful exchange of views and it is my intention to hold further meetings of this kind.

86 Cooperation between the United Nations and regional organizations takes a number of forms. At least five can be identified:

(a) *Consultation:* this has been well-established for some time. In some cases it is governed by formal agreements and reports are made to the General Assembly; in other cases it is less formal. The purpose is to exchange views on conflicts that both the United Nations and the regional organization may be trying to solve;

(b) *Diplomatic support:* the regional organization participates in the peacemaking activities of the United Nations and supports them by diplomatic initiatives (in a manner analogous to groups of "Friends" as described above) and/or by providing technical input, as the Organization for Security and Cooperation in Europe (OSCE) does, for instance, on constitutional issues relating to Abkhazia. In the same way, the United Nations can support the regional organization in its efforts (as it does for OSCE over Nagorny Karabakh);

(c) *Operational support:* the most developed example is the provision by NATO of air power to support the United Nations Protection Force (UNPROFOR) in the former Yugoslavia. For its part, the United Nations can provide technical advice to regional organizations that undertake peace-keeping operations of their own;

(d) *Co-deployment:* United Nations field missions have

been deployed in conjunction with the Economic Community of West African States (ECOWAS) in Liberia and with the Commonwealth of Independent States (CIS) in Georgia. If those experiments succeed, they may herald a new division of labour between the United Nations and regional organizations, under which the regional organization carries the main burden but a small United Nations operation supports it and verifies that it is functioning in a manner consistent with positions adopted by the Security Council. The political, operational and financial aspects of the arrangement give rise to questions of some delicacy. Member States may wish at some stage to make an assessment, in the light of experience in Liberia and Georgia, of how this model might be followed in the future;

(e) *Joint operations:* the example is the United Nations Mission in Haiti, the staffing, direction and financing of which are shared between the United Nations and the Organization of American States (OAS). This arrangement has worked, and it too is a possible model for the future that will need careful assessment.

87 The capacity of regional organizations for peacemaking and peace-keeping varies considerably. None of them has yet developed a capacity which matches that of the United Nations, though some have accumulated important experience in the field and others are developing rapidly. The United Nations is ready to help them in this respect when requested to do so and when resources permit. Given their varied capacity, the differences in their structures, mandates and decision-making processes and the variety of forms that cooperation with the United Nations is already taking, it would not be appropriate to try to establish a universal model for their relationship with the United Nations. Nevertheless it is possible to identify certain principles on which it should be based.

88 Such principles include:

(a) Agreed mechanisms for consultation should be established, but need not be formal;

(b) The primacy of the United Nations, as set out in the Charter, must be respected. In particular, regional organizations should not enter into arrangements that assume a level of United Nations support not yet submitted to or approved by its Member States. This is an area where close and early consultation is of great importance;

(c) The division of labour must be clearly defined and agreed in order to avoid overlap and institutional rivalry where the United Nations and a regional organization are both working on the same conflict. In such cases it is also particularly important to avoid a multiplicity of mediators;

(d) Consistency by members of regional organizations who are also Member States of the United Nations is needed in dealing with a common problem of interest to both organizations, for example, standards for peace-keeping operations.

89 Non-governmental organizations also play an important role in all United Nations activities discussed in the present paper. To date, 1,003 non-governmental organizations have been granted consultative status with the United Nations and many of them have accredited representatives at United Nations Headquarters in New York and/or the United Nations Office at Geneva. The changed nature of United Nations operations in the field has brought non-governmental organizations into a closer relationship with the United Nations, especially in the provision of humanitarian relief in conflict situations and in post-conflict peace-building. It has been necessary to devise procedures that do not compromise their non-governmental status but do ensure that their efforts are properly coordinated with those of the United Nations and its programmes, funds, offices and agencies. Non-governmental organizations have also had great success in mobilizing public support and funds for humanitarian relief in countries affected by international or domestic conflict.

90 Within the United Nations system there are three levels at which coordination is required: within the United Nations Secretariat; between United Nations Headquarters and the head offices of other funds, programmes, offices and agencies of the United Nations system; and in the field.

91   The multifunctional nature of both peace-keeping and peace-building has made it necessary to improve coordination within the Secretariat, so that the relevant departments function as an integrated whole under my authority and control. Proposals the Secretary-General makes to the General Assembly or the Security Council on peace and security issues need to be based on coordinated inputs from the Departments of Political Affairs, Peace-keeping Operations, Humanitarian Affairs and Administration and Management and others. Guidance to the field must similarly be coordinated, in order to ensure that chiefs of missions do not receive conflicting instructions from different authorities within the Secretariat.

92   In an international bureaucracy interdepartmental cooperation and coordination come even less naturally than they do in a national environment. It has required some effort to ensure that the above objectives are met. I have entrusted the main responsibility in this regard to my Task Force on United Nations Operations and to interdepartmental groups at the working level on each major conflict where the organization is playing a peacemaking or peace-keeping role.

93   Improved coordination is equally necessary within the United Nations system as a whole. The responsibilities involved in multifunctional peace-keeping operations and in peace-building transcend the competence and expertise of any one department, programme, fund, office or agency of the United Nations. Short-term programmes are needed for cease-fires, demobilization, humanitarian relief and refugee return; but it is the longer-term programmes that help rebuild societies and put them back on the path of development. Short-term and long-term programmes need to be planned and implemented in a coordinated way if they are to contribute to the consolidation of peace and development. The mechanism for ensuring a more effective and equitable application of sanctions, which I have recommended earlier in the present position paper, will equally

require close coordination between a large number of players on the United Nations stage.

94 Such coordination has to date proved difficult to achieve. Each of the agencies concerned has its own intergovernmental legislative body and its own mandate. In the past, there also has been insufficient interaction, in both directions, between those responsible in the Secretariat for designing and implementing peacemaking, peace-keeping and peace-building activities and the international financial institutions, who often have an all-important say in making sure that the necessary resources are available.

95 As regards coordination in the field, the current practice when a peace-keeping operation is deployed is to entrust this task to a special representative of the Secretary-General. Cambodia, El Salvador and Mozambique are successful examples, not least because of the cooperation extended to my Special Representatives by the various other components of the United Nations system.

96 For my part, I shall maintain my efforts in the Administrative Committee on Coordination and in my bilateral relations with the executive heads of the various funds, programmes, offices and agencies to achieve better coordination within the United Nations system in the context of peace and security. Governments of Member States can support those efforts. Many of the problems of coordination arise from the mandates decreed for the agencies by discrete intergovernmental bodies. As such, they defy the capacity for inter-Secretariat coordination. I accordingly recommend that Governments instruct their representatives in the various intergovernmental bodies to ensure that proper coordination is recognized to be an essential condition for the Organization's success and that it is not made hostage to inter-institutional rivalry and competition.

V. Financial resources

97 None of the instruments discussed in the present paper can be used unless Governments provide the necessary financial

resources. There is no other source of funds. The failure of Member States to pay their assessed contributions for activities they themselves have voted into being makes it impossible to carry out those activities to the standard expected. It also calls in question the credibility of those who have willed the ends but not the means – and who then criticize the United Nations for its failures. On 12 October 1994, I put to the Member States a package of proposals, ideas and questions on finance and budgetary procedures that I believe can contribute to a solution (UN document A/49/PV.28).

98   The financial crisis is particularly debilitating as regards peace-keeping. The shortage of funds, in particular for reconnaissance and planning, for the start-up of operations and for the recruitment and training of personnel imposes severe constraints on the Organization's ability to deploy, with the desired speed, newly approved operations. Peace-keeping is also afflicted by Member States' difficulties in providing troops, police and equipment on the scale required by the current volume of peace-keeping activity.

99   Meanwhile, there is continuing damage to the credibility of the Security Council and of the Organization as a whole when the Council adopts decisions that cannot be carried out because the necessary troops are not forthcoming. The continuing problems with regard to the safe areas in Bosnia and Herzegovina and the expansion of UNAMIR in response to genocide in Rwanda are cases in point. In the future it would be advisable to establish the availability of the necessary troops and equipment before it is decided to create a new peace-keeping operation or assign a new task to an existing one.

100 Peace-building is another activity that is critically dependent on Member States' readiness to make the necessary resources available. It can be a long-term process and expensive – except in comparison with the cost of peacemaking and peace-keeping if the conflict should recur. One lesson learned in recent years is that, in putting together the peace-building elements in a comprehensive settlement plan, the United Nations should consult the international financial institutions in good time to ensure that the cost of implementing the plan is taken into account in the design of the economic plans of the Government concerned. The problems in this area are aggravated by many donors' reluctance to finance crucial elements such as the conversion of guerrilla movements into political parties, the creation of new police forces or the provision of credit for the purchase of land in "arms for land" programmes.

101 Compensation to Member States affected by sanctions on their neighbours or economic partners will also be possible only if the richer Member States recognize both the moral argument that such countries should not be expected to bear alone costs resulting from action collectively decided upon by the international community and the practical argument that such compensation is necessary to encourage those States to cooperate in applying decisions taken by the Security Council. I recognize that the sums involved will be large but I am convinced that they must be made available if the Council is to continue to rely on sanctions.

VI. Conclusion

102 The present position paper, submitted to the Member States at the opening of the United Nations Fiftieth Anniversary year, is intended to serve as a contribution to the continuing campaign to strengthen a common capacity to deal with threats to peace and security.

103 The times call for thinking afresh, for striving together and for creating new ways to overcome crises. This is because the different world that emerged when the cold war ceased is still a world not fully understood. The changed face of conflict today requires us to be perceptive, adaptive, creative and courageous, and to address simultaneously the immediate as well as the root causes of conflict, which all too often lie in the absence of economic opportunities and social inequities. Perhaps above all it requires a deeper commitment to cooperation and true multilateralism than humanity has ever achieved before.

104 This is why the pages of the present paper reiterate the need for hard decisions. As understanding grows of the challenges to peace and security, hard decisions, if postponed, will appear in retrospect as having been relatively easy when measured against the magnitude of tomorrow's troubles.

105 There is no reason for frustration or pessimism. More progress has been made in the past few years towards using the United Nations as it was designed to be used than many could ever have predicted. The call to decision should be a call to confidence and courage.

Notes

1/ UN document A/48/935. See also An Agenda for Development, *United Nations publication, Sales No. E.95.I.16*

2/ Official Records of the General Assembly, Forty-seventh Session, Supplement No. 27 *(A/47/27), appendix I.*

3/ *See* The United Nations Disarmament Yearbook, vol. 5: 1980 *(United Nations publication, Sales No. G.81.IX.4), appendix VII.*

An Agenda for Peace

Preventive diplomacy,
peacemaking and peace-keeping

Report of the Secretary-General
pursuant to the statement adopted by
the Summit Meeting of the Security Council
on 31 January 1992
A/47/277-S/24111, 17 June 1992

Introduction

1   IN ITS STATEMENT of 31 January 1992, adopted at the conclusion of the first meeting held by the Security Council at
the level of Heads of State and Government, I was invited to prepare,
for circulation to the Members of the United Nations by 1 July 1992,
an "analysis and recommendations on ways of strengthening and
making more efficient within the framework and provisions of the
Charter the capacity of the United Nations for preventive diplomacy,
for peacemaking and for peace-keeping.[1/]

2   The United Nations is a gathering of sovereign States and what
it can do depends on the common ground that they create between
them. The adversarial decades of the cold war made the original
promise of the Organization impossible to fulfil. The January 1992
Summit therefore represented an unprecedented recommitment, at the
highest political level, to the Purposes and Principles of the Charter.

3   In these past months a conviction has grown, among nations
large and small, that an opportunity has been regained to achieve the
great objectives of the Charter – a United Nations capable of maintaining international peace and security, of securing justice and
human rights and of promoting, in the words of the Charter, "social
progress and better standards of life in larger freedom". This opportunity must not be squandered. The Organization must never again
be crippled as it was in the era that has now passed.

4   I welcome the invitation of the Security Council, early in my tenure as Secretary-General, to prepare this report. It draws upon ideas and proposals transmitted to me by Governments, regional agencies, non-governmental organizations, and institutions and individuals from many countries. I am grateful for these, even as I emphasize that the responsibility for this report is my own.

5   The sources of conflict and war are pervasive and deep. To reach them will require our utmost effort to enhance respect for human rights and fundamental freedoms, to promote sustainable economic and social development for wider prosperity, to alleviate distress and to curtail the existence and use of massively destructive weapons. The United Nations Conference on Environment and Development, the largest summit ever held, has just met at Rio de Janeiro. Next year will see the second World Conference on Human Rights. In 1994 Population and Development will be addressed. In 1995 the World Conference on Women will take place, and a World Summit for Social Development has been proposed. Throughout my term as Secretary-General I shall be addressing all these great issues. I bear them all in mind as, in the present report, I turn to the problems that the Council has specifically requested I consider: preventive diplomacy, peacemaking and peace-keeping – to which I have added a closely related concept, post-conflict peace-building.

6   The manifest desire of the membership to work together is a new source of strength in our common endeavour. Success is far from certain, however. While my report deals with ways to improve the Organization's capacity to pursue and preserve peace, it is crucial for all Member States to bear in mind that the search for improved mechanisms and techniques will be of little significance unless this new spirit of commonality is propelled by the will to take the hard decisions demanded by this time of opportunity.

7   It is therefore with a sense of moment, and with gratitude, that I present this report to the Members of the United Nations.

I. The changing context

8 In the course of the past few years the immense ideological barrier that for decades gave rise to distrust and hostility – and the terrible tools of destruction that were their inseparable companions – has collapsed. Even as the issues between States north and south grow more acute, and call for attention at the highest levels of government, the improvement in relations between States east and west affords new possibilities, some already realized, to meet successfully threats to common security.

9 Authoritarian regimes have given way to more democratic forces and responsive Governments. The form, scope and intensity of these processes differ from Latin America to Africa to Europe to Asia, but they are sufficiently similar to indicate a global phenomenon. Parallel to these political changes, many States are seeking more open forms of economic policy, creating a world wide sense of dynamism and movement.

10 To the hundreds of millions who gained their independence in the surge of decolonization following the creation of the United Nations, have been added millions more who have recently gained freedom. Once again new States are taking their seats in the General Assembly. Their arrival reconfirms the importance and indispensability of the sovereign State as the fundamental entity of the international community.

11 We have entered a time of global transition marked by uniquely contradictory trends. Regional and continental associations of States are evolving ways to deepen cooperation and ease some of the contentious characteristics of sovereign and nationalistic rivalries. National boundaries are blurred by advanced communications and global commerce, and by the decisions of States to yield some sovereign prerogatives to larger, common political associations. At the same time, however, fierce new assertions of nationalism and sovereignty spring up, and the cohesion of States is threatened by brutal ethnic, religious, social, cultural or linguistic strife. Social peace is challenged on the one hand by new assertions of discrimination and exclusion and, on the other, by acts of terrorism seeking to undermine evolution and change through democratic means.

12   The concept of peace is easy to grasp; that of international security is more complex, for a pattern of contradictions has arisen here as well. As major nuclear Powers have begun to negotiate arms reduction agreements, the proliferation of weapons of mass destruction threatens to increase and conventional arms continue to be amassed in many parts of the world. As racism becomes recognized for the destructive force it is and as apartheid is being dismantled, new racial tensions are rising and finding expression in violence. Technological advances are altering the nature and the expectation of life all over the globe. The revolution in communications has united the world in awareness, in aspiration and in greater solidarity against injustice. But progress also brings new risks for stability: ecological damage, disruption of family and community life, greater intrusion into the lives and rights of individuals.

13   This new dimension of insecurity must not be allowed to obscure the continuing and devastating problems of unchecked population growth, crushing debt burdens, barriers to trade, drugs and the growing disparity between rich and poor. Poverty, disease, famine, oppression and despair abound, joining to produce 17 million refugees, 20 million displaced persons and massive migrations of peoples within and beyond national borders. These are both sources and consequences of conflict that require the ceaseless attention and the highest priority in the efforts of the United Nations. A porous ozone shield could pose a greater threat to an exposed population than a hostile army. Drought and disease can decimate no less mercilessly than the weapons of war. So at this moment of renewed opportunity, the efforts of the Organization to build peace, stability and security must encompass matters beyond military threats in order to break the fetters of strife and warfare that have characterized the past. But armed conflicts today, as they have throughout history, continue to bring fear and horror to humanity, requiring our urgent involvement to try to prevent, contain and bring them to an end.

14   Since the creation of the United Nations in 1945, over 100 major conflicts around the world have left some 20 million dead. The United Nations was rendered powerless to deal with many of these crises because of the vetoes – 279 of them – cast in the Security Council, which were a vivid expression of the divisions of that period.

15 With the end of the cold war there have been no such vetoes since 31 May 1990, and demands on the United Nations have surged. Its security arm, once disabled by circumstances it was not created or equipped to control, has emerged as a central instrument for the prevention and resolution of conflicts and for the preservation of peace. Our aims must be:

- To seek to identify at the earliest possible stage situations that could produce conflict, and to try through diplomacy to remove the sources of danger before violence results;
- Where conflict erupts, to engage in peacemaking aimed at resolving the issues that have led to conflict;
- Through peace-keeping, to work to preserve peace, however fragile, where fighting has been halted and to assist in implementing agreements achieved by the peacemakers;
- To stand ready to assist in peace-building in its differing contexts: rebuilding the institutions and infrastructures of nations torn by civil war and strife; and building bonds of peaceful mutual benefit among nations formerly at war;
- And in the largest sense, to address the deepest causes of conflict: economic despair, social injustice and political oppression. It is possible to discern an increasingly common moral perception that spans the world's nations and peoples, and which is finding expression in international laws, many owing their genesis to the work of this Organization.

16 This wider mission for the world Organization will demand the concerted attention and effort of individual States, of regional and non-governmental organizations and of all of the United Nations system, with each of the principal organs functioning in the balance and harmony that the Charter requires. The Security Council has been assigned by all Member States the primary responsibility for the maintenance of international peace and security under the Charter. In its broadest sense this responsibility must be shared by the General Assembly and by all the functional elements of the world Organization. Each has a special and indispensable role to play in an integrated approach to human security. The Secretary-General's contribution rests on the pattern of trust and cooperation established between him and the deliberative organs of the United Nations.

17 The foundation-stone of this work is and must remain the State. Respect for its fundamental sovereignty and integrity are crucial to any common international progress. The time of absolute and exclusive sovereignty, however, has passed; its theory was never matched by reality. It is the task of leaders of States today to understand this and to find a balance between the needs of good internal governance and the requirements of an ever more interdependent world. Commerce, communications and environmental matters transcend administrative borders; but inside those borders is where individuals carry out the first order of their economic, political and social lives. The United Nations has not closed its door. Yet if every ethnic, religious or linguistic group claimed statehood, there would be no limit to fragmentation, and peace, security and economic well-being for all would become ever more difficult to achieve.

18 One requirement for solutions to these problems lies in commitment to human rights with a special sensitivity to those of minorities, whether ethnic, religious, social or linguistic. The League of Nations provided a machinery for the international protection of minorities. The General Assembly soon will have before it a declaration on the rights of minorities. That instrument, together with the increasingly effective machinery of the United Nations dealing with human rights, should enhance the situation of minorities as well as the stability of States.

19   Globalism and nationalism need not be viewed as opposing trends, doomed to spur each other on to extremes of reaction. The healthy globalization of contemporary life requires in the first instance solid identities and fundamental freedoms. The sovereignty, territorial integrity and independence of States within the established international system, and the principle of self-determination for peoples, both of great value and importance, must not be permitted to work against each other in the period ahead. Respect for democratic principles at all levels of social existence is crucial: in communities, within States and within the community of States. Our constant duty should be to maintain the integrity of each while finding a balanced design for all.

II. Definitions

20   The terms preventive diplomacy, peacemaking and peace-keeping are integrally related and as used in this report are defined as follows:

- Preventive diplomacy is action to prevent disputes from arising between parties, to prevent existing disputes from escalating into conflicts and to limit the spread of the latter when they occur.
- Peacemaking is action to bring hostile parties to agreement, essentially through such peaceful means as those foreseen in Chapter VI of the Charter of the United Nations.
- Peace-keeping is the deployment of a United Nations presence in the field, hitherto with the consent of all the parties concerned, normally involving United Nations military and/or police personnel and frequently civilians as well. Peace-keeping is a technique that expands the possibilities for both the prevention of conflict and the making of peace.

21   The present report in addition will address the critically

related concept of post-conflict peace-building – action to identify
and support structures which will tend to strengthen and solidify
peace in order to avoid a relapse into conflict. Preventive diplomacy
seeks to resolve disputes before violence breaks out; peacemaking
and peace-keeping are required to halt conflicts and preserve peace
once it is attained. If successful, they strengthen the opportunity for
post-conflict peace-building, which can prevent the recurrence of
violence among nations and peoples.

22   These four areas for action, taken together, and carried out
with the backing of all Members, offer a coherent contribution towards
securing peace in the spirit of the Charter. The United Nations has
extensive experience not only in these fields, but in the wider realm of
work for peace in which these four fields are set. Initiatives on decolonization, on the environment and sustainable development, on population, on the eradication of disease, on disarmament and on the
growth of international law – these and many others have contributed
immeasurably to the foundations for a peaceful world. The world has
often been rent by conflict and plagued by massive human suffering
and deprivation. Yet it would have been far more so without the continuing efforts of the United Nations. This wide experience must be
taken into account in assessing the potential of the United Nations in
maintaining international security not only in its traditional sense, but
in the new dimensions presented by the era ahead.

III. Preventive diplomacy

23   The most desirable and efficient employment of diplomacy
is to ease tensions before they result in conflict – or, if conflict
breaks out, to act swiftly to contain it and resolve its underlying
causes. Preventive diplomacy may be performed by the
Secretary-General personally or through senior staff or specialized
agencies and programmes, by the Security Council or the General
Assembly, and by regional organizations in cooperation with the
United Nations. Preventive diplomacy requires measures to create

confidence; it needs early warning based on information gathering and informal or formal fact-finding; it may also involve preventive deployment and, in some situations, demilitarized zones.

Measures to build confidence

24   Mutual confidence and good faith are essential to reducing the likelihood of conflict between States. Many such measures are available to Governments that have the will to employ them. Systematic exchange of military missions, formation of regional or subregional risk reduction centres, arrangements for the free flow of information, including the monitoring of regional arms agreements, are examples. I ask all regional organizations to consider what further confidence-building measures might be applied in their areas and to inform the United Nations of the results. I will undertake periodic consultations on confidence-building measures with parties to potential, current or past disputes and with regional organizations, offering such advisory assistance as the Secretariat can provide.

Fact-finding

25   Preventive steps must be based upon timely and accurate knowledge of the facts. Beyond this, an understanding of developments and global trends, based on sound analysis, is required. And the willingness to take appropriate preventive action is essential. Given the economic and social roots of many potential conflicts, the information needed by the United Nations now must encompass economic and social trends as well as political developments that may lead to dangerous tensions.

(a) An increased resort to fact-finding is needed, in accordance with the Charter, initiated either by the Secretary-General, to enable him to meet his responsibilities under the Charter, including Article 99, or by the Security Council or the General Assembly. Various forms may be employed selectively as the situation requires. A request by a State for the sending of a United Nations fact-finding mission to its territory should be considered without undue delay.

(b) Contacts with the Governments of Member States can provide the Secretary-General with detailed information on issues of concern. I ask that all Member States be ready to provide the information needed for effective preventive diplomacy. I will supplement my own contacts by regularly sending senior officials on missions for consultations in capitals or other locations. Such contacts are essential to gain insight into a situation and to assess its potential ramifications.

(c) Formal fact-finding can be mandated by the Security Council or by the General Assembly, either of which may elect to send a mission under its immediate authority or may invite the Secretary-General to take the necessary steps, including the designation of a special envoy. In addition to collecting information on which a decision for further action can be taken, such a mission can in some instances help to defuse a dispute by its presence, indicating to the parties that the Organization, and in particular the Security Council, is actively seized of the matter as a present or potential threat to international security.

(d) In exceptional circumstances the Council may meet away from Headquarters as the Charter provides, in order not only to inform itself directly, but also to bring the authority of the Organization to bear on a given situation.

Early warning

26   In recent years the United Nations system has been developing a valuable network of early warning systems concerning environmental threats, the risk of nuclear accident, natural disasters, mass movements of populations, the threat of famine and the spread

of disease. There is a need, however, to strengthen arrangements in such a manner that information from these sources can be synthesized with political indicators to assess whether a threat to peace exists and to analyse what action might be taken by the United Nations to alleviate it. This is a process that will continue to require the close cooperation of the various specialized agencies and functional offices of the United Nations. The analyses and recommendations for preventive action that emerge will be made available by me, as appropriate, to the Security Council and other United Nations organs. I recommend in addition that the Security Council invite a reinvigorated and restructured Economic and Social Council to provide reports, in accordance with Article 65 of the Charter, on those economic and social developments that may, unless mitigated, threaten international peace and security.

27   Regional arrangements and organizations have an important role in early warning. I ask regional organizations that have not yet sought observer status at the United Nations to do so and to be linked, through appropriate arrangements, with the security mechanisms of this Organization.

Preventive deployment

28   United Nations operations in areas of crisis have generally been established after conflict has occurred. The time has come to plan for circumstances warranting preventive deployment, which could take place in a variety of instances and ways. For example, in conditions of national crisis there could be preventive deployment at the request of the Government or all parties concerned, or with their consent; in inter-State disputes such deployment could take place when two countries feel that a United Nations presence on both sides of their border can discourage hostilities; furthermore, preventive deployment could take place when a country feels threatened and requests the deployment of an appropriate United Nations presence along its side of the border alone. In each situation, the mandate and composition of the United Nations presence would need to be carefully devised and be clear to all.

29   In conditions of crisis within a country, when the Government requests or all parties consent, preventive deployment could help in a number of ways to alleviate suffering and to limit or control violence. Humanitarian assistance, impartially provided, could be of critical importance; assistance in maintaining security, whether through military, police or civilian personnel, could save lives and develop conditions of safety in which negotiations can be held; the United Nations could also help in conciliation efforts if this should be the wish of the parties. In certain circumstances, the United Nations may well need to draw upon the specialized skills and resources of various parts of the United Nations system; such operations may also on occasion require the participation of non-governmental organizations.

30   In these situations of internal crisis the United Nations will need to respect the sovereignty of the State; to do otherwise would not be in accordance with the understanding of Member States in accepting the principles of the Charter. The Organization must remain mindful of the carefully negotiated balance of the guiding principles annexed to General Assembly resolution 46/182 of 19 December 1991. Those guidelines stressed, *inter alia*, that humanitarian assistance must be provided in accordance with the principles of humanity, neutrality and impartiality; that the sovereignty, territorial integrity and national unity of States must be fully respected in accordance with the Charter of the United Nations; and that, in this context, humanitarian assistance should be provided with the consent of the affected country and, in principle, on the basis of an appeal by that country. The guidelines also stressed the responsibility of States to take care of the victims of emergencies occurring on their territory and the need for access to those requiring humanitarian assistance. In the light of these guidelines, a Government's request for United Nations involvement, or consent to it, would not be an infringement of that State's sovereignty or be contrary to Article 2, paragraph 7, of the Charter which refers to matters essentially within the domestic jurisdiction of any State.

31 In inter-State disputes, when both parties agree, I recommend that if the Security Council concludes that the likelihood of hostilities between neighbouring countries could be removed by the preventive deployment of a United Nations presence on the territory of each State, such action should be taken. The nature of the tasks to be performed would determine the composition of the United Nations presence.

32 In cases where one nation fears a cross-border attack, if the Security Council concludes that a United Nations presence on one side of the border, with the consent only of the requesting country, would serve to deter conflict, I recommend that preventive deployment take place. Here again, the specific nature of the situation would determine the mandate and the personnel required to fulfil it.

Demilitarized zones

33 In the past, demilitarized zones have been established by agreement of the parties at the conclusion of a conflict. In addition to the deployment of United Nations personnel in such zones as part of peace-keeping operations, consideration should now be given to the usefulness of such zones as a form of preventive deployment, on both sides of a border, with the agreement of the two parties, as a means of separating potential belligerents, or on one side of the line, at the request of one party, for the purpose of removing any pretext for attack. Demilitarized zones would serve as symbols of the international community's concern that conflict be prevented.

IV. Peacemaking

34 Between the tasks of seeking to prevent conflict and keeping the peace lies the responsibility to try to bring hostile parties to agreement by peaceful means. Chapter VI of the Charter sets forth a comprehensive list of such means for the resolution of conflict.

These have been amplified in various declarations adopted by the General Assembly, including the Manila Declaration of 1982 on the Peaceful Settlement of International Disputes[2/] and the 1988 Declaration on the Prevention and Removal of Disputes and Situations Which May Threaten International Peace and Security and on the Role of the United Nations in this Field.[3/] They have also been the subject of various resolutions of the General Assembly, including resolution 44/21 of 15 November 1989 on enhancing international peace, security and international cooperation in all its aspects in accordance with the Charter of the United Nations. The United Nations has had wide experience in the application of these peaceful means. If conflicts have gone unresolved, it is not because techniques for peaceful settlement were unknown or inadequate. The fault lies first in the lack of political will of parties to seek a solution to their differences through such means as are suggested in Chapter VI of the Charter, and second, in the lack of leverage at the disposal of a third party if this is the procedure chosen. The indifference of the international community to a problem, or the marginalization of it, can also thwart the possibilities of solution. We must look primarily to these areas if we hope to enhance the capacity of the Organization for achieving peaceful settlements.

35 The present determination in the Security Council to resolve international disputes in the manner foreseen in the Charter has opened the way for a more active Council role. With greater unity has come leverage and persuasive power to lead hostile parties towards negotiations. I urge the Council to take full advantage of the provisions of the Charter under which it may recommend appropriate procedures or methods for dispute settlement and, if all the parties to a dispute so request, make recommendations to the parties for a pacific settlement of the dispute.

36 The General Assembly, like the Security Council and the Secretary-General, also has an important role assigned to it under the Charter for the maintenance of international peace and security. As a universal forum, its capacity to consider and recommend appropriate action must be recognized. To that end it is essential to promote its utilization by all Member States so as to bring greater influence to bear in pre-empting or containing situations which are likely to threaten international peace and security.

37 Mediation and negotiation can be undertaken by an individual designated by the Security Council, by the General Assembly or by the Secretary-General. There is a long history of the utilization by the United Nations of distinguished statesmen to facilitate the processes of peace. They can bring a personal prestige that, in addition to their experience, can encourage the parties to enter serious negotiations. There is a wide willingness to serve in this capacity, from which I shall continue to benefit as the need arises. Frequently it is the Secretary-General himself who undertakes the task. While the mediator's effectiveness is enhanced by strong and evident support from the Council, the General Assembly and the relevant Member States acting in their national capacity, the good offices of the Secretary-General may at times be employed most effectively when conducted independently of the deliberative bodies. Close and continuous consultation between the Secretary-General and the Security Council is, however, essential to ensure full awareness of how the Council's influence can best be applied and to develop a common strategy for the peaceful settlement of specific disputes.

The World Court

38 The docket of the International Court of Justice has grown fuller but it remains an under-used resource for the peaceful adjudication of disputes. Greater reliance on the Court would be an important contribution to United Nations peacemaking. In this connection, I call attention to the power of the Security Council under Articles 36 and 37 of the Charter to recommend to Member States the submission of a dispute to the International Court of Justice, arbitration or other dispute-settlement mechanisms. I recommend that the Secretary-General be authorized, pursuant to Article 96, paragraph 2, of the Charter, to take advantage of the advisory competence of the Court and that other United Nations organs that already enjoy such authorization turn to the Court more frequently for advisory opinions.

39 I recommend the following steps to reinforce the role of the International Court of Justice:

(a) All Member States should accept the general jurisdiction of the International Court under Article 36 of its Statute, without any reservation, before the end of the United Nations Decade of International Law in the year 2000. In instances where domestic structures prevent this, States should agree bilaterally or multilaterally to a comprehensive list of matters they are willing to submit to the Court and should withdraw their reservations to its jurisdiction in the dispute settlement clauses of multilateral treaties;

(b) When submission of a dispute to the full Court is not practical, the Chambers jurisdiction should be used;

(c) States should support the Trust Fund established to assist countries unable to afford the cost involved in bringing a dispute to the Court, and such countries should take full advantage of the Fund in order to resolve their disputes.

Amelioration through assistance

40 Peacemaking is at times facilitated by international action to ameliorate circumstances that have contributed to the dispute or conflict. If, for instance, assistance to displaced persons within a society is essential to a solution, then the United Nations should be able to draw upon the resources of all agencies and programmes concerned. At present, there is no adequate mechanism in the United Nations through which the Security Council, the General Assembly or the Secretary-General can mobilize the resources needed for such positive leverage and engage the collective efforts of the United Nations system for the peaceful resolution of a conflict. I have raised this concept in the Administrative Committee on

Coordination, which brings together the executive heads of United Nations agencies and programmes; we are exploring methods by which the inter-agency system can improve its contribution to the peaceful resolution of disputes.

Sanctions and special economic problems

41 In circumstances when peacemaking requires the imposition of sanctions under Article 41 of the Charter, it is important that States confronted with special economic problems not only have the right to consult the Security Council regarding such problems, as Article 50 provides, but also have a realistic possibility of having their difficulties addressed. I recommend that the Security Council devise a set of measures involving the financial institutions and other components of the United Nations system that can be put in place to insulate States from such difficulties. Such measures would be a matter of equity and a means of encouraging States to cooperate with decisions of the Council.

Use of military force

42 It is the essence of the concept of collective security as contained in the Charter that if peaceful means fail, the measures provided in Chapter VII should be used, on the decision of the Security Council, to maintain or restore international peace and security in the face of a "threat to the peace, breach of the peace, or act of aggression". The Security Council has not so far made use of the most coercive of these measures – the action by military force foreseen in Article 42. In the situation between Iraq and Kuwait, the Council chose to authorize Member States to take measures on its behalf. The Charter, however, provides a detailed approach which now merits the attention of all Member States.

43 Under Article 42 of the Charter, the Security Council has the authority to take military action to maintain or restore international peace and security. While such action should only be taken

when all peaceful means have failed, the option of taking it is essential to the credibility of the United Nations as a guarantor of international security. This will require bringing into being, through negotiations, the special agreements foreseen in Article 43 of the Charter, whereby Member States undertake to make armed forces, assistance and facilities available to the Security Council for the purposes stated in Article 42, not only on an ad hoc basis but on a permanent basis. Under the political circumstances that now exist for the first time since the Charter was adopted, the long-standing obstacles to the conclusion of such special agreements should no longer prevail. The ready availability of armed forces on call could serve, in itself, as a means of deterring breaches of the peace since a potential aggressor would know that the Council had at its disposal a means of response. Forces under Article 43 may perhaps never be sufficiently large or well enough equipped to deal with a threat from a major army equipped with sophisticated weapons. They would be useful, however, in meeting any threat posed by a military force of a lesser order. I recommend that the Security Council initiate negotiations in accordance with Article 43, supported by the Military Staff Committee, which may be augmented if necessary by others in accordance with Article 47, paragraph 2, of the Charter. It is my view that the role of the Military Staff Committee should be seen in the context of Chapter VII, and not that of the planning or conduct of peace-keeping operations.

Peace-enforcement units

   44   The mission of forces under Article 43 would be to respond to outright aggression, imminent or actual. Such forces are not likely to be available for some time to come. Cease-fires have often been agreed to but not complied with, and the United Nations has sometimes been called upon to send forces to restore and maintain the cease-fire. This task can on occasion exceed the mission of peace-keeping forces and the expectations of peace-keeping force contributors. I recommend that the Council consider the utilization

of peace-enforcement units in clearly defined circumstances and with their terms of reference specified in advance. Such units from Member States would be available on call and would consist of troops that have volunteered for such service. They would have to be more heavily armed than peace-keeping forces and would need to undergo extensive preparatory training within their national forces. Deployment and operation of such forces would be under the authorization of the Security Council and would, as in the case of peace-keeping forces, be under the command of the Secretary-General. I consider such peace-enforcement units to be warranted as a provisional measure under Article 40 of the Charter. Such peace-enforcement units should not be confused with the forces that may eventually be constituted under Article 43 to deal with acts of aggression or with the military personnel which Governments may agree to keep on stand-by for possible contribution to peace-keeping operations.

45   Just as diplomacy will continue across the span of all the activities dealt with in the present report, so there may not be a dividing line between peacemaking and peace-keeping. Peacemaking is often a prelude to peace-keeping – just as the deployment of a United Nations presence in the field may expand possibilities for the prevention of conflict, facilitate the work of peacemaking and in many cases serve as a prerequisite for peace-building.

V. Peace-keeping

46   Peace-keeping can rightly be called the invention of the United Nations. It has brought a degree of stability to numerous areas of tension around the world.

Increasing demands
47   Thirteen peace-keeping operations were established between the years 1945 and 1987; 13 others since then. An esti-

mated 528,000 military, police and civilian personnel had served under the flag of the United Nations until January 1992. Over 800 of them from 43 countries have died in the service of the Organization. The costs of these operations have aggregated some $8.3 billion till 1992. The unpaid arrears towards them stand at over $800 million, which represents a debt owed by the Organization to the troop-contributing countries. Peace-keeping operations approved at present are estimated to cost close to $3 billion in the current 12-month period, while patterns of payment are unacceptably slow. Against this, global defence expenditures at the end of the last decade had approached $1 trillion a year, or $2 million per minute.

48 The contrast between the costs of United Nations peace-keeping and the costs of the alternative, war – between the demands of the Organization and the means provided to meet them – would be farcical were the consequences not so damaging to global stability and to the credibility of the Organization. At a time when nations and peoples increasingly are looking to the United Nations for assistance in keeping the peace – and holding it responsible when this cannot be so – fundamental decisions must be taken to enhance the capacity of the Organization in this innovative and productive exercise of its function. I am conscious that the present volume and unpredictability of peace-keeping assessments poses real problems for some Member States. For this reason, I strongly support proposals in some Member States for their peace-keeping contributions to be financed from defence, rather than foreign affairs, budgets and I recommend such action to others. I urge the General Assembly to encourage this approach.

49 The demands on the United Nations for peace-keeping, and peace-building, operations will in the coming years continue to challenge the capacity, the political and financial will and the creativity of the Secretariat and Member States. Like the Security Council, I welcome the increase and broadening of the tasks of peace-keeping operations.

New departures in peace-keeping

50 The nature of peace-keeping operations has evolved rapidly in recent years. The established principles and practices of peace-keeping have responded flexibly to new demands of recent years, and the basic conditions for success remain unchanged: a clear and practicable mandate; the cooperation of the parties in implementing that mandate; the continuing support of the Security Council; the readiness of Member States to contribute the military, police and civilian personnel, including specialists, required; effective United Nations command at Headquarters and in the field; and adequate financial and logistic support. As the international climate has changed and peace-keeping operations are increasingly fielded to help implement settlements that have been negotiated by peacemakers, a new array of demands and problems has emerged regarding logistics, equipment, personnel and finance, all of which could be corrected if Member States so wished and were ready to make the necessary resources available.

Personnel

51 Member States are keen to participate in peace-keeping operations. Military observers and infantry are invariably available in the required numbers, but logistic units present a greater problem, as few armies can afford to spare such units for an extended period. Member States were requested in 1990 to state what military personnel they were in principle prepared to make available; few replied. I reiterate the request to all Member States to reply frankly and promptly. Stand-by arrangements should be confirmed, as appropriate, through exchanges of letters between the Secretariat and Member States concerning the kind and number of skilled personnel they will be prepared to offer the United Nations as the needs of new operations arise.

52 Increasingly, peace-keeping requires that civilian political officers, human rights monitors, electoral officials, refugee and humanitarian aid specialists and police play as central a role as the

military. Police personnel have proved increasingly difficult to obtain in the numbers required. I recommend that arrangements be reviewed and improved for training peace-keeping personnel – civilian, police, or military – using the varied capabilities of Member State Governments, of non-governmental organizations and the facilities of the Secretariat. As efforts go forward to include additional States as contributors, some States with considerable potential should focus on language training for police contingents which may serve with the Organization. As for the United Nations itself, special personnel procedures, including incentives, should be instituted to permit the rapid transfer of Secretariat staff members to service with peace-keeping operations. The strength and capability of military staff serving in the Secretariat should be augmented to meet new and heavier requirements.

Logistics

53   Not all Governments can provide their battalions with the equipment they need for service abroad. While some equipment is provided by troop-contributing countries, a great deal has to come from the United Nations, including equipment to fill gaps in under-equipped national units. The United Nations has no standing stock of such equipment. Orders must be placed with manufacturers, which creates a number of difficulties. A pre-positioned stock of basic peace-keeping equipment should be established, so that at least some vehicles, communications equipment, generators, etc., would be immediately available at the start of an operation. Alternatively, Governments should commit themselves to keeping certain equipment, specified by the Secretary-General, on stand-by for immediate sale, loan or donation to the United Nations when required.

54   Member States in a position to do so should make air- and sea-lift capacity available to the United Nations free of cost or at lower than commercial rates, as was the practice until recently.

VI. Post-conflict peace-building

55 Peacemaking and peace-keeping operations, to be truly successful, must come to include comprehensive efforts to identify and support structures which will tend to consolidate peace and advance a sense of confidence and well-being among people. Through agreements ending civil strife, these may include disarming the previously warring parties and the restoration of order, the custody and possible destruction of weapons, repatriating refugees, advisory and training support for security personnel, monitoring elections, advancing efforts to protect human rights, reforming or strengthening governmental institutions and promoting formal and informal processes of political participation.

56 In the aftermath of international war, post-conflict peace-building may take the form of concrete cooperative projects which link two or more countries in a mutually beneficial undertaking that can not only contribute to economic and social development but also enhance the confidence that is so fundamental to peace. I have in mind, for example, projects that bring States together to develop agriculture, improve transportation or utilize resources such as water or electricity that they need to share, or joint programmes through which barriers between nations are brought down by means of freer travel, cultural exchanges and mutually beneficial youth and educational projects. Reducing hostile perceptions through educational exchanges and curriculum reform may be essential to forestall a re-emergence of cultural and national tensions which could spark renewed hostilities.

57 In surveying the range of efforts for peace, the concept of peace-building as the construction of a new environment should be viewed as the counterpart of preventive diplomacy, which seeks to avoid the breakdown of peaceful conditions. When conflict breaks out, mutually reinforcing efforts at peacemaking and peace-keeping come into play. Once these have achieved their objectives, only sustained, cooperative work to deal with underlying economic, social, cultural and humanitarian problems can place an achieved peace on a durable foundation. Preventive diplomacy is to avoid a crisis;

post-conflict peace-building is to prevent a recurrence.

58   Increasingly it is evident that peace-building after civil or
international strife must address the serious problem of land mines,
many tens of millions of which remain scattered in present or former combat zones. De-mining should be emphasized in the terms of
reference of peace-keeping operations and is crucially important in
the restoration of activity when peace-building is under way: agriculture cannot be revived without de-mining and the restoration of
transport may require the laying of hard surface roads to prevent
re-mining. In such instances, the link becomes evident between
peace-keeping and peace-building. Just as demilitarized zones may
serve the cause of preventive diplomacy and preventive deployment
to avoid conflict, so may demilitarization assist in keeping the peace
or in post-conflict peace-building, as a measure for heightening the
sense of security and encouraging the parties to turn their energies
to the work of peaceful restoration of their societies.

59   There is a new requirement for technical assistance which
the United Nations has an obligation to develop and provide when
requested: support for the transformation of deficient national structures and capabilities, and for the strengthening of new democratic
institutions. The authority of the United Nations system to act in this
field would rest on the consensus that social peace is as important
as strategic or political peace. There is an obvious connection
between democratic practices – such as the rule of law and transparency in decision-making – and the achievement of true peace
and security in any new and stable political order. These elements of
good governance need to be promoted at all levels of international
and national political communities.

VII. Cooperation with regional arrangements and organizations

60   The Covenant of the League of Nations, in its Article 21,
noted the validity of regional understandings for securing the main-

tenance of peace. The Charter devotes Chapter VIII to regional arrangements or agencies for dealing with such matters relating to the maintenance of international peace and security as are appropriate for regional action and consistent with the Purposes and Principles of the United Nations. The cold war impaired the proper use of Chapter VIII and indeed, in that era, regional arrangements worked on occasion against resolving disputes in the manner foreseen in the Charter.

61   The Charter deliberately provides no precise definition of regional arrangements and agencies, thus allowing useful flexibility for undertakings by a group of States to deal with a matter appropriate for regional action which also could contribute to the maintenance of international peace and security. Such associations or entities could include treaty-based organizations, whether created before or after the founding of the United Nations, regional organizations for mutual security and defence, organizations for general regional development or for cooperation on a particular economic topic or function, and groups created to deal with a specific political, economic or social issue of current concern.

62   In this regard, the United Nations has recently encouraged a rich variety of complementary efforts. Just as no two regions or situations are the same, so the design of cooperative work and its division of labour must adapt to the realities of each case with flexibility and creativity. In Africa, three different regional groups – the Organization of African Unity, the League of Arab States and the Organization of the Islamic Conference – joined efforts with the United Nations regarding Somalia. In the Asian context, the Association of South-East Asian Nations and individual States from several regions were brought together with the parties to the Cambodian conflict at an international conference in Paris, to work with the United Nations. For El Salvador, a unique arrangement – "The Friends of the Secretary-General" – contributed to agreements reached through the mediation of the Secretary-General. The end of the war in Nicaragua involved a highly complex effort which was initiated by leaders of the region and conducted by individual States, groups of States and the Organization of American States. Efforts undertaken by the European Community and its member States, with the support of States participating in the Conference on Security and Cooperation in Europe, have been of central importance in dealing with the crisis in the Balkans and neighbouring areas.

63 In the past, regional arrangements often were created because of the absence of a universal system for collective security; thus their activities could on occasion work at cross-purposes with the sense of solidarity required for the effectiveness of the world Organization. But in this new era of opportunity, regional arrangements or agencies can render great service if their activities are undertaken in a manner consistent with the Purposes and Principles of the Charter, and if their relationship with the United Nations, and particularly the Security Council, is governed by Chapter VIII.

64 It is not the purpose of the present report to set forth any formal pattern of relationship between regional organizations and the United Nations, or to call for any specific division of labour. What is clear, however, is that regional arrangements or agencies in many cases possess a potential that should be utilized in serving the functions covered in this report: preventive diplomacy, peace-keeping, peacemaking and post-conflict peace-building. Under the Charter, the Security Council has and will continue to have primary responsibility for maintaining international peace and security, but regional action as a matter of decentralization, delegation and cooperation with United Nations efforts could not only lighten the burden of the Council but also contribute to a deeper sense of participation, consensus and democratization in international affairs.

65 Regional arrangements and agencies have not in recent decades been considered in this light, even when originally designed in part for a role in maintaining or restoring peace within their regions of the world. Today a new sense exists that they have contributions to make. Consultations between the United Nations and regional arrangements or agencies could do much to build international consensus on the nature of a problem and the measures required to address it. Regional organizations participating in complementary efforts with the United Nations in joint undertakings would encourage States outside the region to act supportively. And should the Security Council choose specifically to authorize a regional arrangement or organization to take the lead in addressing a crisis within its region, it could serve to lend the weight of the United Nations to the validity of the regional effort. Carried forward in the spirit of the Charter, and as envisioned in Chapter VIII, the approach outlined here could strengthen a general sense that democratization is being encouraged at all levels in the task of maintaining international peace and security, it being essential to continue to recognize that the primary responsibility will continue to reside in the Security Council.

VIII. Safety of personnel

66 When United Nations personnel are deployed in conditions of strife, whether for preventive diplomacy, peacemaking, peace-keeping, peace-building or humanitarian purposes, the need arises to ensure their safety. There has been an unconscionable increase in the number of fatalities. Following the conclusion of a cease-fire and in order to prevent further outbreaks of violence, United Nations guards were called upon to assist in volatile conditions in Iraq. Their presence afforded a measure of security to United Nations personnel and supplies and, in addition, introduced an element of reassurance and stability that helped to prevent renewed conflict. Depending upon the nature of the situation, different configurations and compositions of security deployments will need to be considered. As the variety and scale of threat widens, innovative measures will be required to deal with the dangers facing United Nations personnel.

67 Experience has demonstrated that the presence of a United Nations operation has not always been sufficient to deter hostile action. Duty in areas of danger can never be risk-free; United

Nations personnel must expect to go in harm's way at times. The courage, commitment and idealism shown by United Nations personnel should be respected by the entire international community. These men and women deserve to be properly recognized and rewarded for the perilous tasks they undertake. Their interests and those of their families must be given due regard and protected.

68   Given the pressing need to afford adequate protection to United Nations personnel engaged in life-endangering circumstances, I recommend that the Security Council, unless it elects immediately to withdraw the United Nations presence in order to preserve the credibility of the Organization, gravely consider what action should be taken towards those who put United Nations personnel in danger. Before deployment takes place, the Council should keep open the option of considering in advance collective measures, possibly including those under Chapter VII when a threat to international peace and security is also involved, to come into effect should the purpose of the United Nations operation systematically be frustrated and hostilities occur.

IX. Financing

69   A chasm has developed between the tasks entrusted to this Organization and the financial means provided to it. The truth of the matter is that our vision cannot really extend to the prospect opening before us as long as our financing remains myopic. There are two main areas of concern: the ability of the Organization to function over the longer term; and immediate requirements to respond to a crisis.

70   To remedy the financial situation of the United Nations in all its aspects, my distinguished predecessor repeatedly drew the attention of Member States to the increasingly impossible situation that has arisen and, during the forty-sixth session of the General Assembly, made a number of proposals. Those proposals which remain before the Assembly, and with which I am in broad agreement, are the following:

Proposal one: This suggested the adoption of a set of measures to deal with the cash flow problems caused by the exceptionally high level of unpaid contributions as well as with the problem of inadequate working capital reserves:

(a) Charging interest on the amounts of assessed contributions that are not paid on time;

(b) Suspending certain financial regulations of the United Nations to permit the retention of budgetary surpluses;

(c) Increasing the Working Capital Fund to a level of $250 million and endorsing the principle that the level of the Fund should be approximately 25 per cent of the annual assessment under the regular budget;

(d) Establishment of a temporary Peace-keeping Reserve Fund, at a level of $50 million, to meet initial expenses of peace-keeping operations pending receipt of assessed contributions;

(e) Authorization to the Secretary-General to borrow commercially, should other sources of cash be inadequate.

Proposal two: This suggested the creation of a Humanitarian Revolving Fund in the order of $50 million, to be used in emergency humanitarian situations. The proposal has since been implemented.

Proposal three: This suggested the establishment of a United Nations Peace Endowment Fund, with an initial target of $1 billion. The Fund would be created by a combination of assessed and voluntary contributions, with the latter being sought from Governments, the private sector as well as individuals. Once the Fund reached its target level, the proceeds from the investment of its principal would be used to finance the initial costs of authorized peace-keeping operations, other conflict resolution measures and related activities.

71   In addition to these proposals, others have been added in recent months in the course of public discussion. These ideas include: a levy on arms sales that could be related to maintaining an Arms Register by the United Nations; a levy on international air

travel, which is dependent on the maintenance of peace; authorization for the United Nations to borrow from the World Bank and the International Monetary Fund – for peace and development are interdependent; general tax exemption for contributions made to the United Nations by foundations, businesses and individuals; and changes in the formula for calculating the scale of assessments for peace-keeping operations.

72   As such ideas are debated, a stark fact remains: the financial foundations of the Organization daily grow weaker, debilitating its political will and practical capacity to undertake new and essential activities. This state of affairs must not continue. Whatever decisions are taken on financing the Organization, there is one inescapable necessity: Member States must pay their assessed contributions in full and on time. Failure to do so puts them in breach of their obligations under the Charter.

73   In these circumstances and on the assumption that Member States will be ready to finance operations for peace in a manner commensurate with their present, and welcome, readiness to establish them, I recommend the following:

(a) Immediate establishment of a revolving peace-keeping reserve fund of $50 million;

(b) Agreement that one third of the estimated cost of each new peace-keeping operation be appropriated by the General Assembly as soon as the Security Council decides to establish the operation; this would give the Secretary-General the necessary commitment authority and assure an adequate cash flow; the balance of the costs would be appropriated after the General Assembly approved the operation's budget;

(c) Acknowledgement by Member States that, under exceptional circumstances, political and operational considerations may make it necessary for the Secretary-General to employ his authority to place contracts without competitive bidding.

74   Member States wish the Organization to be managed with

the utmost efficiency and care. I am in full accord. I have taken important steps to streamline the Secretariat in order to avoid duplication and overlap while increasing its productivity. Additional changes and improvements will take place. As regards the United Nations system more widely, I continue to review the situation in consultation with my colleagues in the Administrative Committee on Coordination. The question of assuring financial security to the Organization over the long term is of such importance and complexity that public awareness and support must be heightened. I have therefore asked a select group of qualified persons of high international repute to examine this entire subject and to report to me. I intend to present their advice, together with my comments, for the consideration of the General Assembly, in full recognition of the special responsibility that the Assembly has, under the Charter, for financial and budgetary matters.

X. An Agenda for Peace

75   The nations and peoples of the United Nations are fortunate in a way that those of the League of Nations were not. We have been given a second chance to create the world of our Charter that they were denied. With the cold war ended we have drawn back from the brink of a confrontation that threatened the world and, too often, paralysed our Organization.

76   Even as we celebrate our restored possibilities, there is a need to ensure that the lessons of the past four decades are learned and that the errors, or variations of them, are not repeated. For there may not be a third opportunity for our planet which, now for different reasons, remains endangered.

77   The tasks ahead must engage the energy and attention of all components of the United Nations system – the General Assembly and other principal organs, the agencies and programmes. Each has, in a balanced scheme of things, a role and a responsibility.

78   Never again must the Security Council lose the collegiality

that is essential to its proper functioning, an attribute that it has gained after such trial. A genuine sense of consensus deriving from shared interests must govern its work, not the threat of the veto or the power of any group of nations. And it follows that agreement among the permanent members must have the deeper support of the other members of the Council, and the membership more widely, if the Council's decisions are to be effective and endure.

79   The Summit Meeting of the Security Council of 31 January 1992 provided a unique forum for exchanging views and strengthening cooperation. I recommend that the Heads of State and Government of the members of the Council meet in alternate years, just before the general debate commences in the General Assembly. Such sessions would permit exchanges on the challenges and dangers of the moment and stimulate ideas on how the United Nations may best serve to steer change into peaceful courses. I propose in addition that the Security Council continue to meet at the Foreign Minister level, as it has effectively done in recent years, whenever the situation warrants such meetings.

80   Power brings special responsibilities, and temptations. The powerful must resist the dual but opposite calls of unilateralism and isolationism if the United Nations is to succeed. For just as unilateralism at the global or regional level can shake the confidence of others, so can isolationism, whether it results from political choice or constitutional circumstance, enfeeble the global undertaking. Peace at home and the urgency of rebuilding and strengthening our individual societies necessitates peace abroad and cooperation among nations. The endeavours of the United Nations will require the fullest engagement of all of its Members, large and small, if the present renewed opportunity is to be seized.

81   Democracy within nations requires respect for human rights and fundamental freedoms, as set forth in the Charter. It requires as well a deeper understanding and respect for the rights of minorities and respect for the needs of the more vulnerable groups of society, especially women and children. This is not only a political matter. The social stability needed for productive growth is nurtured by

conditions in which people can readily express their will. For this, strong domestic institutions of participation are essential. Promoting such institutions means promoting the empowerment of the unorganized, the poor, the marginalized. To this end, the focus of the United Nations should be on the "field", the locations where economic, social and political decisions take effect. In furtherance of this I am taking steps to rationalize and in certain cases integrate the various programmes and agencies of the United Nations within specific countries. The senior United Nations official in each country should be prepared to serve, when needed, and with the consent of the host authorities, as my Representative on matters of particular concern.

82 Democracy within the family of nations means the application of its principles within the world Organization itself. This requires the fullest consultation, participation and engagement of all States, large and small, in the work of the Organization. All organs of the United Nations must be accorded, and play, their full and proper role so that the trust of all nations and peoples will be retained and deserved. The principles of the Charter must be applied consistently, not selectively, for if the perception should be of the latter, trust will wane and with it the moral authority which is the greatest and most unique quality of that instrument. Democracy at all levels is essential to attain peace for a new era of prosperity and justice.

83 Trust also requires a sense of confidence that the world Organization will react swiftly, surely and impartially and that it will not be debilitated by political opportunism or by administrative or financial inadequacy. This presupposes a strong, efficient and independent international civil service whose integrity is beyond question and an assured financial basis that lifts the Organization, once and for all, out of its present mendicancy.

84 Just as it is vital that each of the organs of the United Nations employ its capabilities in the balanced and harmonious fashion envisioned in the Charter, peace in the largest sense cannot be accomplished by the United Nations system or by Governments alone. Non-governmental organizations, academic institutions, parliamentarians, business and professional communities, the media and the public at large must all be involved. This will strengthen the world Organization's ability to reflect the concerns and interests of its widest constituency, and those who become more involved can carry the word of United Nations initiatives and build a deeper understanding of its work.

85 Reform is a continuing process, and improvement can have no limit. Yet there is an expectation, which I wish to see fulfilled, that the present phase in the renewal of this Organization should be complete by 1995, its Fiftieth Anniversary. The pace set must therefore be increased if the United Nations is to keep ahead of the acceleration of history that characterizes this age. We must be guided not by precedents alone, however wise these may be, but by the needs of the future and by the shape and content that we wish to give it.

86 I am committed to broad dialogue between the Member States and the Secretary-General. And I am committed to fostering a full and open interplay between all institutions and elements of the Organization so that the Charter's objectives may not only be better served, but that this Organization may emerge as greater than the sum of its parts. The United Nations was created with a great and courageous vision. Now is the time, for its nations and peoples, and the men and women who serve it, to seize the moment for the sake of the future.

Notes

1/   *See S/23500, statement by the President of the Council, section entitled "Peace-making and peace-keeping". [Reproduced on page 117]*

2/   *General Assembly resolution 37/10, annex.*

3/   *General Assembly resolution 43/51, annex.*

Section Two
RELATED
UN DOCUMENTS

LIST OF REPRODUCED DOCUMENTS

Resolutions of the General Assembly

An Agenda for Peace:
preventive diplomacy and related matters
A/RES/47/120 A, 18 December 1992

The General Assembly,

Recalling the statement of 31 January 1992, adopted at the conclusion of the first meeting held by the Security Council at the level of Heads of State and Government,[1/*] in which the Secretary-General was invited to prepare, for circulation to the States Members of the United Nations by 1 July 1992, an "analysis and recommendations on ways of strengthening and making more efficient within the framework and provisions of the Charter the capacity of the United Nations for preventive diplomacy, for peacemaking and for peace-keeping",

Welcoming the timely presentation of the forward-looking report of the Secretary-General entitled *An Agenda for Peace,*[2/] in response to the summit meeting of the Security Council, as a set of recommendations that deserve close examination by the international community,

Recognizing the need to maintain the increased interest in and momentum for revitalization of the Organization to meet the challenges of the new phase of international relations in order to fulfil the purposes and principles of the Charter of the United Nations,

Stressing that the implementation of the concepts and proposals contained in *An Agenda for Peace* should be in strict conformity with the provisions of the Charter, in particular its purposes and principles,

Recalling also its resolution 2625 (XXV) of 24 October 1970, the annex to which contains the Declaration on Principles of International Law concerning Friendly Relations and Cooperation among States in accordance with the Charter of the United Nations, and its resolution 43/51 of 5 December 1988, the annex to which contains the Declaration on the Prevention and Removal of Disputes

---

* *Footnotes have been placed at the end of each reproduced document.*

and Situations Which May Threaten International Peace and Security and on the Role of the United Nations in this Field,

Emphasizing that international peace and security must be seen in an integrated manner and that the efforts of the Organization to build peace, justice, stability and security must encompass not only military matters, but also, through its various organs within their respective areas of competence, relevant political, economic, social, humanitarian, environmental and developmental aspects,

Stressing the need for international action to strengthen the socio-economic development of Member States as one of the means of enhancing international peace and security and, in this regard, recognizing the need to complement an Agenda for Peace with an Agenda for Development,

Acknowledging that timely application of preventive diplomacy is the most desirable and efficient means of easing tensions before they result in conflict,

Recognizing that preventive diplomacy may require such measures as confidence-building, early-warning, fact-finding and other measures in which consultations with Member States, discretion, confidentiality, objectivity and transparency should be combined as appropriate,

Emphasizing the need to strengthen the capacity of the United Nations in the field of preventive diplomacy, through, *inter alia*, allocating appropriate staff resources and financial resources for preventive diplomacy, in order to assist Member States to resolve their differences in a peaceful manner,

Reaffirming the fundamental importance of a sound and secure financial basis for the United Nations in order, *inter alia*, to enable the Organization to play an effective role in preventive diplomacy,

Emphasizing the importance of cooperation between the United Nations and regional arrangements and organizations for preventive diplomacy within their respective areas of competence,

Emphasizing also that respect for the principles of sovereignty, territorial integrity and political independence of States is crucial to any common endeavour to promote international peace and security,

Recalling further other resolutions adopted by the Assembly during its forty-seventh session concerning various aspects of an Agenda for Peace,

Emphasizing the need for all organs and bodies of the United Nations, as appropriate, to intensify their efforts to strengthen the role of the Organization in preventive diplomacy, peacemaking, peace-keeping and peace-building and to continue the discussion of the report of the Secretary-General with a view to adequate action being taken,

Stressing the need for adequate protection of personnel involved in preventive diplomacy, peacemaking, peace-keeping and humanitarian operations, in accordance with relevant norms and principles of international law,

Noting the definition of preventive diplomacy provided by the Secretary-General in his report entitled *An Agenda for Peace,*[2/]

I. Peaceful settlement of disputes

Emphasizing the need to promote the peaceful settlement of disputes,

1. *Invites* Member States to seek solutions to their disputes at an early stage through such peaceful means as provided for in the Charter of the United Nations;

2. *Decides* to explore ways and means for a full utilization of the provisions of the Charter whereby the General Assembly may recommend measures for the peaceful adjustment of any situation, regardless of origin, which is deemed likely to impair the general welfare or friendly relations among nations;

3. *Encourages* the Security Council to utilize fully the provisions of Chapter VI of the Charter on procedures and methods for peaceful settlement of disputes and to call upon the parties concerned to settle their disputes peacefully;

4. *Encourages* the Secretary-General and the Security Council to engage at an early stage in close and continu-

ous consultation in order to develop, on a case-by-case basis, an appropriate strategy for the peaceful settlement of specific disputes, including the participation of other organs, organizations and agencies of the United Nations system, as well as regional arrangements and organizations as appropriate, and invites the Secretary-General to report to the General Assembly on such consultations;

II. Early-warning, collection of information and analysis

Recognizing the need to strengthen the capacity of the United Nations for early-warning, collection of information and analysis,

1. *Encourages* the Secretary-General to set up an adequate early-warning mechanism for situations which are likely to endanger the maintenance of international peace and security, in close cooperation with Member States and United Nations agencies, as well as regional arrangements and organizations, as appropriate, making use of the information available to these organizations and/or received from Member States, and to keep Member States informed of the mechanism established;

2. *Invites* the Secretary-General to strengthen the capacity of the Secretariat for the collection of information and analysis to serve better the early-warning needs of the Organization and, to that end, encourages the Secretary-General to ensure that staff members receive proper training in all aspects of preventive diplomacy, including the collection and analysis of information;

3. *Invites* Member States and regional arrangements and organizations to provide timely early-warning information, on a confidential basis when appropriate, to the Secretary-General;

4. *Encourages* the Secretary-General to continue, in accordance with Article 99 of the Charter of the United

Nations, to bring to the attention of the Security Council, at his discretion, any matter which in his opinion may threaten the maintenance of international peace and security, together with his recommendations thereon;

5. *Invites* Member States to support the efforts of the Secretary-General in preventive diplomacy, including by providing assistance he may require;

6. *Encourages* the Secretary-General, in accordance with the relevant provisions of the Charter, to notify the General Assembly, as appropriate, of any situation which is potentially dangerous or might lead to international friction or dispute;

7. *Invites* the Secretary-General to bring to the attention of Member States concerned, at an early stage, any matter which in his opinion may adversely affect relations between States;

III. Fact-finding

Recalling the statements made by the President of the Security Council, on behalf of the Council, on 29 October[3/] and 30 November 1992,[4/] and its own resolutions 1967 (XVIII) of 16 December 1963, 2104 (XX) of 20 December 1965, 2182 (XXI) of 12 December 1966 and 2329 (XXII) of 18 December 1967 on the question of methods of fact-finding,

1. *Reaffirms* its resolution 46/59 of 9 December 1991, the annex to which contains the Declaration on Fact-finding by the United Nations in the Field of the Maintenance of International Peace and Security, particularly its guidelines;

2. *Recommends* to the Secretary-General that he should continue to utilize the services of eminent and qualified experts in fact-finding and other missions, selected on

as wide a geographical basis as possible, taking into
account candidates with the highest standards of efficiency, competence and integrity;

3. *Invites* Member States to submit names of suitable individuals whom the Secretary-General might wish to use
at his discretion in fact-finding and other missions;

4. *Recommends* that a request by a Member State for the
dispatch of a fact-finding mission to its territory should
be considered expeditiously;

5. *Invites* the Secretary-General to continue to dispatch
fact-finding and other missions in a timely manner in
order to assist him in the proper discharge of his functions under the Charter of the United Nations;

IV. Confidence-building measures

Recognizing that the application of appropriate confidence-
building measures, consistent with national security needs, would
promote mutual confidence and good faith, which are essential to
reducing the likelihood of conflicts between States and enhancing
prospects for the peaceful settlement of disputes,

Recalling its resolutions 43/78 H of 7 December 1988 and
45/62 F of 4 December 1990, as well as its resolution 47/54 D of 9
December 1992 on the implementation of the guidelines for appropriate types of confidence-building measures,

Recognizing that confidence-building measures may
encompass both military and non-military matters, including political, economic and social matters,

Stressing the need to encourage Member States, and regional
arrangements and organizations where relevant and in a manner consistent with their mandates, to play a leading role in developing confidence-building measures appropriate to the region concerned and
to coordinate their efforts in this regard with the United Nations in
accordance with Chapter VIII of the Charter of the United Nations,

1. *Invites* Member States and regional arrangements and organizations to inform the Secretary-General through appropriate channels about their experiences in confidence-building measures in their respective regions;
2. *Supports* the intention of the Secretary-General to consult on a regular basis with Member States and regional arrangements and organizations on further confidence-building measures;
3. *Encourages* the Secretary-General to consult with parties to existing or potential disputes, the continuance of which is likely to endanger the maintenance of international peace and security, and with other interested Member States and regional arrangements and organizations, as appropriate, on the possibility of initiating confidence-building measures in their respective regions and to keep Member States informed thereon in consultation with the parties concerned;
4. *Commends* such confidence-building measures as the promotion of openness and restraint in the production, procurement and deployment of armaments, the systematic exchange of military missions, the possible formation of regional risk reduction centres, arrangements for the free flow of information and the monitoring of regional arms control and disarmament agreements;

V. Humanitarian assistance

Recalling its resolution 45/100 of 14 December 1990 on humanitarian assistance to victims of natural disasters and similar emergency situations and its resolution 46/182 of 19 December 1991 on the strengthening of the coordination of emergency humanitarian assistance of the United Nations,

Welcoming the increasing role of the United Nations system in providing humanitarian assistance,

Noting that, in certain circumstances, programmes of impartially-provided humanitarian assistance and peace-keeping operations can be mutually supportive,

1. *Encourages* the Secretary-General to continue to strengthen the capacity of the Organization in order to ensure coordinated planning and execution of humanitarian assistance programmes, drawing upon the specialized skills and resources of all parts of the United Nations system, as well as those of non-governmental organizations, as appropriate;

2. *Also encourages* the Secretary-General to continue to address the question of coordination, when necessary, between humanitarian assistance programmes and peace-keeping or related operations, preserving the non-political, neutral and impartial character of humanitarian action;

3. *Invites* the Secretary-General to bring to the attention of appropriate organs of the United Nations any situation requiring urgent humanitarian assistance in order to prevent its deterioration, which might lead to international friction or dispute;

VI. Resources and logistical aspects of preventive diplomacy

Recognizing the need for adequate resources in support of the United Nations efforts in preventive diplomacy,

1. *Invites* Member States to provide political and practical support to the Secretary-General in his efforts for the peaceful settlement of disputes, including early-warning, fact-finding, good offices and mediation;

2. *Also invites* Member States, on a voluntary basis, to provide the Secretary-General with any necessary additional expertise and logistical resources that he might

require for the successful execution of these functions of increasing importance;

VII. Role of the General Assembly in preventive diplomacy

Emphasizing that, together with the Security Council and the Secretary-General, it has an important role in preventive diplomacy,

Recognizing that, having an important role in preventive diplomacy, it has to work in close cooperation and coordination with the Security Council and the Secretary-General in accordance with the Charter of the United Nations and consistent with their respective mandates and responsibilities,

Decides to explore ways and means to support the recommendations of the Secretary-General in his report entitled *An Agenda for Peace*[2/] to promote the utilization of the General Assembly, in accordance with the relevant provisions of the Charter of the United Nations, by Member States so as to bring greater influence to bear in pre-empting or containing any situation which is potentially dangerous or might lead to international friction or dispute;

VIII. Future work

Bearing in mind that owing to time constraints it could not examine all the proposals contained in the report of the Secretary-General entitled *An Agenda for Peace*,[2/]

1. *Decides* to continue early in 1993 its examination of other recommendations on preventive diplomacy and related matters contained in the report of the Secretary-General entitled *An Agenda for Peace*, including preventive deployment, demilitarized zones and the International Court of Justice, as well as implementa-

tion of the provisions of Article 50 of the Charter of the United Nations, in conformity with the Charter and taking into account the relevant developments and practices in the competent organs of the United Nations;

2. *Also decides* to discuss and consider other proposals contained in *An Agenda for Peace*.

1/ S/23500.
2/ A/47/277-S/24111.
3/ S/24728.
4/ S/24872.

An Agenda for Peace
A/RES/47/120 B, 20 September 1993

The General Assembly,

Recalling its resolution 47/120 A of 18 December 1992 entitled "An Agenda for Peace: preventive diplomacy and related matters",

Reaffirming its resolution 46/59 of 9 December 1991, the annex to which contains the Declaration on Fact-finding by the United Nations in the Field of the Maintenance of International Peace and Security,

Recalling also its resolution 46/182 of 19 December 1991 on the strengthening of the coordination of humanitarian emergency assistance of the United Nations,

Recalling further its resolution 47/71 of 14 December 1992 on the comprehensive review of the whole question of peace-keeping operations in all their aspects,

Emphasizing that, together with the Security Council and the Secretary-General, it has an important role in preventive diplomacy,

Recognizing that it has to work in close cooperation and coordination with the Security Council and the Secretary-General in accordance with the Charter of the United Nations and consistent with their respective mandates and responsibilities,

I. Role of the General Assembly

Recalling the relevant provisions of the Charter of the United Nations relating to the functions and powers of the General Assembly,

Recalling also the report of the Secretary-General entitled *An Agenda for Peace*,[1/] which refers to the utilization of these functions and powers,

1. *Resolves* to make full and effective use of the functions and powers set out in Articles 10 and 14 of the Charter of the United Nations, in conformity with other relevant provisions of the Charter;

2. *Decides* to consider the use of existing or new machinery, including subsidiary organs under Article 22 of the Charter, to facilitate consideration of any situation coming within the scope of Article 14 of the Charter, with a view to recommending measures for the peaceful adjustment of such a situation;

3. *Also decides* to consider appropriate ways and means consistent with the Charter to improve cooperation among the competent United Nations organs in order to strengthen the role of the United Nations in the promotion of peace, including the possibility that the General Assembly receives reports, as appropriate, from the Secretary-General on matters related to the items on its agenda or on other matters within its competence;

II. Preventive deployment and demilitarized zones

Taking note of paragraphs 28 to 33 on preventive deployment and demilitarized zones contained in the report of the Secretary-General entitled *An Agenda for Peace*,[1] within the larger context of preventive diplomacy, as well as the views expressed on these issues by Member States,

Stressing that the implementation of any concepts and proposals on preventive deployment and demilitarized zones contained in *An Agenda for Peace* should be undertaken in accordance with the provisions of the Charter of the United Nations, in particular its purposes and principles, and other relevant principles of international law,

Welcoming the instances of effective use of United Nations preventive deployment and the establishment of demilitarized zones,

Stressing the importance of appropriate consultations with Member States and transparency in any decision-making concerning the undertaking of preventive deployment or the establishment of a demilitarized zone,

Recognizing that a United Nations preventive deployment or the establishment of demilitarized zones could promote the prevention or containment of conflicts, the continuance of which is likely to endanger the maintenance of international peace and security,

Emphasizing that respect for the principles of sovereignty, territorial integrity and political independence of States and non-intervention in matters which are essentially within the domestic jurisdiction of any State is crucial to any common endeavour to promote international peace and security,

Bearing in mind that, as each situation in which preventive deployment may be undertaken or a demilitarized zone established has its own special characteristics, it is of the utmost importance to make decisions on such measures on a case-by-case basis with due regard to all relevant factors and circumstances, including consultations with Member States,

Recognizing the need to preserve the impartiality of the United Nations when engaged in preventive deployment or in the establishment of demilitarized zones,

Recognizing also that preventive deployment and the establishment of demilitarized zones are evolving concepts,

1. *Acknowledges* the importance of considering, on a case-by-case basis, the use of preventive deployment and/or the establishment of demilitarized zones as a means to prevent existing or potential disputes from escalating into conflicts and to promote efforts to achieve the peaceful settlement of such disputes, the continuance of which is likely to endanger the maintenance of international peace and security;

2. *Reaffirms* that a United Nations preventive deployment and/or the establishment of a demilitarized zone should be undertaken with the consent of and, in principle, on

the basis of a request by the Member State or Member
States involved, having taken into account the positions
of other States concerned and all other relevant factors;

3. *Also reaffirms* that a United Nations preventive deployment and/or the establishment of a demilitarized zone
should be undertaken in accordance with the provisions
of the Charter of the United Nations, in particular its
purposes and principles and other relevant principles of
international law, also taking into account relevant
General Assembly and Security Council resolutions;

4. *Invites* the competent organs of the United Nations,
within their respective mandates, to consider implementing preventive deployment and/or the establishment of a
demilitarized zone with the objective of preventing conflict and of promoting efforts to achieve the peaceful settlement of disputes, and to continue to examine practical, operational and financial aspects of such preventive
deployment and demilitarized zones with a view to
increasing their efficacy and effectiveness;

III. Use of the International Court of Justice in the peaceful settlement of disputes

Emphasizing the role of the International Court of Justice
under the Charter of the United Nations in the peaceful settlement
of disputes,

1. *Encourages* States to consider making greater use of the
International Court of Justice for the peaceful settlement of disputes;

2. *Recommends* that States consider the possibility of
accepting the jurisdiction of the International Court of
Justice, including through the dispute settlement clauses
of multilateral treaties;

3. *Notes* that the use of chambers of the International

Court of Justice for dealing with particular cases submitted to the Court by the parties is a means of providing increased use of the Court for the peaceful settlement of disputes;

4. *Requests* States to consider making, if possible on a regular basis, contributions to the Trust Fund of the Secretary-General to assist States in resolving their disputes through the International Court of Justice, and invites the Secretary-General to report periodically both on the financial status and the utilization of the Fund;

5. *Recalls* that the General Assembly or the Security Council may request the International Court of Justice to give an advisory opinion on any legal question, and that other organs of the United Nations and specialized agencies, which may at any time be so authorized by the General Assembly, may also request advisory opinions of the Court on legal questions arising within the scope of their activities;

6. *Decides* to keep under examination all the recommendations of the Secretary-General concerning the International Court of Justice, including those related to the use of the advisory competence of the Court;

IV. Special economic problems arising from the implementation of preventive or enforcement measures

Recalling Article 50 of the Charter of the United Nations, which entitles States that find themselves confronted with special economic problems arising from the carrying out of preventive or enforcement measures taken by the Security Council against any other State to consult the Council with regard to a solution to those problems,

Recalling also the recommendation of the Secretary-General in his report entitled *An Agenda for Peace* that the Security

Council devise a set of measures involving the financial institutions and other components of the United Nations system that can be put in place to insulate States from such difficulties and his view that such measures would be a matter of equity and a means of encouraging States to cooperate with decisions of the Council,

Recalling further the statement made on 30 December 1992 by the President of the Security Council,[2/] in which the Council expressed its determination to consider this matter further and invited the Secretary-General to consult with the heads of international financial institutions, other components of the United Nations system and Member States of the United Nations, and to report to the Council as early as possible,

Recalling its resolution 47/120 A entitled "An Agenda for Peace: preventive diplomacy and related matters", in which it decided to continue early in 1993 its examination of other recommendations contained in the report of the Secretary-General entitled *An Agenda for Peace*, including implementation of the provisions of Article 50 of the Charter, in conformity with the Charter and taking into account the relevant developments and practices in the competent organs of the United Nations,

Stressing the importance of economic and other measures not involving the use of armed forces in maintaining international peace and security, in accordance with Article 41 of the Charter,

Recalling Article 49 of the Charter, which requires the Members of the United Nations to join in affording mutual assistance in carrying out the measures decided upon by the Security Council,

Noting that the implementation of Article 50 of the Charter has been addressed recently in several forums, including the General Assembly and its subsidiary organs and the Security Council,

Recognizing that, in the conditions of economic interdependence that exist today, the implementation of preventive or enforcement measures under Chapter VII of the Charter against any State continues to create special economic problems for certain other States,

Recalling that Member States have engaged previously in consultations with bodies established by the Security Council regarding special economic problems confronted by them as a result of the implementation of preventive or enforcement measures against Iraq and the Federal Republic of Yugoslavia (Serbia and Montenegro),

Concerned that certain States continue to be confronted with adverse economic problems owing to the implementation of preventive and enforcement measures under Chapter VII of the Charter,

Recognizing the need for appropriate means to find solutions to these problems as soon as possible,

1. *Decides* to continue its examination of ways to implement Article 50 of the Charter of the United Nations, with a view to finding solutions to the special economic problems of other Member States when preventive or enforcement measures are decided upon by the Security Council against a State;

2. *Invites* the Security Council to consider what could be done within the United Nations system and involving international financial institutions with regard to solutions to the special economic problems of States arising from the carrying out of the measures imposed by the Council and to consider, *inter alia*, the following measures:

    (a) Strengthening of the consultative process for studying, reporting on and suggesting solutions to the special economic problems, with a view to minimizing such economic problems through consultations with States adversely affected or, as appropriate, with States likely to be adversely affected as a result of their implementing the preventive or enforcement measures, as well as with the Secretary-General, the principal organs, programmes and agencies of the United Nations, and international financial institutions;

    (b) Other measures, in consultation with Member States

and, as appropriate, with international financial institutions, such as voluntary funds to provide assistance to States experiencing special economic problems arising from carrying out the measures imposed by the Security Council, additional credit lines, assistance for the promotion of exports of the affected countries, assistance for technical cooperation projects in such countries and/or assistance for the promotion of investment in the affected countries;

3. *Also invites* the committees of the Security Council and other bodies entrusted with the task of monitoring the implementation of preventive and enforcement measures to take into account, in discharging their mandates, the need to avoid unnecessary adverse consequences for other Member States, without prejudice to the effectiveness of such measures;

4. *Requests* the Secretary-General to report annually to the General Assembly on the implementation of Article 50 of the Charter;

V. Post-conflict peace-building

Noting that post-conflict peace-building is a new and evolving concept,

Recognizing the need for sustained cooperative efforts by the United Nations to deal with the underlying economic, social, cultural and humanitarian causes and effects of conflicts in order to promote a durable foundation for peace,

Recalling the provisions of Article 55 of the Charter of the United Nations,

Recognizing also that the concept of post-conflict peace-building is aimed at the creation of a new environment to forestall the recurrence of conflicts,

Bearing in mind that each situation in which post-conflict peace-building may be undertaken is unique and therefore should be considered on a case-by-case basis,

Bearing in mind also that post-conflict peace-building should complement efforts at peacemaking and peace-keeping in order to consolidate peace and advance a sense of confidence and well-being among people and States,

1. *Acknowledges* the usefulness of the proposals of the Secretary-General contained in paragraphs 55 to 59 of his report entitled *An Agenda for Peace*[1], particularly in relation to the range of activities for post-conflict peace-building;

2. *Emphasizes* that post-conflict peace-building should be carried out in accordance with the Charter of the United Nations, in particular the principles of sovereign equality and political independence of States, territorial integrity, and non-intervention in matters that are essentially within the domestic jurisdiction of any State;

3. *Recalls* that each State has the right freely to choose and develop its political, social, economic and cultural systems;

4. *Stresses* that activities related to post-conflict peace-building should be carried out within a well-defined time-frame;

5. *Also stresses* that post-conflict peace-building be undertaken on the basis of agreements ending conflicts or reached after conflicts, or at the request of the Government or Governments concerned;

6. *Emphasizes* the need for measures to promote peace and cooperation among previously conflicting parties;

7. *Stresses* the need for coordinated action by relevant components of the United Nations system, including the contributions that the international financial institutions can make in the area of socio-economic development in post-conflict peace-building;

8. *Also stresses* the importance for post-conflict peace-building of contributions from diverse sources, includ-

ing components of the United Nations system, regional organizations, Member States and non-governmental organizations;

9. *Requests* the Secretary-General to inform the General Assembly of requests relating to post-conflict peace-building by the Government or Governments concerned, or emanating from peace agreements ending conflicts or reached after conflicts by parties concerned;

10. *Affirms* its readiness to support, as appropriate, post-conflict peace-building;

VI. Cooperation with regional arrangements and organizations

Recognizing the importance of the role of regional organizations and arrangements in dealing with such matters relating to the maintenance of international peace and security as are appropriate for regional action, and the need to enhance, in this respect, cooperation between such organizations and arrangements and the United Nations,

Recalling Chapter VIII of the Charter of the United Nations and its acknowledgement of the role of regional arrangements and agencies in dealing with such matters relating to the maintenance of international peace and security as are appropriate for regional action, provided that such arrangements or agencies and their activities are consistent with the purposes and principles of the United Nations,

Taking into account the experience gained and the favourable results achieved by regional organizations in the peaceful settlement of disputes in different parts of the world,

1. *Recognizes* that regional organizations, arrangements and agencies can, in their fields of competence and in accordance with the Charter of the United Nations, make important contributions to the maintenance of international peace and security, preventive diplomacy,

peacemaking, peace-keeping and post-conflict peace-building;

2. *Encourages* regional organizations, arrangements and agencies to consider, as appropriate, in their fields of competence, ways and means for promoting closer cooperation and coordination with the United Nations with the objective of contributing to the fulfilment of the purposes and principles of the Charter;

3. *Also encourages* the Secretary-General to continue his efforts at promoting cooperation between the United Nations and regional organizations, arrangements and agencies, in accordance with the Charter;

VII. Safety of personnel

Recalling its resolution 47/72 of 14 December 1992 on protection of peace-keeping personnel, and all other relevant resolutions,

Bearing in mind the concern expressed by the Secretary-General over the safety of United Nations personnel in his report entitled *An Agenda for Peace*,[1]

Also recalling the relevant resolutions of the Security Council,

Taking note with appreciation of the statement made on 31 March 1993 by the President of the Security Council on the protection of United Nations forces and personnel,[3]

Noting with appreciation the work done by the Special Committee on Peace-keeping Operations on the issue of the status and safety of United Nations peace-keeping personnel,

Gravely concerned about the growing number of fatalities and injuries among United Nations peace-keeping and other personnel resulting from deliberate hostile actions in dangerous areas of deployment,

1. *Welcomes* the report of the Secretary-General on the security of United Nations operations;[4]

2. *Decides* to consider further steps to enhance the status and safety of United Nations personnel involved in United Nations operations, taking into account the need for concerted action by all relevant bodies of the United Nations in this regard.

1/ *A/47/277-S/24111.*
2/ *See S/25493.*
3/ *A/48/173.*
4/ *A/48/349-S/26358.*

Question of responsibility for attacks on United Nations and associated personnel and measures to ensure that those responsible for such attacks are brought to justice
A/RES/48/37, 9 December 1993

The General Assembly,

Recalling the report of the Secretary-General entitled *An Agenda for Peace*[1/] and General Assembly resolution 47/120 B of 20 September 1993,

Recalling also its resolution 47/72 of 14 December 1992,

Gravely concerned at the increasing number of attacks on United Nations personnel that have caused death or serious injury,

Recalling further the statement made by the President of the Security Council, on behalf of the Council, on 31 March 1993,[2/] in which the Security Council, *inter alia*, recognized the need for all relevant bodies of the Organization to take concerted action to enhance the safety and security of United Nations forces and personnel,

Recalling the report of the Special Committee on Peacekeeping Operations,[3/]

Having considered the report of the Secretary-General of 27 August 1993 on the security of United Nations operations,[4/]

Recalling also Security Council resolution 868 (1993) of 29 September 1993,

Noting with appreciation the draft proposals submitted by the delegations of New Zealand[5/] and Ukraine[6/] under this item,

Welcoming the oral report of the Chairman of the Working Group established under the item,[7/]

1. *Decides* to establish an Ad Hoc Committee open to all Member States to elaborate an international convention dealing with the safety and security of United Nations and associated personnel, with particular reference to responsibility for attacks on such personnel;

2. *Decides also* that the Ad Hoc Committee shall be autho-

rized to hold a session from 28 March to 8 April 1994 and, if the Committee itself so decides, to hold a further session from 1 to 12 August 1994, to prepare the text of a draft convention, taking into account any suggestions and proposals from States, as well as comments and suggestions that the Secretary-General may wish to provide on this subject, and bearing in mind views expressed during the debate on this item at the forty-eighth session of the General Assembly;

3. *Requests* the Secretary-General to provide the Ad Hoc Committee with the necessary facilities for the performance of its work;

4. *Requests* the Ad Hoc Committee to report to the General Assembly at its forty-ninth session on progress made towards the elaboration of the draft convention;

5. *Recommends* that at its forty-ninth session a working group be re-established in the framework of the Sixth Committee in the event that further work is required for the elaboration of the draft convention;

6. *Decides* to include in the provisional agenda of its forty-ninth session the item entitled "Question of responsibility for attacks on United Nations and associated personnel and measures to ensure that those responsible for such attacks are brought to justice".

1/ *A/47/277-S/24111.*
2/ *See S/25493.*
3/ *A/48/173.*
4/ *A/48/349-S/26358.*
5/ *A/C.6/48/L.2.*
6/ *A/C.6/48/L.3.*
7/ *See A/C.6/48/SR.29.*

Comprehensive review of the whole question of peace-keeping operations in all their aspects
A/RES/48/42, 10 December 1993

The General Assembly,

Recalling its resolution 2006 (XIX) of 18 February 1965 and all other relevant resolutions,

Recalling in particular its resolutions 47/71 and 47/72 of 14 December 1992,

Welcoming the progress made by the Special Committee on Peace-keeping Operations during its recent sessions,

Convinced that peace-keeping operations constitute a considerable part of the efforts by the United Nations to maintain international peace and security and to enhance the effectiveness of the United Nations in this regard,

Recognizing that the peacemaking activities of the Secretary-General and of organs of the United Nations, which are actions to bring hostile parties to agreement essentially through peaceful means such as those foreseen in Chapter VI of the Charter of the United Nations, constitute an essential function of the United Nations and are among the important means for the prevention, containment and resolution of disputes, the continuance of which is likely to endanger the maintenance of international peace and security,

Emphasizing that respect for the principles of sovereignty, territorial integrity and political independence of States and non-intervention in matters which are essentially within the domestic jurisdiction of any States is crucial to any common endeavour to promote international peace and security,

Taking note of the statement by the President of the Security Council of 28 May 1993 and the recommendations contained therein,[1/]

Convinced that in order to ensure the effectiveness of peace-keeping operations it is necessary that they have precise and clearly defined mandates,

Taking into account that the increase in activities in the field of United Nations peace-keeping requires both increasing and better managed human, financial and material resources for the Organization,

   Aware of the extremely difficult financial situation of the United Nations as described in the report of the Secretary-General[2/] and of the heavy burden on all the troop contributors, many of which are developing countries,

   Taking note of the report of the Secretary-General on the work of the Organization,[3/] having examined the report of the Special Committee on Peace-keeping Operations,[4/] and being aware of the relevant parts of the report of the Joint Inspection Unit on staffing of the United Nations peace-keeping and related missions (civilian component),[5/]

   1.   *Welcomes* the report of the Special Committee on Peace-keeping Operations[4/];

Resources

   2.   *Notes with appreciation* the initiative of the Secretary-General in establishing a stand-by forces planning team and looks forward to periodic reports on that initiative;

   3.   *Recommends* that contact between the Secretariat and Member States should be enhanced with a view to clarifying the military and civilian needs for United Nations peace-keeping operations and such capabilities of Member States as could be made available for those operations;

   4.   *Encourages* Member States, to the extent that their domestic arrangements permit, to develop, in cooperation with the Secretariat, arrangements for military, police and civilian personnel to participate in peace-keeping operations and to notify the Secretary-General of the existence and the modalities of such arrangements on an ongoing basis;

   5.   *Calls upon* the Secretary-General to develop a proposal for regularly updated data banks recording the type and availability of resources Member States could provide, as described in paragraph 4 above, as well as individuals with skills appropriate for civilian

peace-keeping duties, and invites the Secretary-General to propose such other measures as he believes necessary to meet the urgent need for timely availability of personnel qualified to serve in the full spectrum of civilian peace-keeping capacities;

6. *Stresses* the need for the United Nations to be given the resources commensurate with its growing responsibilities in the area of peace-keeping, particularly with regard to the resources needed for the start-up phase of such operations;

7. *Takes note* of the recommendations of the Secretary-General concerning the timely provision of basic peace-keeping equipment,[6/] and suggests the development of a limited revolving reserve of such equipment within existing resources;

8. *Invites* the Secretary-General to consult in advance with Member States on their willingness to earmark certain equipment specified by the Secretary-General for immediate sale, loan or donation to the United Nations when required;

9. *Encourages* Member States to make available air- and sea-lift resources to the United Nations at the best available rates in accordance with the Financial Regulations and Rules of the United Nations;

10. *Requests* the Secretariat to develop guidelines concerning the disposition of United Nations equipment upon the termination of a peace-keeping operation;

Finances

11. *Recalls* that the financing of peace-keeping operations is the collective responsibility of all Member States in accordance with Article 17, paragraph 2, of the Charter of the United Nations, notes the report of the Secretary-General on improving the financial situation of the United Nations, reiterates its call upon all Member States to pay their assessed contributions in full and on time, and encourages States to make voluntary contributions in accordance with the Financial Regulations and Rules of the United Nations;

12. *Invites* the Secretary-General to review, as appropriate, the applicable United Nations financial and administrative regulations

concerning peace-keeping operations, and to that end urges that steps be taken to strengthen lateral communication and the distribution of information within the Secretariat;

13. *Requests* that the Secretary-General improve the financial control mechanisms relative to peace-keeping by strengthening the system of audit and inspection, including external controls, stresses the need to ensure that appropriate accountability is maintained, and in that regard notes with appreciation recent steps to strengthen the capacity for independent oversight and investigation;

14. *Stresses* the need to delegate the appropriate degree of financial and administrative authority to Force Commanders or Special Representatives while ensuring that measures relating to responsibility and accountability are strengthened in order to increase the missions' capacity to adjust to new situations and specific requirements;

15. *Notes* that a number of military officers have been made available on loan on a non-reimbursable basis to the Secretariat at its request, and welcomes the efforts of the Secretary-General to implement financial arrangements, within existing resources, which would enable all Member States to contribute to such a system in the future and would ease the costs borne by Member States contributing those officers;

16. *Calls* upon the Secretariat to prepare comprehensive budget estimates for all new and ongoing peace-keeping operations in a timely fashion in order to allow for a thorough examination by the Advisory Committee on Administrative and Budgetary Questions and the General Assembly;

17. *Stresses also* the importance of reimbursing all outstanding dues of troop-contributing or other participating States without delay, and notes the report of the Secretary-General in that regard;

18. *Reaffirms* the competence of the General Assembly for the appropriation and apportionment of the costs of United Nations peace-keeping operations, and notes the importance for the Security Council to be aware of, *inter alia*, the availability of adequate physical and material resources and the cost implications before it establishes new peace-keeping operations;

19. *Considers* that the issue of supplementing diversified financial resources to the assessed contributions should be studied further in all the appropriate United Nations forums;

20. *Encourages* the consideration in the appropriate forums of further measures that could improve the financing of peace-keeping operations, including the feasibility of an improved billing system;

21. *Requests* the Secretary-General to consult with Member States during his current review of the rates of reimbursement for depreciation of contingent-owned equipment deployed at the request of the United Nations;

22. *Requests* the Secretariat to compile all the existing financial and administrative rules, regulations, practices and procedures relating to peace-keeping into a comprehensive document available to Member States;

23. *Welcomes* the creation of the Peace-keeping Reserve Fund, notes the importance of adequate resources for peace-keeping start-up costs and that sufficient resources have not been made available for this purpose, stresses that the Fund should be supplied with the amount specified in its resolution 47/217 of 23 December 1992, thereby making the Fund operational as soon as possible, and emphasizes that the Fund should, in the future, serve as an essential source of funds for peace-keeping start-up costs;

Organization and effectiveness

24 *Suggests* that the Security Council and the Secretary-General should continue to analyse a given situation very carefully before the establishment of a United Nations peace-keeping operation, that a realistic mandate, including clear objectives and a time-frame for the resolution of the problem, as appropriate, should be formulated in each case, conducive to the furtherance of the political process and that the Security Council should review periodically the effectiveness of current operations with a view to ensuring that they are consistent with the objectives and the mandates as approved by the Council, and affirms that no change in the mandate, character or duration of peace-keeping operations authorized by the

Security Council is possible except through a specific decision of the Council;

25 *Notes* with appreciation the steps taken by the Secretary-General to strengthen and reform those units of the Secretariat dealing with peace-keeping, as outlined in his report on the implementation of the recommendations contained in "An Agenda for Peace";

26. *Stresses* the need for the Secretariat to deal effectively and efficiently with planning, launching, managing and providing administrative and logistics support to peace-keeping operations, and urges the Secretary-General, as the chief administrative officer of the Organization, in consultation with Member States, to initiate a comprehensive review of the role, tasks and functions, including civilian functions, of the various units of the Secretariat with a view to identifying the optimum Secretariat structure in that respect and to assuring the unity of command and control indispensable for successful peace-keeping by assigning executive responsibility for all aspects of a peace-keeping operation to the Department of Peace-keeping Operations of the Secretariat;

27. *Also stresses* the importance of coordination of all aspects of the planning process in peace-keeping operations, and suggests that the emergency relief coordinator should be fully consulted in the overall planning of a peace-keeping operation when the mandate for such an operation contains a humanitarian component and in other cases should be consulted at an early stage when close coordination between humanitarian and peace-keeping activities is required;

28. *Notes* the transfer of the Field Operations Division from the Department of Administration and Management to the Department of Peace-keeping Operations, and encourages the Secretary-General to continue his efforts to strengthen and make more effective the planning, management and administrative support for peace-keeping operations and the capability of the Secretariat for overall evaluation and analysis of peace-keeping operations from their initial stages to their conclusion;

29. *Urges* the Secretary-General in his review of Secretariat capabilities to improve information flow and to enhance coordina-

tion and communication between United Nations Headquarters and field missions in order to manage peace-keeping operations effectively and inform Member States as appropriate;

30. *Requests* the Secretary-General to keep Member States informed on organizational responsibilities of the various units of those Secretariat departments responsible for peace-keeping operations;

31. *Invites* the Secretary-General to identify a focal point for contact by Member States seeking information on all facets, including operational, logistics and administrative matters, of ongoing and planned peace-keeping operations;

32. *Also invites* the Secretary-General to continue arrangements and procedures for providing additional personnel on a short-term basis in order to ensure that the Secretariat can respond effectively and efficiently to fluctuations in its workload, particularly when new operations are planned and launched, and to keep the Member States informed of such procedures;

33. *Once again invites* the Secretary-General to consider means whereby Special Representatives, Force Commanders and other key personnel of newly approved missions are identified and involved in the planning process at the earliest possible time;

34. *Welcomes* the establishment in the Department of Peace-keeping Operations of a situation centre functioning twenty-four hours a day, seven days a week, which will be equipped with appropriately standardized communication and information management systems so as to enhance the management of all peace-keeping operations, and requests the Secretary-General to keep under review the efficiency and efficacy of the situation centre;

35. *Also welcomes* the initiative of the Secretariat in establishing a logistics doctrine and procedures project charged with developing a set of guidelines of United Nations logistics doctrine and procedures in order to standardize logistics practices and procedures and thereby enhance the efficiency and effectiveness of logistics support to peace-keeping operations;

36. *Requests* the Secretary-General to consider, in the ongoing restructuring of the Secretariat, the inclusion of a logistics plan-

ning capability in the Department of Peace-keeping Operations which would consider all aspects of support required for peace-keeping operations;

37. Stresses that the conclusion of a status-of-forces agreement between the United Nations and a host State is of the utmost importance when deploying peace-keeping operations and calls upon host States to give their fullest cooperation in that regard, and recommends that after the establishment of a peace-keeping operation by the Security Council the concerned Member States should cooperate fully with the operation in the implementation of its mandate;

38. Also requests the Secretary-General to include in the status-of-forces agreement between the United Nations and host States requirements for host States to treat United Nations peace-keeping forces at all times with full respect for the principles and relevant Articles of the Charter, for United Nations peace-keeping forces to respect local laws and regulations and for both parties to such an agreement to act at all times in accordance with the provisions of the status-of-forces agreement and the principles and relevant Articles of the Charter;

39. Notes the importance of concluding arrangements between the United Nations and troop contributors before deployment occurs and urges implementation of the agreements along the lines of the model agreement outlined in the report of the Secretary-General of 23 May 1991;[7/]

40. Further requests the Secretary-General to include, in the agreements to be concluded with States providing contingents, a clause by which those States would ensure that the members of their contingents serving in United Nations peace-keeping operations were fully acquainted with the principles and rules of relevant international law, in particular international humanitarian law and the purposes and principles of the Charter;

41. Stresses the importance of the institution of appropriate rules of engagement, on a case-by-case basis, for all United Nations peace-keeping operations;

42. Also notes the recent increase in the number of peace-keeping operations, and requests the Secretary-General to prepare a detailed report on operations that have significant difficulties in implementing their mandates by highlighting the root causes of such difficulties and suggesting possible measures to address them;

43. *Requests* the Secretary-General, once again, to report periodically to Member States on the performance of all peace-keeping operations;

44. *Welcomes* the increasingly frequent informal consultations between the Secretariat and contributing States, strongly recommends the continuation of such consultations on peace-keeping operations from their initial stages to their conclusion and strongly encourages the presence of the President of the Security Council and other members of the Council, as appropriate, at such consultations;

45. *Recognizes* that the training of peace-keeping personnel is primarily the responsibility of Member States;

46. *Also welcomes* the establishment of a focal point for peace-keeping training in the Department of Peace-keeping Operations, and recommends that the focal point act as the coordinating centre for the relationship between the United Nations and national and regional training facilities;

47. *Requests* the Secretary-General to review and improve arrangements for training civilian, police and military peace-keeping personnel, using the appropriate capabilities of Member States, regional organizations and arrangements, in accordance with their constitutional mandates and Chapter VIII of the Charter, and of non-governmental organizations and the Secretariat;

48. *Acknowledges* the increasing challenge of forging large and cohesive peace-keeping missions from many and diverse contingents, stresses the need for the effective training of civilian, police and military personnel before deployment, and in that regard urges the Secretary-General to develop, in consultation with Member States, official United Nations guidelines combined with performance goals for individuals and units, so that peace-keepers can be trained within a national framework in accordance with agreed-upon common standards, skills, practices and procedures;

49. Also requests the Secretary-General to develop and publish peace-keeping training guidelines, manuals and other relevant training material, including material for correspondence instruction, in order to assist Member States in preparing their civilian, police and military personnel for peace-keeping operations in a standardized and cost-effective manner;

50. Further requests the Secretary-General, in close consultation with Member States, to initiate, within resources which may be allocated for training purposes, a trial programme designed to train national peace-keeping trainers as a supplement to national training programmes, as well as to develop a proposal to strengthen the leadership cadre available for peace-keeping by training potential Force Commanders and senior military and civilian personnel for peace-keeping leadership and management duties;

51. Recommends that training for peace-keeping operations be included, as appropriate, in the training of those military, civilian and police personnel being sent on peace-keeping operations, and encourages Member States that have already developed such training to share information and experience with other Member States;

52. Strongly recommends that peace-keeping operations personnel be made generally aware of relevant local laws and customs of the host State and of the importance of respecting them;

53. Encourages troop contributors to consider arrangements between themselves for the loan and/or exchange of peace-keeping operations experts to enhance operational effectiveness through sharing of information and experience gained in peace-keeping operations;

54. Once again requests the Secretary-General to consider establishing a training programme for key staff personnel of peace-keeping operations with a view to creating a pool of trained personnel with knowledge of the United Nations system and its working procedures;

55. Recognizes that public information on peace-keeping operations, particularly an understanding of their mandates, is important, and calls for significant enhancement of the press and public information function for peace-keeping missions and in particular for rapid deployment at the start of a peace-keeping operation of a robust and professional media outreach programme in the area of operation commensurate with the scope and needs of the missions;

56. *Requests* the Secretary-General, in consultation with Member States, to establish guidelines for the public information function of peace-keeping operations;

57. *Requests* the Secretariat immediately to make all necessary arrangements for the reissue of *The Blue Helmets*[8/] in 1995;

58. *Also requests* the Secretariat to take the appropriate steps to record, in a dignified and yet simple manner in a public area of the United Nations Headquarters, the names of those who have given their lives in the service of United Nations peace-keeping operations;

59. *Welcomes* the intention of the Secretariat to establish a memorial dedicated to those peace-keepers who have given their lives in the service of peace;

Issues arising from An Agenda for Peace

60. *Recalls* its resolutions 47/120 A of 18 December 1992 and 47/120 B of 20 September 1993, and takes note of the report of the Secretary-General on the implementation of the recommendations contained in *An Agenda for Peace*, welcomes the efforts of the Secretary-General to take appropriate steps through preventive diplomacy and, recognizing the need for those steps to be based on timely and accurate knowledge of relevant facts, encourages him to strengthen the capability of the Secretariat to secure and analyse all relevant information from as wide a variety of sources as possible in accordance with the relevant provisions of the Charter, urges Member States to assist the Secretary-General in this regard, and requests the Secretary-General to keep the Member States regularly informed of such capabilities and mechanisms;

61. *Reaffirms* its resolution 47/120 B, in particular section II, entitled "Preventive deployment and demilitarized zones", and in this context recalls the importance of considering, on a case-by-case basis, the use of preventive deployment and/or the establishment of

demilitarized zones as a means to prevent existing or potential disputes from escalating into conflicts and to promote efforts to achieve the peaceful settlement of such disputes, the continuance of which is likely to endanger the maintenance of international peace and security;

62. *Encourages,* in accordance with Chapter VIII of the Charter, the involvement of Member States through regional organizations and arrangements, as appropriate, in accordance with their respective areas of competence and the purposes and principles of the United Nations;

63. *Welcomes* efforts by the Secretary-General to develop, in consultation with Member States, a set of guidelines governing cooperation between the United Nations and regional organizations;

64. *Notes* the existing cooperation between the United Nations and regional organizations, in particular in the area of peace-keeping;

65. *Requests* the Secretary-General, in accordance with Chapter VIII of the Charter, to consider ways to provide advice and assistance, in a variety of forms such as advisory services, seminars and conferences, to regional organizations and arrangements in their respective areas of competence, so as to enhance their capacity to cooperate with the United Nations in the field of peace-keeping operations;

66. *Resolves* to continue consideration of these items;

Status and safety of United Nations peace-keeping personnel

67. *Urges* all Member States in whose territory United Nations peace-keeping operations are conducted to provide, in accordance with relevant Articles of the Charter and other instruments, comprehensive support to all United Nations peace-keeping operations personnel in fulfilling their functions, as well as to take all necessary measures to ensure respect for and guarantee the safety and security of those personnel;

68. *Considers* that any State in whose territory a United Nations peace-keeping operation is conducted should act promptly to deter and prosecute all those responsible for attacks and other acts of violence

against all personnel of United Nations peace-keeping operations;

69. *Notes* the particular difficulties and dangers that can arise when United Nations peace-keeping operations are conducted in situations where no authority exercises jurisdiction or discharges responsibilities with regard to ensuring the safety and security of United Nations personnel, and in such an eventuality agrees that measures appropriate to the particular circumstances and in accordance with the purposes and principles of the United Nations should be considered by the Security Council and other appropriate bodies of the United Nations;

70. *Emphasizes* the importance of all relevant information on conditions in the field of operations for the safety of United Nations peace-keepers, and invites the Secretariat to adopt measures to secure and analyse such information from as wide a variety of sources as possible for immediate transmission to field missions;

71. *Considers* that it is the responsibility of host countries to disseminate to their populations necessary information on the role of peace-keeping operations and the inviolability of the safety of peace-keepers, including the information the United Nations may make available for that purpose;

72. *Also considers* that host countries are required to provide all available information in a timely manner to the United Nations and the respective peace-keeping missions in the field on any potential dangers that might jeopardize the safety of the peace-keepers, and that that requirement should be clearly specified in the status-of-forces agreements;

73. *Urges* the Secretary-General to review the current arrangements of compensation for death, injury, disability or illness attributable to peace-keeping service with a view to developing equitable and appropriate arrangements, and to ensure expeditious reimbursement;

74. *Recognizes* that conditions in the field require practical steps aimed at enhancing the necessary operational, political and legal environment to deal effectively with the problem of the growing vulnerability of United Nations operations personnel deployed in the field;

75. Requests the Secretary-General to take concrete steps to improve the physical security of all United Nations peace-keeping personnel deployed in the field, including all aspects related to material, organizational, operational and other aspects of safety;

76. Welcomes the report of the Secretary-General on current measures and new proposals to ensure and enhance the security of United Nations operations[9/] and will consider what further steps might be taken to enhance their status and safety, taking into account the need for concerted action by all relevant bodies of the United Nations, and in that context welcomes Security Council resolution 868 (1993) of 29 September 1993, in which connection the General Assembly:

(a) Will give consideration to promoting the elaboration of a declaration that would, *inter alia*, reaffirm the principles of international law and the obligations of Member States concerning the status and safety of United Nations personnel;

(b) Calls upon the Security Council to include in mandates for the deployment of United Nations personnel specific provisions recalling the obligations of Member States and the expectations of the United Nations concerning the status and safety of United Nations personnel;

(c) Notes that a legally binding international instrument to reinforce the existing arrangements regarding the status and safety of United Nations personnel is being considered by the Sixth Committee;

77. Recommends that, should any of the proposals contained in the present resolution result in budgetary implications for the biennium 1994-1995, such additional costs should be accommodated within the appropriation level approved by the General Assembly for this biennium;

78. Decides that the Special Committee on Peace-keeping Operations, in accordance with its mandate, should continue its efforts for a comprehensive review of the whole question of peace-keeping operations in all their aspects;

79. *Requests* the Secretary-General to ensure that full conference services, including translation of official documents and simultaneous translation into all official languages, are provided to the Special Committee and its working group whenever they meet, normally for up to one month in April and May;

80. *Requests* the Special Committee to submit a report on its work to the General Assembly at its forty-ninth session;

81. *Invites* Member States to submit further observations and suggestions on peace-keeping operations to the Secretary-General by 1 March 1994, outlining practical proposals on specific items in order to allow for more detailed consideration by the Special Committee;

82. *Also requests* the Secretary-General to prepare, within existing resources, a compilation of the above-mentioned observations and suggestions and to submit it to the Special Committee by 30 March 1994;

83. *Decides* to include in the provisional agenda of its forty-ninth session the item entitled "Comprehensive review of the whole question of peace-keeping operations in all their aspects".

1/ *S/25859.*
2/ *A/48/503 and Add.1.*
3/ *A/48/1.*
4/ *A/48/173.*
5/ *A/48/421, annex.*
6/ *See A/47/965-S/25944.*
7/ *A/46/185 and Corr.1, annex.*
8/ *United Nations publication, Sales No. E.90.I.18.*
9/ *A/48/349-S/26358.*

Statements by the President of the Security Council on behalf of the Council

Statement by the President of the Security Council
S/23500, 31 January 1992

At the conclusion of the 3046th meeting of the Security Council, held at the level of Heads of State and Government on 31 January 1992 in connection with the item entitled "The responsibility of the Security Council in the maintenance of international peace and security", the President of the Security Council issued the following statement on behalf of the members of the Council.

The members of the Security Council have authorized me to make the following statement on their behalf.

The Security Council met at United Nations Headquarters in New York on 31 January 1992, for the first time at the level of heads of State and Government. The members of the Council considered, within the framework of their commitment to the Charter of the United Nations, "The responsibility of the Security Council in the maintenance of international peace and security".[1/]

The members of the Security Council consider that their meeting is a timely recognition of the fact that there are new favourable international circumstances under which the Security Council has begun to fulfil more effectively its primary responsibility for the maintenance of international peace and security.

A time of change

This meeting of the Council takes place at a time of momentous change. The ending of the cold war has raised hopes for a safer, more equitable and more humane world. Rapid progress has been made, in many regions of the world, towards democracy and responsive forms of government, as well as towards achieving the Purposes set out in the Charter of the United Nations. The completion of the dismantling of apartheid in South Africa would constitute a major contribution to these Purposes and positive trends, including to the encouragement of respect for human rights and fundamental freedoms.

Last year, under the authority of the United Nations, the international community succeeded in enabling Kuwait to regain its sovereignty and territorial integrity, which it had lost as a result of Iraqi aggression. The resolutions adopted by the Council remain essential to the restoration of peace and stability in the region and must be fully implemented. At the same time the members of the Council are concerned by the humanitarian situation of the innocent civilian population of Iraq.

The members of the Council support the Middle East peace process, facilitated by the Russian Federation and the United States of America, and hope that it will be brought to a successful conclusion on the basis of Council resolutions 242 (1967) of 22 November 1967 and 338 (1973) of 22 October 1973.

The members of the Council welcome the role the United Nations has been able to play under the Charter in progress towards settling long-standing regional disputes, and will work for further progress towards their resolution. They applaud the valuable contribution being made by United Nations peace-keeping forces now operating in Asia, Africa, Latin America and Europe.

The members of the Council note that United Nations peace-keeping tasks have increased and broadened considerably in recent years. Election monitoring, human rights verification and the repatriation of refugees have in the settlement of some regional conflicts, at the request or with the agreement of the parties concerned, been integral parts of the Security Council's effort to maintain international peace and security. They welcome these developments.

The members of the Council also recognize that change, however welcome, has brought new risks for stability and security. Some of the most acute problems result from changes to State structures. The members of the Council will encourage all efforts to help achieve peace, stability and cooperation during these changes.

The international community therefore faces new challenges

in the search for peace. All Member States expect the United Nations to play a central role at this crucial stage. The members of the Council stress the importance of strengthening and improving the United Nations to increase its effectiveness. They are determined to assume fully their responsibilities within the United Nations Organization in the framework of the Charter.

The absence of war and military conflicts amongst States does not in itself ensure international peace and security. The non-military sources of instability in the economic, social, humanitarian and ecological fields have become threats to peace and security. The United Nations membership as a whole, working through the appropriate bodies, needs to give the highest priority to the solution of these matters.

Commitment to collective security

The members of the Council pledge their commitment to international law and to the Charter of the United Nations. All disputes between States should be peacefully resolved in accordance with the provisions of the Charter.

The members of the Council reaffirm their commitment to the collective security system of the Charter to deal with threats to peace and to reverse acts of aggression.

The members of the Council express their deep concern over acts of international terrorism and emphasize the need for the international community to deal effectively with all such acts.

Peacemaking and peace-keeping

To strengthen the effectiveness of these commitments, and in order that the Security Council should have the means to discharge its primary responsibility under the Charter of the United Nations for the maintenance of international peace and security, the members of the Council have decided on the following approach.

They invite the Secretary-General to prepare, for circulation to the Members of the United Nations by 1 July 1992, his analysis and recommendations on ways of strengthening and making more efficient within the framework and provisions of the Charter the capacity of the United Nations for preventive diplomacy, for peacemaking and for peace-keeping.

The Secretary-General's analysis and recommendations could cover the role of the United Nations in identifying potential crises and areas of instability as well as the contribution to be made by regional organizations in accordance with Chapter VIII of the Charter in helping the work of the Council. They could also cover the need for adequate resources, both material and financial. The Secretary-General might draw on lessons learned in recent United Nations peace-keeping missions to recommend ways of making more effective Secretariat planning and operations. He could also consider how greater use might be made of his good offices, and of his other functions under the Charter.

Disarmament, arms control and weapons of mass destruction

The members of the Council, while fully conscious of the responsibilities of other organs of the United Nations in the fields of disarmament, arms control and non-proliferation, reaffirm the crucial contribution which progress in these areas can make to the maintenance of international peace and security. They express their commitment to take concrete steps to enhance the effectiveness of the United Nations in these areas.

The members of the Council underline the need for all Member States to fulfil their obligations in relation to arms control and disarmament; to prevent the proliferation in all its aspects of all weapons of mass destruction; to avoid excessive and destabilizing accumulations and transfers of arms; and to resolve peacefully in accordance with the Charter any problems concerning these matters threatening or disrupting the maintenance of regional and global stability. They emphasize the importance of the early ratification and implementation by the States concerned of all international and regional arms control arrangements, especially the Strategic Arms Reduction Talks and the Treaty on Conventional Armed Forces in Europe.

The proliferation of all weapons of mass destruction constitutes a threat to international peace and security. The members of the Council commit themselves to working to prevent the spread of technology related to the research for or production of such weapons and to take appropriate action to that end.

On nuclear proliferation, the members of the Council note the importance of the decision of many countries to adhere to the Treaty on the Non-Proliferation of Nuclear Weapons of 1 July 1968[2/] and emphasize the integral role in the implementation of that Treaty of fully effective International Atomic Energy Agency safeguards, as well as the importance of effective export controls. They will take appropriate measures in the case of any violations notified to them by the Agency.

On chemical weapons, the members of the Council support the efforts of the Third Review Conference of the Parties to the Convention on the Prohibition of the Development, Production and Stockpiling of Bacteriological (Biological) and Toxin Weapons and on their Destruction, held at Geneva from 9 to 27 September 1991, with a view to reaching agreement on the conclusion, by the end of 1992, of a universal convention, including a verification regime, to prohibit chemical weapons.

On conventional armaments, they note the General Assembly's vote in favour of a United Nations register of arms transfers as a first step, and in this connection recognize the importance of all States providing all the information called for in the General Assembly's resolution.[3/]

In conclusion, the members of the Council affirm their determination to build on the initiative of their meeting in order to secure positive advances in promoting international peace and security. They agree that the Secretary-General has a crucial role to play. The members of the Council express their deep appreciation to the outgoing Secretary-General, His Excellency Mr. Javier Pérez de Cuéllar, for his outstanding contribution to the work of the United Nations, culminating in the signature of the El Salvador peace agreements.[4/] They welcome the new Secretary-General, Mr.

Boutros Boutros-Ghali, and note with satisfaction his intention to strengthen and improve the functioning of the United Nations. They pledge their full support to him, and undertake to work closely with him and his staff in fulfilment of their shared objectives, including a more efficient and effective United Nations system.

The members of the Council agree that the world now has the best chance of achieving international peace and security since the founding of the United Nations. They undertake to work in close cooperation with other United Nations Member States in their own efforts to achieve this, as well as to address urgently all the other problems, in particular those of economic and social development, requiring the collective response of the international community. They recognize that peace and prosperity are indivisible and that lasting peace and stability require effective international cooperation for the eradication of poverty and the promotion of a better life for all in larger freedom.

1/ *The meeting was chaired by the Prime Minister of the United Kingdom of Great Britain and Northern Ireland as the President of the Security Council for January. Statements were made by:*
   His Excellency Dr. Franz Vranitzky, Federal Chancellor of Austria,
   His Excellency Mr. Wilfried Martens, Prime Minister of Belgium,
   His Excellency Dr. Carlos Alberto Wahnon de Carvalho Veiga, Prime Minister of Cape Verde,
   His Excellency Mr. Li Peng, Premier of the State Council of China,
   His Excellency Dr. Rodrigo Borja-Cevallos, Constitutional President of Ecuador,
   His Excellency Mr. François Mitterrand, President of France,
   His Excellency Dr. Géza Jeszenszky, Minister for Foreign Affairs and Personal Emissary of the Prime Minister of Hungary,
   His Excellency Mr. P. V. Narasimha Rao, Prime Minister of India,
   His Excellency Mr. Kiichi Miyazawa, Prime Minister of Japan,
   His Majesty Hassan II, King of Morocco,
   His Excellency Mr. Boris N. Yeltsin, President of the Russian Federation,
   His Excellency the Rt. Hon. John Major MP, Prime Minister of the United Kingdom of Great Britain and Northern Ireland,
   His Excellency Mr. George Bush, President of the United States of America,
   His Excellency Dr. Carlos Andrés Pérez, President of Venezuela and
   His Excellency Dr. Nathan Shamuyarira, Minister of Foreign Affairs and Personal Emissary of the President of Zimbabwe,
   His Excellency Dr. Boutros Boutros-Ghali, Secretary-General of the United Nations
2/ *United Nations, Treaty Series, vol. 729, No. 10485*
3/ *General Assembly resolution 46/36 L of 9 December 1991*
4/ Official Records of the Security Council, Forty-seventh Year, Supplement for January, February and March 1992, *document S/23501, annex*

Statement by the President of the Security Council
S/24210, 30 June 1992

The Council has noted with interest and appreciation the report of the Secretary-General of 17 June 1992 entitled *An Agenda for Peace*[1] on ways of strengthening and making more efficient within the framework and provisions of the Charter of the United Nations the capacity of the United Nations for preventive diplomacy, for peacemaking and for peace-keeping, prepared pursuant to the statement adopted on 31 January 1992 at the conclusion of the meeting held for the first time by the Security Council at the level of heads of State and Government.[2] It is grateful to the Secretary-General for his report, which is a comprehensive reflection on the ongoing process of strengthening the Organization. In this connection, the Council welcomes the efforts made by the Secretary-General.

In reading the report, the Council has noted a set of interesting proposals addressed to the various organs of the United Nations and to Member States and regional organizations. The Council therefore trusts that all organs and entities, in particular the General Assembly, will devote particular attention to the report and will study and evaluate the elements of the report that concern them.

Within the scope of its competence, the Security Council will, for its part, examine in depth and with due priority the recommendations of the Secretary-General.

The Council also takes this opportunity to reiterate its readiness to cooperate fully with the Secretary-General in the strengthening of the Organization in accordance with the provisions of the Charter.

1/ *S/24111.*
2/ *S/23500.*

Statement by the President of the Security Council
S/24728, 29 October 1992

Pursuant to the President's statement of 30 June 1992,[1/] the Council has begun to examine the Secretary-General's report entitled *An Agenda for Peace*.[2/]

This consideration of the report of the Secretary-General of 17 June 1992 entitled *An Agenda for Peace* [3/] by the Council will be coordinated with the discussions carried out in the General Assembly. The Council welcomes in this regard the contact already established between the Presidents of the two organs and invites the President of the Council to continue and intensify such contacts.

The Council intends to examine the proposals of the Secretary-General which concern it or are addressed to it. For this purpose, the members of the Council have decided to hold a meeting at least once a month on the report, such meetings being prepared for, as necessary, by a working group.

One objective of this examination is to arrive at conclusions which would be considered during a special meeting of the Council, which will determine the date of this meeting, bearing in mind the progress of the work at the present session of the General Assembly, but it hopes to hold the meeting by next spring at the latest.

The Council has followed with close interest the views expressed by Member States in the General Assembly during the general debate as well as during the discussion on item 10 of the agenda of the General Assembly. It has also noted the report of the special session of the Special Committee on Peace-keeping Operations.[4/] It has now identified the Secretary-General's proposals which concern it or are addressed to it.

Without prejudice to the further examination of other proposals of the Secretary-General, and taking into account the greatly increased number and complexity of peace-keeping operations authorized by the Council during recent months, the Council believes that two suggestions contained in *An Agenda for Peace* should be considered at this moment:

> The Council, in accordance with the recommendations contained in paragraph 51 of the Secretary-General's report, encourages Member States to inform the Secretary-General of their willingness to provide forces or capabilities to the United Nations for peace-keeping operations and the type of units or capabilities that might be available at short notice, subject to overriding national defence requirements and the approval of the Governments providing them. It further encourages the Secretariat and those Member States which have indicated such willingness to enter into direct dialogue so as to enable the Secretary-General to know with greater precision what forces or capabilities might be made available to the United Nations for particular peace-keeping operations, and on what time-scale;

> The Council shares the view of the Secretary-General in paragraph 52 of his report concerning the need for an augmentation of the strength and capability of military staff serving in the Secretariat and of civilian staff dealing more generally with peace-keeping matters in the Secretariat. The Council suggests to the Secretary-General that he report to it, as well as to the General Assembly, on this subject as soon as possible. The Secretary-General might consider in his report the establishment in the Secretariat of an enhanced peace-keeping planning staff and an operations centre in order to deal with the growing complexity of initial planning and control of peace-keeping operations in the field. The Council further suggests to Member States that they consider making available to the Secretariat appropriately experienced military or civilian staff, for a fixed period of time, to help with work on peace-keeping operations.

Moreover, the Council intends to study those paragraphs which are addressed to it, including paragraph 41 concerning the special economic problems which may concern other States when sanctions are imposed on a State, paragraphs 64 and 65 concerning the role of regional organizations, and paragraph 25 concerning resort by the United Nations to fact-finding.

1/ *S/24210.*
2/ Official Records of the Security Council, Forty-seventh Year, Supplement for January, February and March 1992, *document S/24111.*
3/ *S/24210.*
4/ *A/47/386.*

Statement by the President of the Security Council
S/24872, 30 November 1992

The members of the Council continued the examination of the report of the Secretary-General of 17 June 1992 entitled *An Agenda for Peace.*[1]

The members of the Council welcome and support the proposals in paragraph 25 of the report of the Secretary-General on fact-finding. They are of the view that an increased resort to fact-finding as a tool of preventive diplomacy, in accordance with the Charter of the United Nations and the United Nations Declaration on Fact-finding for International Security and Peacemaking,[2] particularly its guidelines, can result in the best possible understanding of the objective facts of a situation which will enable the Secretary-General to meet his responsibilities under Article 99 of the Charter and facilitate Security Council deliberations. They agree that various forms of fact-finding can be employed according to the requirements of a situation, and that a request by a State for the dispatch of a fact-finding mission to its territory should be considered without undue delay. They encourage all Member States in a position to do so to provide the Secretary-General with the detailed information needed on issues of concern, so as to facilitate effective preventive diplomacy.

The members of the Council, being aware of the increased responsibilities of the United Nations in the area of preventive diplomacy, invite the Secretary-General to consider the appropriate measures necessary to strengthen the capacity of the Secretariat for information-gathering and in-depth analysis. They also invite Member States and the Secretary-General to consider the secondment of experts to help in this regard. They urge the Secretary-General to take appropriate measures to ensure the availability at short notice of eminent persons who might share, with senior officials of the Secretariat, the burden of fact-finding missions. They note the positive role of regional organizations and arrangements in fact-finding within their areas of competence and welcome its intensification and close coordination with fact-finding efforts by the United Nations.

Bearing in mind the above-mentioned Declaration and the Secretary-General's recommendations in his report, the members of the Council for their part will facilitate and encourage every appropriate use of fact-finding missions on a case-by-case basis and in accordance with the Purposes and Principles of the Charter.

In this context, the members of the Council note and endorse the Secretary-General's view that in some cases a fact-finding mission can help defuse a dispute or situation, indicating to those concerned that the United Nations and in particular the Security Council is actively seized of the matter as a present or potential threat to international peace and security. Such action in the early stages of a potential dispute can be particularly effective. They welcome the Secretary-General's readiness to make full use of his powers under Article 99 of the Charter to draw the attention of the Security Council to any matter which in his opinion may threaten international peace and security. They note with satisfaction the recent greater use of fact-finding missions, as exemplified by the missions to Moldova, Nagorny-Karabakh, Georgia, Uzbekistan and Tajikistan.

The members of the Council intend to continue their work on the Secretary-General's report as indicated in the President's statement of 29 October 1992.[3]

---

[1]   Official Records of the Security Council, Forty-seventh Year, Supplement for January, February and March 1992, *document S/24111.*

[2]   *General Assembly resolution 46/59 of 9 December 1991, annex.*

[3]   *S/24728.*

Statement by the President of the Security Council
S/25036, 30 December 1992

In pursuance of the President's statement of 29 October 1992[1] in connection with the Secretary-General's report entitled *An Agenda for Peace*,[2] according to which "the Council intends to study those paragraphs which are addressed to it, including paragraph 41 concerning the special economic problems which may concern other States when sanctions are imposed on a State", the Security Council examined the question of special economic problems of States as a result of sanctions imposed under Chapter VII of the Charter of the United Nations.

The Council shares the observation made by the Secretary-General in paragraph 41 of his report that when such sanctions are imposed under Chapter VII of the Charter, it is important that States confronted with special economic problems have the right to consult the Council regarding such problems, as provided in Article 50 of the Charter. The Council agrees that appropriate consideration should be given to their situation.

The Council notes the Secretary-General's recommendation that the Council devise a set of measures, involving the financial institutions and other components of the United Nations system, that can be put in place to insulate States from such difficulties.

The Council, while noting that this matter is being considered in other forums of the United Nations, expresses its determination to consider this matter further and invites the Secretary-General to consult the heads of the international financial institutions, other components of the United Nations system and Member States, and to report to the Security Council as early as possible.

The Council intends to continue its work on the Secretary-General's report as indicated in the President's statement of 29 October 1992.

1/ *S/24728.*
2/ Official Records of the Security Council, Forty-seventh Year, Supplement for January, February and March 1992, *document S/24111.*

Statement by the President of the Security Council
S/25184, 28 January 1993

The Security Council has continued its examination of the Secretary-General's report entitled *An Agenda for Peace.*[1/] The Council notes with appreciation the views of the Secretary-General, as presented in paragraphs 63, 64 and 65 of his report, concerning cooperation with regional arrangements and organizations.

Bearing in mind the relevant provisions of the Charter of the United Nations, the pertinent activities of the General Assembly and the challenges to international peace and security in the new phase of international relations, the Council attaches great importance to the role of regional arrangements and organizations and recognizes the need to coordinate their efforts with those of the United Nations in the maintenance of international peace and security.

While reaffirming its primary responsibility for the maintenance of international peace and security and being aware of the variety of mandate, scope and composition of regional arrangements and organizations, the Council encourages and, where appropriate, supports such regional efforts as undertaken by regional arrangements and organizations within their respective areas of competence in accordance with the purposes and principles of the Charter of the United Nations.

The Council therefore invites, within the framework of Chapter VIII of the Charter, regional arrangements and organizations to study, on a priority basis, the following:

- ways and means to strengthen their functions to maintain international peace and security within their areas of competence, paying due regard to the characteristics of their respective regions. Taking into account the matters of which the Council has been seized and in accordance with the Charter, they might consider, in particular, preventive diplomacy including fact-finding, confidence-building, good offices and peace-building and, where appropriate, peace-keeping;

- ways and means further to improve coordination of their efforts with those of the United Nations. Being aware of the variety of mandate, scope and composition of the regional arrangements and organizations, the Council stresses that the forms of interaction of these arrangements and organizations with the United Nations should be flexible and adequate to each specific situation. These may include, in particular, exchange of information and consultations with the Secretary-General or, where appropriate, his special representative, with a view to enhancing the United Nations capability including monitoring and early-warning; participating as observers in the sessions and the work of the General Assembly; secondment of officials to the United Nations Secretariat; making timely and specific requests for United Nations involvement; and a readiness to provide necessary resources.

The Council requests the Secretary-General:

- to transmit this statement to those regional arrangements and organizations which have received a standing invitation to participate in the sessions and the work of the General Assembly as observers, and to other regional arrangements and organizations, with a view to promoting the aforementioned studies and encouraging the replies to the United Nations;
- to submit to the Council as soon as possible and preferably by the end of April 1993 a report concerning the replies from the regional arrangements and organizations.

The Council invites the States which are members of regional arrangements and organizations to play a constructive role in the consideration by their respective arrangements or organizations of ways and means to improve coordination with the United Nations.

In discharging its responsibilities, the Council will take into account the replies as well as the specific nature of the issue and the characteristics of the region concerned. The Council considers it important to establish such forms of cooperation between the United Nations and the regional arrangements and organizations, in the area of maintaining peace and security, that are appropriate to each specific situation.

The Council, noting the constructive relationship it has maintained with the League of Arab States, the European Community, the Organization of the Islamic Conference, the Organization of American States and the Organization of African Unity, supports the intention of the Secretary-General as described in paragraph 27 of his report to ask regional arrangements and organizations that have not yet sought observer status at the United Nations to do so.

The Council notes the importance of the understanding reached at the Conference on Security and Cooperation in Europe to consider the CSCE a regional arrangement in the sense of Chapter VIII of the Charter of the United Nations and of the further examination within the framework of the CSCE of the practical implications of this understanding. The Council welcomes the role of the CSCE, together with the European Community, in the implementation of action required to carry out the pertinent resolutions of the Council.

The Council intends to continue its consideration of the report of the Secretary-General, as indicated in the President's statement of 29 October 1992.[2]

1/ Official Records of the Security Council, Forty-seventh Year, Supplement for January, February and March 1992, *document S/24111.*

2/ *S/24728; see* Official Records of the Security Council, Forty-seventh Year, Resolutions and Decisions of the Security Council, 1992, *p. 102.*

Statement by the President of the Security Council
S/25344, 26 February 1993

The Security Council has continued its examination of the report of the Secretary-General entitled *An Agenda for Peace*.[1]

The Council welcomes the observations contained in *An Agenda for Peace* concerning the question of humanitarian assistance and its relationship to peacemaking, peace-keeping and peace-building, in particular those contained in paragraphs 29, 40 and 56 to 59. It notes that in some particular circumstances there may be a close relationship between acute needs for humanitarian assistance and threats to international peace and security.

In this respect, the Council notes the Secretary-General's assessment that the impartial provision of humanitarian assistance could be of critical importance in preventive diplomacy.

Recalling its statement on fact-finding[2] in connection with *An Agenda for Peace*, the Council recognizes the importance of humanitarian concerns in conflict situations and thus recommends that the humanitarian dimension should be incorporated in the planning and dispatching of fact-finding missions. It also recognizes the need to include this aspect in connection with information-gathering and analysis, and encourages Member States concerned to provide the Secretary-General and the Governments concerned with relevant humanitarian information.

The Council notes with concern the incidence of humanitarian crises, including mass displacements of population, becoming or aggravating threats to international peace and security. In this connection, it is important to include humanitarian considerations and indicators within the context of early-warning information capacities as referred to in paragraphs 26 and 27 of *An Agenda for Peace*. The Council emphasizes the role of the Department of Humanitarian Affairs in coordinating the activities of the various agencies and functional offices of the United Nations. It believes that this capacity should be utilized systematically at a pre-emergency phase to facilitate planning for action to assist Governments in averting crises that could affect international peace and security.

The Council notes the ongoing and constructive collaboration between the United Nations and various regional arrangements and organizations, within their respective areas of competence, in identifying and addressing humanitarian emergencies, in order to solve crises in a manner appropriate to each specific situation. The Council also notes the important role which is being played by nongovernmental organizations, in close cooperation with the United Nations, in the provision of humanitarian assistance in emergency situations around the world. The Council commends this cooperation and invites the Secretary-General further to explore ways in which this cooperation can be advanced in order to enhance the capacity of the United Nations to prevent and respond to emergency situations.

The Council expresses concern about the increased incidence of deliberate obstruction of delivery of humanitarian relief and violence against humanitarian personnel, as well as misappropriation of humanitarian assistance, in many parts of the world, in particular in the former Yugoslavia, Iraq and Somalia, where the Council has called for secure access to affected populations for the purpose of providing humanitarian assistance. The Council stresses the need for adequate protection of personnel involved in humanitarian operations, in accordance with relevant norms and principles of international law. The Council believes that this matter requires urgent attention.

The Council believes that humanitarian assistance should help establish the basis for enhanced stability through rehabilitation and development. The Council thus notes the importance of adequate planning in the provision of humanitarian assistance in order to improve prospects for rapid improvement of the humanitarian situation. It also notes, however, that humanitarian considerations may become or continue to be relevant during periods in which the results of peacemaking and peace-keeping efforts are beginning to be consolidated. The Council thus recognizes the importance of ensuring a smooth transition from relief to development, and notes that the provision of coordinated humanitarian assistance is among the basic peace-building tools available to the Secretary-General. In particular, it fully endorses the Secretary-General's observations in paragraph 58 of *An Agenda for Peace* regarding the problem of land mines and invites him to address this as a matter of special concern.

The Council intends to continue its consideration of the report of the Secretary-General, as indicated in the President's statement of 29 October 1992.[3]

[1]   Official Records of the Security Council, Forty-seventh Year, Supplement for January, February and March 1992, *document S/24111.*

[2]   *S/24872; see* Official Records of the Security Council, Forty-seventh Year, Resolutions and Decisions of the Security Council, 1992, *p. 103.*

[3]   *S/24728; see* Official Records of the Security Council, Forty-seventh Year, Resolutions and Decisions of the Security Council, 1992, *p. 102.*

Statement by the President of the Security Council
S/25493, 31 March 1993

The Security Council has continued its examination of the reort of the Secretary-General entitled *An Agenda for Peace*,[1/] including the problem identified in paragraphs 66 to 68 – the safety of United Nations forces and personnel deployed in conditions of strife. The Council has considered this question with regard to persons deployed in connection with a Council mandate.

The Council commends the Secretary-General for drawing attention to this problem, including the unconscionable increase in the number of fatalities and incidents of violence involving United Nations forces and personnel. The Council shares fully the Secretary-General's concerns.

The Council recognizes that increasingly it has found it necessary, in discharging its responsibility for the maintenance of international peace and security, to deploy United Nations forces and personnel in situations of real danger. The Council greatly appreciates the courage and commitment of these dedicated people who accept considerable personal risk in order to implement the mandates of this Organization.

The Council recalls that it has been necessary on a number of occasions to condemn incidents directed against United Nations forces and personnel. It deplores the fact that, despite its repeated calls, incidents of violence continue.

The Council considers that attacks and other acts of violence, whether actual or threatened, including obstruction or detention of persons, against United Nations forces and personnel are wholly unacceptable and may require the Council to take further measures to ensure the safety and security of such forces and personnel.

The Council reiterates its demand that States and other parties to various conflicts take all possible steps to ensure the safety and security of United Nations forces and personnel. It further demands that States act promptly and effectively to deter, prosecute and punish all those responsible for attacks and other acts of violence against such forces and personnel.

The Council notes the particular difficulties and dangers that can arise where United Nations forces and personnel are deployed in situations where the State or States concerned are unable to exercise jurisdiction in order to ensure the safety and security of such forces and personnel, or where a State is unwilling to discharge its responsibilities in this regard. In such an eventuality, the Council may consider measures appropriate to the particular circumstances to ensure that persons responsible for attacks and other acts of violence against United Nations forces and personnel are held to account for their actions.

The Council requests the Secretary-General to report as soon as possible on the existing arrangements for the protection of United Nations forces and personnel, and the adequacy thereof, taking into account, *inter alia*, relevant multilateral instruments and status of forces agreements concluded between the United Nations and host countries, as well as comments he may receive from Member States, and to make such recommendations as he considers appropriate for enhancing the safety and security of United Nations forces and personnel.

The Council will consider the matter further in the light of the Secretary-General's report and of work done in the General Assembly and its subsidiary bodies, including, in particular, the Special Committee on Peace-keeping Operations established pursuant to General Assembly resolution 2006 (XIX). In that regard, the Council recognizes the need for all relevant bodies of the Organization to take concerted action to enhance the safety and security of United Nations forces and personnel.

The Council intends to continue its consideration of the report of the Secretary-General entitled *An Agenda for Peace*, as indicated in the President's statement of 29 October 1992.[2]

1/ Official Records of the Security Council, Forty-seventh Year, Supplement for January, February and March 1992, *document S/24111.*

2/ *S/24728; see* Official Records of the Security Council, Forty-seventh Year, Resolutions and Decisions of the Security Council, 1992, *p. 102.*

Statement by the President of the Security Council
S/25696, 30 April 1993

Continuing its examination of the report of the Secretary-General entitled *An Agenda for Peace*,[1/] the Security Council during the month of April 1993, emphasizing the importance of building strong foundations for peace in all countries and regions of the world, considered the subject of post-conflict peace-building.

The Council supports the view that the United Nations, in order to meet its responsibilities in the context of international peace and security, should view its objectives in respect of economic and social cooperation and development with the same sense of responsibility and urgency as its commitments in the political and security areas.

The Council stresses that, in examining the question of post-conflict peace-building, it wishes to highlight the importance and the urgency of the work of the United Nations in the field of development cooperation, without prejudice to the recognized priorities for the activities of the United Nations in that field as defined by the competent bodies.

The Council took note of the Secretary-General's observation that, to be truly successful, peacemaking and peace-keeping operations 'must come to include comprehensive efforts to identify and support structures which will tend to consolidate peace and advance a sense of confidence and well-being among people'. It agreed that in addition to the specific measures mentioned by the Secretary-General in paragraph 55 of his report, *An Agenda for Peace*, activities such as disarming and demobilization of belligerent forces and their reintegration into society, electoral assistance, the restoration of national security through formation of national defence and police forces and mine-clearing, where appropriate and within the framework of comprehensive settlements of conflict situations, strengthen national political structures and enhance institutional and administrative capabilities and are important in restoring a sound basis for sustainable peace.

The Council further agrees that in the aftermath of an international conflict, peace-building may, *inter alia*, include measures and cooperative projects linking two or more countries in mutually beneficial undertakings which contribute not only to economic, social and cultural development but also enhance the mutual understanding and confidence that are so fundamental to peace.

In discharging its responsibilities in the prevention of breaches of peace and in the resolution of conflicts, the Council encourages coordinated action by other components of the United Nations system to remedy the underlying causes of threats to peace and security. The Council is convinced that the organizations and agencies of the United Nations system, in the development and implementation of their programmes, need to be constantly sensitive to the goal of strengthening international peace and security as envisaged in Article 1 of the Charter of the United Nations.

The Council recognizes that post-conflict peace-building, in the context of overall efforts to build the foundations of peace, in order to be effective, also needs adequate financial resources. The Council therefore recognizes that it is important for Member States and financial and other United Nations bodies and agencies, as well as other organizations outside the United Nations system, to make all possible efforts to have adequate funding available for specific projects, such as the earliest possible return of refugees and displaced persons to their homes of origin, in post-conflict situations.

The Security Council, as the organ having primary responsibility for the maintenance of international peace and security, fully recognizes, as stated in paragraph 59 of *An Agenda for Peace*, that social peace is as important as strategic or political peace and supports the Secretary-General's view that there is a new requirement for technical assistance for the purposes described in that paragraph.

The Council intends to continue its consideration of the report of the Secretary-General entitled *An Agenda for Peace*, as indicated in the President's statement of 29 October 1992.[2]

---

[1] Official Records of the Security Council, Forty-seventh Year, Supplement for January, February and March 1992, *document S/24111.*

[2] *S/24728; see* Official Records of the Security Council, Forty-seventh Year, Resolutions and Decisions of the Security Council, 1992, *p. 102.*

Statement by the President of the Security Council
S/25859, 28 May 1993

In accordance with its statement of 29 October 1992,[1] the Security Council held a special meeting devoted to the report of the Secretary-General entitled *An Agenda for Peace*.[2] This meeting concluded the present stage of the examination of this report by the Council. On this occasion, the Council wishes to express once again its gratitude to the Secretary-General for this report.

The Security Council recommends that all States make participation in and support for international peace-keeping a part of their foreign and national security policy. It considers that United Nations peace-keeping operations should be conducted in accordance with the following operational principles consistent with the provisions of the Charter of the United Nations: a clear political goal with a precise mandate subject to periodic review and to change in its character or duration only by the Council itself; the consent of the Government and, where appropriate, the parties concerned, save in exceptional cases; support for a political process or for the peaceful settlement of the dispute; impartiality in implementing Security Council decisions; readiness of the Council to take appropriate measures against parties which do not observe its decisions; and the right of the Council to authorize all means necessary for United Nations forces to carry out their mandate and the inherent right of United Nations forces to take appropriate measures for self-defence. In this context, the Security Council emphasizes the need for the full cooperation of the parties concerned in implementing the mandates of peace-keeping operations as well as relevant decisions of the Council, and stresses that peace-keeping operations should not be a substitute for a political settlement, nor should they be expected to continue in perpetuity.

The Council has studied thoroughly the recommendations of the Secretary-General contained in *An Agenda for Peace*. It pays tribute to the valuable contributions made by the Special Committee on Peace-keeping Operations and other relevant bodies of the General Assembly. These discussions and consultations make it possible to formulate more clearly the common priorities of the Member States.

In the context of the rapid growth in and new approaches to peace-keeping operations, the Council commends the initial measures taken by the Secretary-General to improve the capacity of the United Nations in this field. It believes that bold new steps are required and invites all Member States to make their views known to the Secretary-General. It also invites the Secretary-General to submit by September 1993 a further report addressed to all the Members of the United Nations containing specific new proposals for further enhancing these capabilities, including:

- the strengthening and consolidation of the peace-keeping and military structure of the Secretariat, including creation of a plans and current operations directorate reporting to the Under-Secretary-General for Peace-keeping Operations to facilitate planning and to enhance coordination;
- notification by Member States of specific forces or capabilities which, with the approval of their national authorities, they could make available on a case-by-case basis to the United Nations for the full spectrum of peace-keeping or humanitarian operations; in this context the Council welcomes the Secretary-General's effort to ascertain the readiness and availability of Member States' forces or capabilities for peace-keeping operations and encourages Member states to cooperate in this effort;
- the feasibility of maintaining a limited revolving reserve of equipment commonly used in peace-keeping or humanitarian operations;
- elements for inclusion in national military or police training programmes for peace-keeping operations to prepare personnel for a United Nations peace-keeping

    role, including suggestions concerning the feasibility of conducting multinational peace-keeping exercises;

- refinement of standardized procedures to enable forces to work together more effectively;
- developing the non-military elements of peace-keeping operations.

    In view of the mounting cost and complexity of peace-keeping operations, the Security Council also requests the Secretary-General in his report to address measures designed to place them on a more solid and durable financial basis, taking into account where appropriate the Volcker-Ogata report[3/] and addressing the necessary financial and managerial reforms, diversification of funding, and the need to ensure adequate resources for peace-keeping operations and maximum transparency and accountability in the use of resources. In this context the Council recalls that, in accordance with the Charter and the relevant resolutions of the General Assembly, financing of peace-keeping operations is the collective responsibility of all Member States. It calls upon all Member States to pay their assessed contributions in full and on time and encourages those States which can do so to make voluntary contributions.

    The Council expresses gratitude to the soldiers and civilians who have served or are serving in United Nations peace-keeping operations. It pays tribute to the courageous nationals of dozens of States who have been killed or wounded while fulfilling their duty to the United Nations. It also strongly condemns attacks on United Nations peace-keepers and declares its determination to undertake more decisive efforts to ensure the security of United Nations personnel in the course of fulfilling their duties.

    In accordance with Chapter VI of the Charter of the United Nations, the Council notes the need to strengthen the United Nations potential for preventive diplomacy. It welcomes General Assembly resolution 47/120 of 18 December 1992. It notes with satisfaction the increased use of fact-finding missions. It invites Member States to provide the Secretary-General with relevant detailed information on situations of tension and potential crisis. It invites the Secretary-General to consider appropriate measures for strengthening the Secretariat capacity to collect and analyse information. The Council recognizes the importance of new approaches to prevention of conflicts, and supports preventive deployment, on a case-by-case basis, in zones of instability and potential crisis the continuance of which is likely to endanger the maintenance of international peace and security.

The Council underlines the close link which may exist, in many cases, between humanitarian assistance and peace-keeping operations and highly appreciates recent efforts by the Secretary-General aimed at further improvement of coordination among Member States and relevant agencies and organizations, including non-governmental organizations. It reiterates, in this context, its concern that humanitarian personnel should have unimpeded access to those in need.

The Council reaffirms the importance it attaches to the role of regional arrangements and organizations and to coordination between their efforts and those of the United Nations in the maintenance of international peace and security. The Council welcomes the readiness of Member States, acting nationally or through regional organizations or arrangements, to cooperate with the United Nations and other Member States by providing their particular resources and capabilities for peace-keeping purposes. The Council, acting within the framework of Chapter VIII of the Charter, calls upon regional organizations and arrangements to consider ways and means of enhancing their contributions to the maintenance of peace and security. For its part the Council expresses its readiness to support and facilitate, taking into account specific circumstances, peace-keeping efforts undertaken in the framework of regional organizations and arrangements in accordance with Chapter VIII of the Charter. The Council looks forward to the report of the Secretary-General on cooperation between the United Nations and regional organizations.

The Council draws attention to the increasing significance of post-conflict peace-building. It is convinced that in present circumstances peace-building is inseparably linked with the maintenance of peace.

The Council stresses the value of its high-level meetings and expresses its intention to convene such a meeting on the subject of peace-keeping in the near future.

1/ *S/24728; see* Official Records of the Security Council, Forty-seventh Year, Resolutions and Decisions of the Security Council, 1992, *p. 102.*

2/ Official Records of the Security Council, Forty-seventh Year, Supplement for January, February and March 1992, *document S/24111.*

3/ Financing an effective United Nations: a report of the Independent Advisory Group on United Nations Financing *(A/48/460, annex, and Corr.1).*

Statement by the President of the Security Council
S/PRST/1994/22, 3 May 1994

Aware of its primary responsibility for the maintenance of international peace and security, the Security Council has begun its consideration of the report of the Secretary-General entitled *Improving the capacity of the United Nations for peace-keeping* of 14 March 1994.[1] The Security Council welcomes the useful account the report provides of the measures the Secretary-General has taken to strengthen the capacity of the United Nations to undertake peace-keeping operations. The Security Council notes that this report follows the report of the Secretary-General entitled *An Agenda for Peace*[2] and that it responds to the statements made by successive Presidents of the Security Council on *An Agenda for Peace*, including in particular the statement made by the President of the Security Council on 28 May 1993.[3]

The Security Council notes that the report 'Improving the capacity of the United Nations for peace-keeping' has been transmitted to the General Assembly and also notes that the Special Committee on Peace-keeping Operations has made recommendations on the report.

Establishment of Peace-keeping Operations

The Security Council recalls that the statement made by its President on 28 May 1993[3] stated, *inter alia*, that United Nations peace-keeping operations should be conducted in accordance with a number of operational principles, consistent with the provisions of the Charter of the United Nations. In that context, the Security Council is conscious of the need for the political goals, mandate, costs, and, where possible, the estimated time-frame of United Nations peace-keeping operations to be clear and precise, and of the requirement for the mandates of peace-keeping operations to be subject to periodic review. The Council will respond to situations on a case-by-case basis. Without prejudice to its ability to do so and to respond rapidly and flexibly as circumstances require, the Council considers that the following factors, among others, should be taken into account when the establishment of new peace-keeping operations is under consideration:

- whether a situation exists the continuation of which is likely to endanger or constitute a threat to international peace and security;
- whether regional or subregional organizations and arrangements exist and are ready and able to assist in resolving the situation;
- whether a cease-fire exists and whether the parties have committed themselves to a peace process intended to reach a political settlement;
- whether a clear political goal exists and whether it can be reflected in the mandate;
- whether a precise mandate for a United Nations operation can be formulated;
- whether the safety and security of United Nations personnel can be reasonably ensured, including in particular whether reasonable guarantees can be obtained from the principal parties or factions regarding the safety and security of United Nations personnel; in this regard it reaffirms its statement of 31 March 1993[4/] and its resolution 868 (1993) of 29 September 1993.

The Security Council should also be provided with an estimate of projected costs for the start-up phase (initial 90 days) of the operation and the first six months, as well as for the resulting increase in total projected annualized United Nations peace-keeping expenditures, and should be informed of the likely availability of resources for the new operation.

The Security Council emphasizes the need for the full cooperation of the parties concerned in implementing the mandates of peace-keeping operations as well as relevant decisions of the Security Council.

Ongoing Review of Operations

The Security Council notes that the increasing number and complexity of peace-keeping operations, and of situations likely to give rise to proposals for peace-keeping operations, may require measures to improve the quality and speed of the flow of information available to support Council decision-making. The Security Council will keep this question under consideration.

The Security Council welcomes the enhanced efforts made by the Secretariat to provide information to the Council and underlines the importance of further improving the briefing for Council members on matters of special concern.

Communication with Non-Members of the
Security Council (including Troop Contributors)

The Security Council recognizes the implications which its decisions on peace-keeping operations have for the Members of the United Nations and in particular for troop-contributing countries.

The Security Council welcomes the increased communication between members and non-members of the Council and believes that the practice of monthly consultations between the President of the Security Council and competent groups of Member States on the Council's programme of work (which includes matters relating to peace-keeping operations) should be continued.

The Security Council is conscious of the need for enhanced consultations and exchange of information with troop-contributing countries regarding peace-keeping operations, including their planning, management and coordination, particularly when significant extensions in an operation's mandate are in prospect. Such consultations can take a variety of forms involving Member States, troop-contributing countries, members of the Security Council and the Secretariat.

The Security Council believes that when major events occur regarding peace-keeping operations, including decisions to change or extend a mandate, there is a particular need for members of the Council to seek to exchange views with troop contributors, including by way of informal communications between the Council's President or its members and troop contributors.

The recent practice of the Secretariat convening meetings of troop contributors, in the presence, as appropriate, of Council members, is welcome and should be developed. The Council also encourages the Secretariat to convene regular meetings for troop contributors and Council members to hear reports from Special Representatives of the Secretary-General or Force Commanders and, as appropriate, to make situation reports on peace-keeping operations available at frequent and regular intervals.

The Security Council will keep under review arrangements for communication with non-members of the Council.

Stand-by Arrangements

The Security Council attaches great importance to improving the capacity of the United Nations to meet the need for rapid deployment and reinforcement of peace-keeping operations.

In this context the Security Council welcomes the recommendations in the Secretary-General's report of 14 March 1994 concerning stand-by arrangements and capabilities. The Security Council notes the intention of the Secretary-General to devise stand-by arrangements or capabilities which Member States could maintain at an agreed state of readiness as a possible contribution to a United Nations peace-keeping operation and welcomes the commitments undertaken by a number of Member States.

The Security Council welcomes the request by the Secretary-General to Member States to respond positively to this initiative and encourages Member States to do so in-so-far as possible.

The Security Council encourages the Secretary-General to continue his efforts to include civilian personnel, such as police, in the present stand-by arrangements planning initiative.

The Security Council also encourages the Secretary-General to ensure that the Stand-by Arrangements Management Unit carry on its work, including the periodic updating of the list of units and resources.

The Security Council requests the Secretary-General to report by 30 June 1994 and thereafter at least once a year on progress with this initiative.

The Council will keep this matter under review in order to make recommendations or take decisions required in this regard.

Civilian Personnel

The Security Council welcomes the observations made by the Secretary-General in his report in respect of civilian personnel, including civilian police, and invites Member States to respond positively to requests to contribute such personnel to United Nations peace-keeping operations.

The Security Council attaches importance to full coordination between the different components, military and civilian, of a peace-keeping operation, particularly a multifaceted one. This coordination should extend throughout the planning and implementation of the operation, both at United Nations Headquarters and in the field.

Training

The Security Council recognizes that the training of personnel for peace-keeping operations is essentially the responsibility of Member States, but encourages the Secretariat to continue the development of basic guidelines and performance standards and to provide descriptive materials.

The Security Council notes the recommendations of the Special Committee on Peace-keeping Operations on training of peace-keeping personnel. It invites Member States to cooperate with each other in the provision of facilities for this purpose.

Command and Control

The Security Council stresses that as a leading principle United Nations peace-keeping operations should be under the operational control of the United Nations.

The Security Council welcomes the call by the General

Assembly (resolution 48/43) that the Secretary-General, in cooperation with the members of the Security Council, troop-contributing States and other interested Member States, take urgent action on the question of command and control, notes the comments of the Secretary-General in his report of 14 March 1994 and looks forward to his further report on the matter.

Financial and Administrative Issues

Bearing in mind the responsibilities of the General Assembly under Article 17 of the Charter, the Security Council notes the Secretary-General's observations and recommendations on budgetary matters relating to peace-keeping operations in his report of 14 March 1994 and notes also that his report has been referred to the General Assembly for its consideration.

The Security Council confirms that estimates of the financial implications of peace-keeping operations are required from the Secretariat before decisions on mandates or extensions are taken so that the Council is able to act in a financially responsible way.

Conclusion

The Security Council will give further consideration to the recommendations contained in the report of the Secretary-General.

1/ *S/26450.*

2/ Official Records of the Security Council Forty-seventh Year, Supplement for January, February and March 1992, *document S/24111.*

3/ S/25859; see Official Records of the Security Council Forty-seventh Year, Resolutions and Decisions of the Security Council, 1993, *p.49.*

4/ *S/25493; see* Official Records of the Security Council Forty-seventh Year, Resolutions and Decisions of the Security Council, 1993, *p.47.*

Statement by the President of the Security Council
S/PRST/1994/36, 27 July 1994

The Security Council has considered the report of the Secretary-General of 30 June 1994 concerning stand-by arrangements for peace-keeping,[1] submitted pursuant to the statement by the President of the Council of 3 May 1994.[2]

The Security Council reiterates the importance it attaches to improving the capacity of the United Nations for rapid deployment and reinforcement of peace-keeping operations. The recent history of United Nations peace-keeping operations demonstrates that such an effort is essential.

In this context, the Security Council is grateful for the efforts undertaken by the Secretary-General in respect of stand-by arrangements and welcomes the responses so far received from Member States. It also welcomes the intention of the Secretary-General to maintain a comprehensive database of the offers made, including the technical details of these offers.

The Security Council notes that one of the major limiting factors in the timely deployment of troops for United Nations peace-keeping is the lack of readily available equipment. It stresses the importance of urgently addressing the issue of availability of equipment both in the context of stand-by arrangements and more broadly.

The Security Council notes the Secretary-General's view that the commitments made so far do not yet cover adequately the spectrum of resources required to mount and execute future peace-keeping operations. It also notes that additional commitments are expected from other Member States. In this context, it welcomes the Secretary-General's call to those Member States which are not already doing so to participate in the arrangements.

The Security Council looks forward to a further and more comprehensive report on the progress of the stand-by arrangements initiative.

[1] *S/1994/777.*
[2] *S/PRST/1994/22.*

Statement by the President of the Security Council
S/PRST/1994/62, 4 November 1994

The Security Council has given further consideration to the question of communication between members and non-members of the Council, in particular troop contributing-countries, which was addressed in the statement of the President of the Council of 3 May 1994.[1/] The Council remains conscious of the implications that its decisions on peace-keeping operations have for troop-contributing countries. Having regard to the increase in the number and complexity of such operations, it believes that there is a need for further enhancement, in a pragmatic and flexible manner, of the arrangements for consultation and exchange of information with troop-contributing countries.

To this end, the Security Council has decided in future to follow the procedures set out in this statement:

(a) Meetings should be held as a matter of course between members of the Council, troop-contributing countries and the Secretariat to facilitate the exchange of information and views in good time before the Council takes decisions on the extension or termination of, or significant changes in, the mandate of a particular peace-keeping operation;

(b) Such meetings would be chaired jointly by the Presidency of the Council and a representative of the Secretariat nominated by the Secretary-General;

(c) The monthly tentative forecast of work of the Council made available to Member States will in future include an indication of the expected schedule of such meetings for the month;

(d) In the context of their review of the tentative forecast, the members of the Council will examine this schedule and communicate any suggested changes or proposals as to the timing of meetings to the Secretariat;

(e) Ad hoc meetings chaired jointly by the Presidency of

the Security Council and a representative of the Secretariat nominated by the Secretary-General may be convened in the event of unforeseen developments in a particular peace-keeping operation which could require action by the Council;

(f) Such meetings will be in addition to those convened and chaired solely by the Secretariat for troop contributors to meet with special representatives of the Secretary-General or force commanders or to discuss operational matters concerning particular peace-keeping operations, to which members of the Security Council will also be invited;

(g) An informal paper, including topics to be covered and drawing attention to relevant background documentation, will be circulated by the Secretariat to the participants well in advance of each of the various meetings referred to above;

(h) The time and venue of each meeting with members of the Council and troop contributors to a peace-keeping operation should, where possible, appear in advance in the Journal of the United Nations;

(i) The President of the Council will, in the course of informal consultations of members of the Council, summarize the views expressed by participants at each meeting with troop contributors.

The Security Council recalls that the arrangements described herein are not exhaustive. Consultations may take a variety of forms, including informal communication between the Council President or its members and troop-contributing countries and, as appropriate, with other countries especially affected, for example countries from the region concerned.

The Security Council will keep arrangements for the exchange of information and views with troop contributors under review and stands ready to consider further measures to enhance arrangements in the light of experience.

The Security Council will also keep under review arrangements to improve the quality and speed of the flow of information available to support Council decision-making, bearing in mind the conclusions contained in its statement of 3 May 1994.

1/   *S/PRST/1994/22.*

INDEX

The numbers following the entries refer to paragraph numbers in the texts of the two reports that have been indexed. The letter "A" before the paragraph number refers to the "Supplement to an An Agenda for Peace", which is reproduced on pages 5-38. The letter "B" refers to "An Agenda for Peace", which is reproduced on pages 39-72. The documents in Section Two are not indexed.

Prayer and the Quest for Healing

Prayer and the Quest for Healing

*Our Personal Transformation
and Cosmic Responsibility*

BARBARA FIAND

A Crossroad Book
The Crossroad Publishing Company
New York

The Crossroad Publishing Company
370 Lexington Avenue, New York, NY 10017

Printed in the United States of America

Library of Congress Cataloging-in-Publication Data

Fiand, Barbara.
    Prayer and the quest for healing : our personal transformation and
cosmic responsibility / Barbara Fiand.
      p.   cm.
    Includes bibliographical references.
    ISBN 0-8245-1812-8
    1. Prayer—Christianity.   I. Title.
BV210.2.F49   1999
248.3'2—DC21   99-12732
                                        CIP

1 2 3 4 5 6 7 8 9 10 04 03 02 01 00 99

To
Irene Dugan,
Lois Weber, Ron Terrence Colloty,
and Pat Underhill—
In Gratitude

Contents

vii

Preface

There is an appointed time for everything. . . .
  A time for birth, a time to die;
  a time to plant, and a time to uproot . . .
  A time to seek, and a time to lose;
  a time to keep, and a time to cast away . . .
  a time to be silent, and a time to speak.
    —Ecclesiastes 3:1–6

THERE IS A TIME ALSO FOR PROBING INTO DEPTH and for the courage it takes to do so. This book is for such a time. It involves birthing and dying, to be sure. It struggles with planting and uprooting, keeping and casting away. But, more than anything else, it involves the seeking and losing that are involved when the mind and the heart are open to the new.

This is not a book for the fainthearted. Nor was it intended for those who would prefer to "keep on keeping on." It will involve taking time to reflect slowly, to sit with the issues—"marinating" in them is what I call it in

my classes. "The human heart can go the lengths of God," Christopher Fry insists. He challenges us to "wake, for pity's sake," and take "the longest stride of soul [we] ever took," for our times call us to move into the very depths of God.

For at least a decade now, I have been teaching a course addressing the experience of prayer. Together its participants and I have probed into the reasons for our hunger for God. We have looked at our culture and the apparent destitution of our times. We have also looked at ourselves and asked why and how we pray. We have wondered who God is in our lives and who *we* are that God, in fact, is such a burning issue for us. We have explored the language of prayer, the why of words, and the need for silence and for the empty space within, where God can break in and break through. We have talked about the clutter in our lives and the life-process of emptying out that connects us to the very essence of the transformative process which is creation. We have prayed together and were nurtured in each other's presence. Part 1 of this book remembers these moments of search and of prayer and sets the stage for what is to follow.

Part 2 probes our unity with all of humankind in its brokenness and with the cosmos groaning for redemption. It invites us into a depth encounter with ourselves and urges the acceptance of our call toward continuous conversion. The latter happens from the inside out and is predicated on the recognition of personal need, helpless-

ness, and surrender. Only prayer can bring us to such honesty. This section explores in detail the relation between healing prayer and redemption. It considers the ongoing process of individual, communal, and cosmic transformation as involving a variety of layers. We are connected to each layer, deeply bound up with its healing, as was Jesus, who showed us the way. The encounter with cultural, racial, national, gender, and familial sin is difficult, often excruciatingly painful. Acceptance of our responsibility for, and sharing in, the human condition, however, is essential for genuine forgiveness and reconciliation. Part 2 explores these issues and, I hope, opens up the space for authentic compassion.

Part 3 invites us to expand our horizons. The thoughts and insights emerging in spirituality today and presented in this book do not readily fit into the "wineskins" of what Ó Murchú calls "religious minimalism." They are often interdisciplinary in origin and demand a shift in foundations away from the paradigms of the past which no longer prove adequate for today's learnings. The latter tend to broaden the scope and to provide a desperately needed link between spirit and matter, the sacred and the secular, science and religion. This section offers insights from contemporary science as well as theology that can provide the bridge between previously held perspectives and present-day ideas in spirituality.

Part 3 may be the most intellectually challenging because of the newness of the concepts for some readers.

It could, however, also prove to be an "Aha!" experience for others, for it connects us to the ancient in surprisingly new ways. Science and mysticism are approaching each other these days in a depth search for ultimate meaning that is providing a rich harvest. They offer hope to many who are looking for viable interpretations of what may have grown stale for want of solid grounding in the here-and-now of our age. No one who is longing for a deeper perspective on prayer and spirituality can ignore the new horizons that science and mysticism offer.

This book, like the others I have written, is worth reading only if it invites participation. I have, therefore, once again offered reflections and questions for meditation and discussion at the end of each part. I have also added some suggestions for prayer experiences that build upon the themes discussed. The chapters within the parts vary in length but are generally brief to focus reading and to stimulate thought.

I have tried to write this book in as inclusive a language style as possible in the hope of providing the atmosphere wherein both women and men can see themselves addressed by the issues under discussion. For this pur-pose, any omitted generic female or male pronoun has been added to citations, or else the plural form has been adopted. In the interest of inclusivity, I ask the reader's support and indulgence of what may on occasion prove cumbersome reading.

Once again, there are many to whom I am much

indebted. I want to thank in particular the women and men who attended my classes on the experience of prayer. Your thoughtful questions, enthusiasm, and manifest hunger for God were truly gift to me as well as empowerment in the writing of these pages. This book is for you. Among the many friends who were so very present to me during these months of writing, my special thanks go, once again, to Clare Gebhardt for her invaluable advice and thoughtful reflections, but most of all for her walking with me through these pages, for honest criticism and loving support. My heartfelt thanks also to Joan Marie Sasse, Camilla Burns, Pietra Hagenberger, and Catherine Griffiths for depth insights and powerful life experiences shared. To Kay Brogle and many of my friends who could have legitimately claimed my time, my appreciation for encouragement badly needed at times and for patient endurance. To Sandy Lopez-Isnardi, a special thank you for the art work and, last but never least, to Crossroad Publishing, my gratitude as ever for continued support and encouragement.

PART ONE

Our Hunger for God

The human heart can go the lengths of God.
Dark and cold we may be, but this
Is no winter now. The frozen misery
Of centuries breaks, cracks, begins to move;
The thunder is the thunder of the floes,
The thaw, the flood, the upstart Spring.
Thank God our time is now when wrong
Comes up to face us everywhere,
Never to leave us till we take
The longest stride of soul [we humans] ever took.
Affairs are now soul size.
The enterprise
Is exploration into God.
Where are you making for? It takes
So many thousand years to wake,
But will you wake for pity's sake?
                       —Christopher Fry
                         A Sleep of Prisoners

1

A Shift at Our Core

IN ONE OF HIS MOST SIGNIFICANT WORKS, *THE FIRE and the Rose Are One,* Sebastian Moore claims that original sin—that state of disharmony from which Jesus came to set us free and with which we must struggle, each in our own way, each day, even now—is *the unreality of God.*[1] He suggests that, to the extent to which God and God's unconditional love are *not yet real* in the very core of our hearts, we are still in sin. To the extent to which we do *not as yet realize* that the Holy One pervades our lives, breathes through us, explodes in us, breaks out in us, aches in us, laughs in us, and permeates every fiber of our being with relentless and passionate love, we are still under the control of sin. To the extent to which we still cannot, as Fry would have us, hear "the thunder of the floes," and recognize "the thaw, the flood, the upstart Spring" that announces the end of centuries of frozen misery, sin still holds sway in us and blinds us from the glory that is life.

I have often wondered whether our sojourn here on

earth might not best be understood as a profound dialectic, as a deep wrestling between *our experience of God's reality*, between our encounter with a love that surpasses all understanding, envelopes us, and holds us in the resurrection moment—its truth and its bliss—and *our stubborn insistence on God's unreality*—our doubt and our cynicism—because we, after all, killed God's presence in our midst once, and we continue to deny it to this day in our blind bitterness toward ourselves and others. Our tradition teaches us that salvation is a process, a journey, a race. Some would even have us see it as a battle. Holiness, somehow, is found "on the way" and in the fray. We are assured, over and over again, that this way is Christ, the victorious one, and that prayer means being connected, being "plugged into" the Christ. Prayer, it is said, helps us find our home in Christ's peace. And yet I wonder why there seems to be so little peace even among those who pray. Why is resting in God's love so difficult for us and seemingly so undervalued? Why are so many of us so busy still, "saying our prayers," engaging in spiritual "exercises," and yet experiencing little if any transformation?

The story comes to mind of the young religious who years ago decided to give up on her daily noonday "examen." When asked by her superior why she no longer did this exercise, she simply observed that she did not believe that it was helping her bring about any change. The superior then pointed out to her the numerous religious living in her community who had engaged in this kind of prayer

for thirty, forty, fifty years. Whereupon the young woman noted that this proved her point.

It is my sense that perhaps the time is long overdue for a shift (not a new shift but, truly, a primordial one) at the very core of the God experience in our personal lives, as well as in our tradition. "The frozen misery of centuries," so Christopher Fry assures us, is about to break, to crack, to move. With this shift, I surmise, a movement away from an often blind, task-oriented egocentricity in prayer that has us wallow in God's unreality, to a much-needed and greatly hungered-for ego-transcendence will unleash energies hitherto unfathomed. These energies will effect personal, ecclesial, and even cosmic transformation.

What if we were to experience prayer as something other than primarily an obligation to worship, either communally or privately, imposed on us or endured to "render our dues"? What if we were to let go of the idea of prayer as a desire to establish contact with the deity in order to ask for forgiveness, for healing, for protection? What if we were to see it, rather, as the recognition and the desire to further *what is;* as a dwelling *in,* rather than as an *approaching?* What if prayer were a continuous thanking for the reality that embraces us—a seeing and a celebrating of the Light by which we are surrounded? What if prayer flowed in us very much as our blood does—as a constant "yes" to life and to love, a perpetual affirmation and surrender—not anything we *do,* but rather *everything we are?*

The story is told of the old man in the back of the church who would sit for hours simply gazing, a gentle smile lighting up his countenance. When asked what he was doing, his response was always the same, "Oh, I just look at God, and God looks at me." The gentle serenity that comes with the uncompromised experience of presence is prayer in its deepest possibility. "*Presence* transcends the boundaries of space. It calls us from within even as it encounters us from without. We touch it at our center and from there are moved beyond ourselves. . . . It grounds us and releases us simultaneously, reveals and withholds itself beyond our control."[2]

The Buddhist mystic Thich Nhat Hanh gives words to this experience when he suggests the following centering mantra:

> *I have arrived.*
> *I am home,*
> *In the here,*
> *In the now.*
> *I am solid.*
> *I am free.*
> *In the ultimate*
> *I dwell.*[3]

Prayer is this dwelling. It is the arrival—the coming home, not primarily out of obligation but quite simply because inwardness is our most authentic presence in and to reality.

2

Prayer as a Disposition

PRAYER IS NOT A TASK. PRAYER IS A DISPOSITION, AND this is how Jesus taught it to us. When looking over Matthew's rendition of Jesus' primary lesson on prayer, I noted with interest some of the preliminary observations: "In your prayers do not babble," Jesus warns us. It would seem that for him the use of many words is a waste of time, since God "knows what you need before you ask" (Matt. 6:7–8). With this kind of an introduction, it is difficult to believe that Jesus would have wished us merely to *recite* the prayer he modeled for us with such care.

Perhaps we might consider that when Jesus taught his disciples to pray, his emphasis was on *attitude,* not formula. It seems easy enough to imagine his disciples' admiration for the utter intensity of his prayer life, for his rapture and complete absorption into the Holy. "Teach us to pray," they said. And he, perhaps reflecting for a moment to determine how best he might do that, then began to describe to them the ingredients necessary for any and for all prayer, for their daily recognition of the

Holy One's presence, for their walking on God's earth, and for their dealing with God's people. When Jesus taught his prayer, he taught us a way of being. He modeled a way of seeing that has to permeate our lives, a way of holding ourselves in the context of creation as sacred and in recognition of a Love that permeates the very world we live in.

When you pray, allow the reality of God's unconditional love to embrace you. See God, at all times, as you would a loving parent—as one who cherishes you unconditionally, as one for whom you are utterly important; as one who knows your every need, shelters you in your vulnerability, and wishes you only good. Remember that God has birthed you into being; that God treasures you with infinite tenderness, listens to you with infinite patience, and reaches out to you at every moment of your existence. Dwell in this realization. Allow it to suffuse your very being. Know it in your innermost heart. Live it at your deepest core.

If you do this, your life will be prayer. And you will be filled with the passionate longing that all of God's creatures will come to realize the presence of God in their lives; that Love's reign might be established on earth as, indeed, it exists among the blessed who have passed into eternity already and throughout the universe.

The hunger that fills those who pray is the hunger for justice. They will not be satisfied with pious words of sympathy and condolence when encountering the

oppressed. They will roll up their sleeves and get busy bringing about God's reign, for their prayer opens up to action, and their action yields to prayer. Those who pray are transformers of space, workers—however, wherever— on behalf of the oppressed. Those who pray hold the mission of Jesus, the Christification of the universe, as an uncompromised priority. They know that the will of God has nothing to do with the interests of this world, with the IMF (International Monetary Fund), for example, or the "New World Order," with "first world" and "superpower" interests too often originating in puny minds and puny hearts that can see no further than their own misguided policies. Economies can be of God only when they work genuinely toward feeding the hungry and clothing the naked, when they put their energies toward peacemaking through authentic brotherhood and sisterhood and leave weapons out of it.

To be filled with the sense of God's abiding faithfulness means being consumed with the desire for God's recognition everywhere and by all. One's life becomes a prayer for justice. To be filled with the sense of God's abiding faithfulness means wanting the whole world to benefit from the love energy that courses through creation. It means developing a listening and discerning heart and bringing it into all of life's situations to influence every decision we make from the great to the small. It provides us also with a sense of trust that *God's providence will give us what we need for each day and will help us share what we have with*

those who have less. Prayer requires childlike trust that the concerns of each day can be worked through, and that God is present in every event and will be at our side. We approach prayer with surrender and gratitude, for God "knows what [we] need before [we] ask."

One of my own spiritual guides pointed out to me not long ago that one of the healthiest ways to petition is to thank. Gratitude assumes the generosity of the Giver, the unconditional love of the Lover. If God knows what we need before we ask, and if God loves us more than we can possibly love ourselves, then it is a foregone conclusion that God will provide us with what we need. Our prayer, therefore, overflows with thanksgiving. We live in a disposition of trust, expectancy, and celebration.

All prayer also needs to be prayer for forgiveness as well as for the grace to forgive, and the latter is predicated on the recognition of the former. It would seem, however, highly unlikely that we, in our brokenness, would want God to model God's forgiveness on ours. The wording of the Lord's Prayer may confuse this issue sometimes. Jesus here shows an uncanny insight into the human psyche and its need to encounter its "shadow side." He invites us to contemplate our own sins and presents the call to forgiveness within the framework of personal brokenness and the need for repentance. Compassion, contrary to condescension, is built on the memory of personal failure. If I've "been there, done that" myself (in other words, have betrayed my integrity in different but equally serious

ways), I can hold others in love and understanding and lift them up. The most serious offense against forgiveness is forgetfulness. It breeds self-righteousness and hardens the heart. "Never say 'never'" (i.e., "I would never . . .") is a lesson often learned only through a long process of letting go and of "ego deflation," but it is essential for authentic humility and for the compassion that allows us to experience God.

The disposition required for all prayer, finally, demands *a very keen awareness of the negative and of evil, as well as a depth plea for God's protection:* "I throw in my lot with you, O God. Protect me from anyone who, or anything which, would steer me away from you or oppose the fulfillment of your will in me (not least of which is my own inner darkness and propensity to betray you)." A keen sense of the reality of the human condition in which we are held and of powers beyond human control that can effectively work against the good for which we yearn makes the woman or man of prayer thoroughly realistic and, at the same time, utterly God-dependent—with the serene confidence that good will ultimately prevail.

The prayer that Jesus taught us is meant to be an all-pervasive phenomenon. It was never intended to be rattled off when nothing else comes to mind. It was meant to be lived and to be carried in our hearts as an abiding treasure that permeates every fiber of our being and directs all our actions. When we pray with its vision, we are changed, and we can change the world.

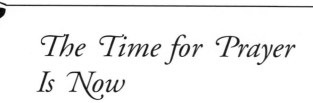

3

The Time for Prayer Is Now

PERHAPS NO TIME IN HISTORY IS IN GREATER need of prayer, and of the healing and peace that come through it, than our present time. In the pivotal moments of the centuries—indeed, of the millennia—in which we find ourselves, our past exposes to us decades of misery and violence, of inhumanity and greed. Not only have we experienced wars that have become ever more brutal and unchecked by common standards of decency, but violence now pervades our everyday existence. Our streets are unsafe, our homes and even our schools are places of abuse, of rape, of incest, and even of murder. The outrage we commit against ourselves and each other is equaled only by the devastation we visit upon this planet—the pollution of earth, and sea, and air. Our knowledge is unparalleled in history, yet the wisdom needed to shepherd our discoveries seems often sadly lacking. This is indeed a time in need of prayer, a time hungry for healing.

And yet, might this not also be a time of redemption,

of thaw, of awakening, as Christopher Fry insists? I once saw a poster depicting the old, rusty fender and wheel of a truck that had been tossed away on a garbage dump. Through the debris and in the midst of all the mess and dirt there blossomed a small white flower. The poster spoke of Gerard Manley Hopkins's vision: "The world is charged with the grandeur of God." Where sin and ugliness abound, does not God's power abound even more (Rom. 5:21)?

With what seems to me to be a rare sense of the grace unique for our time, Christopher Fry suggests that, although our moment in history may appear as ripe for despair, "this is no winter now." We live today, and today is our time of grace. What seems to many of us one of the darkest hours for humankind and its earth is, nevertheless, *our* moment for creative response. Today again, as in every other time since the beginning, the Spirit of God moves over the chaos, and, although "wrong comes up to face us everywhere," God will not leave us to ourselves; the Spirit urges us instead to put our hands and our hearts to the task and to take responsibility for the God-quest for which we were created. Fry pleads with us to wake up "for pity's sake." The call could not be clearer, nor our vocation more urgent, to plunge into the greatest depth, to take "the longest stride of soul [we humans] ever took" and "go the lengths of God."

Martin Heidegger's insight that often "sorrow (anguish, pain) gives forth its healing power where we least expect

to find it" (*Der Schmerz verschenkt seine Heilkraft dort, wo wir sie nicht vermuten*) might be very helpful here. Perhaps for those among us who can see through the despair and are willing to look and to listen, hope is beckoning more so today than ever before since the empty tomb. Is it not true that, in spite of the unprecedented evil and seeming hopelessness we encounter in all areas of life, we nevertheless seem to have been given the tools needed for the victory of goodness and compassion? This century's breakthroughs in science alone offer us now, more than at any other time in history, a vision that clearly propels us beyond the divisiveness of individualism (and the dualism that spawned it in times past) toward newness, and wholeness, and creativity. Human self-understanding and psychology's discovery of the unconscious and of human motivation have today opened up for us the opportunity for self-critique heretofore impossible. The growing emancipation and consequent self-appreciation of women and of other oppressed groups have added voices and power to our common quest for a better world, voices that had been forced into silence for centuries and were forgotten or ignored for so long that no one even knew or would have believed they existed.

It would seem that ours is a time of intense spiritual hunger, of deep longing and waiting for God. The human heart has never ached as it is aching today; the human soul has never been as parched with thirst as it is today. And this, I believe, is precisely why we are ready "to go the

lengths of God," and can open ourselves up to the healing, conversion, and reconciliation that prayer engenders.

The archetypal story of conversion, developed through
centuries of myths, legends, and life experiences, speaks
quite plainly of our propensity for, as well as our hankering after, power and glory. It speaks of the unwholesome-
ness of these desires and depicts the opportunity for
conversion in their demise. Our myths warn us that the
strong and ruthless among us will be brought low, either
through age or through the suffering caused by their own
unrecognized darkness—perhaps even through both.
They will encounter personal vulnerability and sin and
will in due time be invited to surrender in order to
become whole.

The wisdom on this topic abounds in every age and
culture—a clear warning, often unheeded, as in our
times, yet never without consequences: "Pride was my
wilderness," Hagar Shipley, Margaret Laurence's protago-
nist in *The Stone Angel*, whispers on her deathbed. "And
the demon that led me there was fear. I was alone, never
anything else, and never free, for I carried my chains
within me, and they spread out from me and shackled all
I touched."[4] Hagar stands for an attitude of invincibility
particularly relevant for our time: the "I can handle it"
attitude of Western society, which imprisons us in our
own selfishness and shuts out the healing that contact
with others—relationship, love—alone can offer. She was
not a "bad" woman. She was proud and self-sufficient,

incapable of reaching beyond herself. On her deathbed the reality of her situation comes to haunt her with excruciating pain. She longs for the freedom she never allowed herself to enjoy, and for the love that is its expression. Hagar has to be brought low before she can recognize her want. One hopes that in the longing, finally recognized, is the moment of grace, her redemption.

More universally symbolic but, because of this, also less personal and in need, therefore, of careful interpretation are the stories from Scripture and the epics of antiquity. The experience of the dying thief on the cross next to Jesus, the parable of the prodigal child, the story of Israel's sojourn in the desert are just some examples that are applicable here and, in ancient Greece, Homer's Odysseus. The many years it took Odysseus to come home to himself are, perhaps, paradigmatic of the "thousand years" from which Fry asks us to wake in his *A Sleep of Prisoners*.

It is my intuition that an epic is, perhaps, being enfleshed once again, in today's reality. What if, with extraordinary urgency, like Laurence's Hagar at the beginning of her end and after years of independence, like the prodigal child, or like Homer's Odysseus, we are being called home to ourselves again as well as being moved beyond ourselves into cosmic responsibility—into the Heart of God? Epics speak of mysterious events in human collective growth, of powerful forces that draw us into our cosmic destiny and help bring us to integrity. These

events can rarely be clearly identified and planned for. They are surmised, rather, and entered in upon with generosity and passion. They are the stuff of thoughtfulness, of intuition—the stuff that prayer is made of.

This book hopes to explore what prayer can do for each of us to help us plumb the depths and take our part in the transformation to which we are called. It is not a book for prisoners asleep, for bystanders, or onlookers. Our task is too serious for that, and our responsibility too grave.

> *[It took] so many thousand years to wake,*
> *[So let us] wake for pity's sake!*

4

Entering the Silence

IN AN ANCIENT AND PRECIOUS LITTLE SPIRITUAL classic of unknown origin the story is told of a poor Russian peasant who, having lost his family as well as all that he owned and being unable to earn a living because of a physical handicap, wanders the roads of his vast country in search of someone who would help him realize in his life the meaning of Paul's exhortation to pray unceasingly (1 Thess. 5:17). "What shall I do?" he asks. "Where can I find a person who will explain this mystery to me? I heard many very good homilies on prayer, but they were all instructions about prayer in general, . . . no one spoke of the way to succeed in prayer." He finally finds help with a spiritual Father who teaches him to practice what today we call the "Jesus Prayer."[5]

There is perhaps no other account in our spiritual tradition that is as poignant and filled with ardent longing for union with God through prayer than is this simple tale. Its mandate is thought-provoking: "Rejoice always,

never cease praying, render constant thanks; such is God's will for you in Christ Jesus" (1 Thess. 5:17).

At first it would seem quite understandable that such an exhortation would evoke puzzlement and a sense of the impossible, for even the recitation of the Jesus Prayer would, of itself, appear like repetitious "babbling" that could easily lead to boredom—a kind of mindless murmuring where content becomes insignificant and meaning is lost. For many of us the rosary falls into the same category, and the recommendation to meditate on the mysteries of redemption while reciting the same prayer over and over again may be an attempt to prevent the boredom that repetition can bring about.

Yet the peasant really did not get bored but seemed to have moved ever more deeply into the mystical. What he did looked like "babbling," but was it that? What is it that has the old woman in the back of the church lose herself for hours in the recitation of the "Hail Mary"? Why do Buddhist monks drone endlessly the prayers of their tradition? What is the point of the mantra or breath prayer, recited (much like the Jesus Prayer but in a rhythmic fashion of numbered syllables) over and over again? Why do we repeat words or make sounds we sometimes may not even understand?

The Russian peasant tells us that his holy words moved him into silence even as he was reciting them. Could it be that this is the *true* reason for speech? Words are spoken,

but meaning falls into the heart and is silent. This is most
eloquently so in depth encounters, as between friends, or
during the recitation of a poem. How much more so in
prayer, for prayer addresses the unspeakable and, by so
doing, points beyond words. Perhaps true prayer uses
words only to enhance stillness and deepen love. Once
again, the words of Martin Heidegger come to mind:
"What is spoken," he says, "is never, and in no language,
what is said" (*Nie ist das Gesprochene und in keiner Sprache
das Gesagte*).

Our world is filled with frequencies for communication. We turn them on; we tune them out. Their inaudi-
bility, however, is not silence. More accurately it is noise
ever waiting to happen—words invading stillness. The
words of prayer are meant for a different sphere and
touch a deeper dimension. Their intent is to create space,
to open up the possibility, to make available the
moment—the now—for the inbreaking of the Holy.
When our worship moves into this space, words and
silence merge. Then, style, method, language, and format
become inconsequential, and prayer dissolves into what
the mystics so often experienced: a simple "Ah!" before
the mystery of it all.

A story I told in *Wrestling with God,* in a slightly different context, comes to mind here and bears repeating.
It comes to us from the Persian mystics. There it was said
that Moses one day heard a shepherd praying to God in
the simple and homely way of shepherds. He spoke of

wanting to help God—of fixing God's shoes and comb-
ing God's hair, of washing God's clothes and picking off
all the lice. He wanted to bring God milk and kiss God's
hands and feet before he went to bed. He wanted to
sweep God's room and keep it neat and tidy. He told God
that all he could say when he thought of God was "Ah!"

Moses, so the mystics tell us, became quite irritated
with the shepherd's apparent disrespect. He told the shepherd that the one who made the earth and sky should not
be addressed that way; that God does not need shoes and
socks and milk; that this kind of talk was blasphemous
and sounded more like a conversation with one's uncle.
Only something that grows needs milk; only someone
with feet needs shoes and socks. Moses suggested that the
shepherd's love was foolish and irreverent and advised
him to use appropriate language.

It is reported that the shepherd repented when he
heard Moses' admonition; that he tore his clothes in sorrow, sighed, and wandered into the desert. Moses, on the
other hand, had a sudden revelation from God, who rep-
rimanded him for separating God from one of God's
own. "Did you come as a prophet to unite or to sever?"
God asked. God pointed out that God has given each
being a unique way of seeing, and knowing, and speaking
wisdom. What seems so wrong to Moses may be quite
right for the shepherd. Purity and impurity, sloth and
diligence in worship, Moses was told, mean nothing to
God, who is apart from all that. Ways of worship are not

to be ranked as better or worse. It is all praise. It is all right. Contrary to Moses' view, it is not God who is glorified in acts of worship; it is the worshiper. *"I do not hear the words they say,"* God instructed him. *"I look inside at the humility. That broken, open lowliness is the reality, not the language. Forget phraseology. I want burning, burning!"* God asked Moses to be friends with his burning, to burn up his thinking and his forms of expression. He suggested that "those who pay attention to manners of speaking are of one sort. *Lovers who burn are another."*[6]

5

Approaches to God

THERE ARE NUMEROUS WELL-WRITTEN AND INFOR-
mative books that speak of diverse prayer styles and
methodology, describe various spiritualities, and identify
which personality types might best fit which type of
prayer. There are others that help with the actual experience of prayer, offer guided meditations, and suggest
steps that can help us breathe, quiet ourselves, concentrate, and center. This book does not need to repeat what
they already offer,[7] although I will, by way of example,
suggest some prayer experiences at the end of each section. What is important to remember as one explores various movements and styles, and what is clearly illustrated
by the Sufi story above, is that there is no "superior" way
to God. I frequently suggest to students of prayer this
simple norm: if it helps to bring you to an awareness of
God's presence, use it. I can still remember the woman
religious in my class who, after years of struggling with
centering prayer and feeling totally inadequate, discovered that her personality would much rather work with

guided imagery. She felt relieved and affirmed. Others will journal. Still others will dance, chant, paint, or do meditative walking. As God communicated to Moses: "Ways of worship are not to be ranked as better or worse. It is all praise. It is all right." ALL GOD WANTS IS BURNING.

It is clear that prayer changes as we change. There is really no sacrosanct way to pray above all others, not even the Psalter. What works for one tradition or culture, for one personality or Enneagram type, may not for another. What works for us when we are young may prove no longer useful as we mature. During moments of crisis we may pray differently from the way we prayed during periods of calm. Centering may be difficult during certain times of life even for the one for whom it is the surest way to stillness at other times. None of this needs to be an indication of failure. The importance of prayer is in the praying, not in the method—and, I might add, in praying regularly. We pray daily so that our day might become prayer.

All of us, of course, move between the two primary orientations of spirituality generally known as cataphatic and apophatic. The former emphasizes imagery, symbols, sensation, words, and feelings. It is essential for public worship, and without it the young could never be introduced to the ways of prayer. Cataphatic spirituality responds to our embodied presence to each other, to the reality around us, to the Holy permeating the world in

which we live and move. It gives itself to singing, to danc-
ing, to art. Cataphatic spirituality fosters color, designs
vestments, writes psalms, creates prayer services that help
us praise, give thanks, and mourn. Cataphatic spirituality
sees God in all things and longs, through metaphor, to
speak of the divine and to proclaim God's goodness.

Apophatic spirituality, on the other hand, while appreciating the former, places its emphasis on the truth of
God that lies behind or is hidden within all sensory or
intellectual representations. It recognizes the limitedness
of human symbols, the inadequacy of words. It notes the
exaggeration in certitude and definitive statements about
the divine and stresses the negativity and darkness that
pervade all human knowing. Apophatic prayer prefers
silence and emphasizes the importance of "unknowing,"
of listening, and of waiting. "I pray God to rid me of
God," the Rhineland Mystic cries and means by the second "God" that he needs to be rid of all the images that
have become sacrosanct and have imprisoned God in the
human mind. The apophatic wants freedom to be open
and utterly empty, for it is there alone that God can be
found.

It is clear that for human interaction and communication images and words are essential. It is equally clear that
they are never adequate. The danger of cataphatic exaggeration is externalism, the endless fascination with
imagery, conceptuality, and words. It can lead to a denial
of mystery even though this is usually quite subtle.

Complicated declarations about God and pious explanations of the holy mysteries can have it seem as if the Holy were ever before us, even as we delude ourselves about containing it indubitably within our propositions. Then, as Karl Rahner would say,

> We talk of God as if we had already slapped [God] on the shoulder—so to speak—and, with regard to [our fellow humans], we feel that we are God's supervisors and more or less [God's] equals. . . . Whenever piety is directed only by an ingenious, complicated intellectuality and conceptuality, with highly complicated theological tenets, it is really a pseudo-piety, however profound it seems to be.[8]

Quite simply, piety is enhanced neither by individual or institutional certitude, nor by doctrinal obsession with correctness. It flows out of a humble heart emptied of all presuppositions, assumptions, and expectations. For this, the apophatic approach is indispensable, since it has us face the ultimate limitations of human speech and helps us embrace the silence which alone can make room for the Holy.

> In the midst of our everyday awareness we are blessed or damned (have it how we will) in regard to that nameless, illimitable eternity. The concepts and words which we use subsequently to talk of this everlastingness to and into which we are constantly referred, *are not the original actual mode of being* of that experience of nameless mystery that surrounds the island of our everyday awareness,

but merely the tiny signs and idols which we erect and have
to erect so that they constantly remind us of *the original,
unthematic, silently offered and proffered, and graciously
silent experience of the strangeness of the mystery in which,
in spite of all the light offered by the everyday awareness of
things, we reside, as if in a dark night and a pathless wilderness.* (There we are in darkness and a desert place—but
one that reminds us of the abyss in whose depths we are
grounded but can never plumb.)[9]

The danger for the apophatic lies in extreme passivity
and a refusal to get involved in the world. If God lies
beyond the tangible, the sensory, the world of nature,
God's mystery, nevertheless, pervades it. There is a *presence*
in the "beyondness" or seeming negativity, a *luminosity*
within the darkness. This *presence* and *luminosity*, however, can be experienced *only through engagement.* We
noted earlier that true prayer uses words only to enhance
stillness. The Russian peasant's holy words moved him
into silence even as he was reciting them. What we see
here is *the merging of the apophatic and the cataphatic.* The
apophatic provides the environment wherein the cataphatic can flourish and, in turn, deepen the stillness
whence it came.

Angelus Silesius hints at this when he observes:

> God, whose love and joy
>   are present everywhere,
> can't come to visit you
>   unless you aren't there.[10]

And again:

> God is a pure no-thing
>   concealed in now and here:
> the less you reach for [God]
>   the more [God] will appear.[11]

The love and joy of God found *everywhere* speak to the cataphatic attitude. They cannot, however, be encountered truly *unless the heart is empty of its own expectations, presuppositions and assumptions.* God simply cannot be reduced to the category of a "thing"—not even a holy "thing" (or "substance," as our Greco-Roman vocabulary is prone to phrase it). Though God's holy mystery breaks through in space and time (cataphatic), the surrender of empty openness, abandonment, freedom from expectations (what elsewhere I have called "releasement"[12]) is essential for an authentic encounter.

6

Human Emptiness

I HAVE OFTEN WONDERED WHY PAUL'S EXHORTATION to the Philippians does not get more prominence in books about prayer: "In your minds," he tells us, "you must be the same as Christ Jesus. His state was divine, yet he did not cling to his equality with God, *but emptied himself* to assume the condition of a slave, *and became as [we] are*" (Phil. 2:5–7). The point here is that when God became incarnate in Jesus, God modeled for us human nature at its most authentic: as empty receptivity, as vulnerability, as surrender. Paul tells us that we need to assume this attitude.

It is my sense that reaching the still point where the cataphatic and the apophatic experiences of God meet within the human person allows this emptying to happen. As persons, so anthropologists tell us, we are "the universe come to consciousness." In us, creation can reflect on its existence and cry out in wonder and in awe. In us, the stars of the heavens, the mountains, and the sea praise their God. But they can do so only because in the

fullness of our personhood we are empty enough to receive them and return them, once again, to their Maker in thanksgiving.[13]

The word "person," as I discussed in *Embraced by Compassion*, symbolizes in its etymology this very point:

> It is interesting to note that the word "person" is derived from the Latin: *personare* (*per*, through; *sonare*, to sound). The etymology of this word reveals much about the wisdom of the ancients in whom language first broke forth and found expression—about their insight into the authenticity and beauty of their own being as receptive, vulnerable, and interdependent. Imaging with our fore-mothers and forefathers into the nature of personhood as that "through which sound flows" invariably returns me to Caryll Houselander's *The Reed of God:* I think of the emptiness of the Mother of God, praised here in the fullness of her humanity as person, and symbolized by a wind instrument, a flute. There are certain distinct characteristics that allow for sound to flow through a flute. First, it would seem that a flute must be *open* to receive the breath of the flutist. It will also have to be hollow or *empty within* so that the air can freely pass through it, so that no blockage will distort or hinder the sound. There will need to be in the overall makeup of the instrument, in its wood or metal and its design, a givenness to receive, a *receptivity* to the breath, and a *responsiveness* to this breath: a capacity to let it be transformed into sound, to let it flow forth from the instrument and allow for music. Openness, emptiness, receptivity, and response

seem essential for a good wind instrument. They are also essential to authentic personhood.[14]

And they are the ingredients for prayer. They do not "come easy," of course, and often years of stripping— sometimes done gently, sometimes done with excruciating pain—precede their emergence. The ego has a tendency to fill itself with seemingly important "identity" issues: our names, our degrees, our connections, our ideas, our viewpoints, our plans and ambitions, our status, our reputation, our profession, to mention only a few. We "putter around" with them, their concerns, and the version of truth they present to us about ourselves. We puff ourselves up because of them and feel offended when others ignore them or forget them. We "worry and fret about many *things*," Jesus warns us, "and yet few are needed, indeed only one," and that is the Word of God, which can be received only when the heart is empty (Luke 10:41–42).

In an extraordinary meditation on the passage from Luke just cited, the German mystic Eckhart asks the fundamental question necessary for anyone longing for depth prayer: What makes it possible for the Word of God to enter the human soul?[15] Eckhart, speaking metaphorically and wishing to exemplify in his response the ready openness and surrender of Mary, the Mother of God, replies as follows: The soul must be both virgin and mother. By "virgin" Eckhart symbolizes emptiness. We

must be as free and open as we were when we as yet were not (*So ledig wie er war, da er noch nicht war* [the German word *ledig* can mean both "unmarried," i.e., virgin, and "free"]). Eckhart here clearly stresses freedom from ego involvement. Ideas and thoughts are, of course, always a part of human consciousness, and empty-mindedness is not what he is recommending. What he wants us to become is *liberated from our obsession with them*. We are empty if they do not bind us. Only then can we receive nature as it is—can we let a river be a river and a mountain, a mountain. Only then can we accept persons—our friends, our children, our sisters and brothers—the way they are and allow our relationships to flourish without the encumbrance of the will to control and to overpower. In the virgin soul, God can be God and can break through into all of creation.

The breakthrough of God, made possible by the empty openness we are discussing, is addressed through the metaphor of motherhood. When we are full, we cannot receive. It is the empty womb (virgin) that allows God to be conceived and gives God room to flourish and grow in the depth of human existence until, as mothers, we can give God forth—praising, appreciating, being so transformed that we can see the glory of God and affirm divine birthing in all of creation.

The interdependence of the apophatic (emptying out—the traditional *via negativa*) and the cataphatic (seeing God in all of creation—*via positiva*) is clearly sym-

bolized here. What may not, however, be so obvious is
that this process is *for all of us*. It *is* what prayer is meant
to bring about, because it is most authentically what the
human person *is* and *was destined for*. Prayer, at its deepest, is meant to bring us home to ourselves. As *virgin-
mothering* it is touching the source of reality as mystery
and allowing us to stand within it in open, vulnerable,
receptive responsiveness. It is most fundamentally a state
of being, *a state we were designed for by a God bursting
forth in love and longing for our love*. Prayer is the open
emptiness we *are*, directed toward God. Prayer is touching the eternal.

7

Our Yes to God's Breakthrough

WE KNOW, OF COURSE, THAT THE OPENNESS WE HAVE been discussing is not an accomplished fact, even though *it is what we are.* Perhaps it would be easier if we understood it as *our fulfillment,* as that toward which we are directed by the creative love of God. We carry the seed of this, our destiny, with us from the mysterious moments of our beginning and are called forth toward its ever deeper realization at every subsequent moment of our life.

The experience here is clearly one of process, of becoming, and of change because, even though empty-openness is in the deepest sense our essence, this is far from recognized in the beginning of our existence, and we come to its realization only slowly, all too slowly. Also, as I mentioned already, our preference often is to obstruct the process of self-emptying through the collecting and gathering of nonessentials. Our hankering is for possessions. We fill ourselves up in order to protect ourselves and our precious identity from the *no-thing*, which much more clearly presences the truth of our existence. We do this

primarily, I believe, because we are so afraid of being *who we are:* "A living incompleteness," as Thomas Merton puts it, "a gap, an emptiness that calls for fulfillment from someone else,"[16] an empty receptivity and open vulnerability before God. Ego building has its perks even if the effort is quite often painful and filled with disappointments. Ego transcendence, on the other hand, threatens us because we do not want to lose anything, and we do not know where the "I" will fit "when this is all over." Francis Thompson's classic poem *The Hound of Heaven*— its recounting of human flight from, and resistance to, the movement into God—is a story for all of us.

There is, perhaps, nothing more experiential for an authentic understanding of the charter events of faith— creation, incarnation, and redemption—than our very own slow and often painful becoming. Most of us see creation as something that happened at the beginning and ended millions of years ago. For us, incarnation occurred some two thousand years ago and brought about redemption through crucifixion. We live a theology of the past. This explains why, for so many, religion has lost its enthusiasm and challenge. After all, we do not live in the past but do so in the now. Creation, incarnation, and redemption address us, therefore, in the present moment and as a unified whole, or they do not address us at all.

I am not implying here that the history of our faith and our remembering it is irrelevant. What I am saying is that this story never ended; that it is ongoing, and that it

is one. Creation, incarnation, redemption—that is, *trans-formation*—occurs in the here-and-now. God's activity involves us intimately and all the time, and prayer establishes the bonds necessary for this involvement. Prayer centers us in the transformative event and, as it furthers our own personal journey into emptiness, it links us also ever more authentically to the depth journey of the universe being propelled into God.

William Johnston, the great writer on Christianity and Zen, claims that the observation that "the Zen master 'sits' for the whole universe" and, therefore, helps in its transformation applies to the person of prayer as well. Speaking of mystical prayer, Johnston observes that when we surrender to it, "the very highest form of human energy is brought into play, a human energy that is nothing other than love at the core of one's being. It is precisely this," he insists, *"that builds the earth. . . .* Here a whole cosmic energy is unleashed and the whole world shakes. More things are wrought by prayer than this world dreams of."[17]

The dynamic we encounter in prayer is the dynamic of creation. "God is not finished with us yet," nor is God finished with the cosmos. God is shaping what we are and are ever more becoming in a continuous process of emergence (creation). This process, at one and the same time, is the enfleshing of God in creation (incarnation) and the furthering of the good and of the well-being of everything that is (redemption). Ours is a living God, not a static

clockmaker. God, therefore, is bursting forth in love all the time, and *we are in the bursting forth*—the Christ event—every day, every moment anew. The salvific plan of God, which is creation, incarnation, and redemption all in one, is being lived in us every moment of our existence and always for the Christification of the world.

Prayer yields us the space for the *yes* to this love explosion into creation. Because "we are the universe come to consciousness," self-aware and free, God's "breaking out" can be realized in us. But it can also be impeded. We have the power to deny God's plan, to ruin creation. We can thwart God's breakthrough in us and in the world. We can interfere with God's continuous incarnation and redemption. We can hurt the Mystical Body. We do so, as I pointed out already, by refusing to accept the reality of all of this, by denying our life-blood, by betraying what we are meant to be as emptiness, as "virgin mothers," where the yes to what is can be spoken, and where creation can sing forth in praise and in thanksgiving.

Our emptiness is the focal point for creative energy. It is so for us; it is so also for the cosmos whose dynamic we articulate. In a recent book by Diarmuid Ó Murchú entitled *Reclaiming Spirituality,* this point is brought home beautifully. After identifying our uniqueness in the evolutionary process in terms of serving "that process in its becoming conscious of itself," Ó Murchú reflects on the creative energy of emptiness that is actually found in space:

From the spiritual perspective, we also need to heed current research on the nature of empty space in the universe. . . . Some 90 per cent of the space in the universe is emptiness, in the sense that it is not occupied by tangible, physical reality. What we now realize is that that *emptiness is in fact fullness*, a reservoir of pure energy that continuously potentiates, begets and holds the entire universal creative process in being. Without the creative vacuum, everything would dissolve into nothingness. *Emptiness is the precondition for the fullness of life in the universe.*[18]

The above highlights our connectedness as well as our extraordinary *similarity* with all of creation. Our *difference* lies in our freedom and in our consequent capacity to flee from the creative paradox. The fullness of emptiness is not easily credible to our complex ways of understanding and readily induces fear. It is my sense, however, that most of life's suffering comes from our resistance, and most of our need for healing springs from the hurt created by it.

Thoughts and Questions
for Meditation

1. To the extent to which God and God's unconditional love are not yet real in the very core of our hearts, sin still holds sway in us and blinds us from the glory that is life.

2. What if prayer were a continuous thanking for the reality that embraces us—a seeing and a celebrating of the Light by which we are surrounded? What if prayer flowed in us very much as our blood does—as a constant yes to life, to love; a perpetual affirmation and surrender—not anything we *do,* but rather *everything we are?*

3. When Jesus taught his prayer, he taught an attitude. He modeled a way of seeing that needs to permeate our lives.

4. The hunger that fills those who pray is the hunger for justice. They will not be satisfied with pious words of sympathy and condolence when encountering the oppressed. They will roll up their sleeves and get busy bringing about God's reign, for their prayer opens up to action, and their action yields to prayer.

5. One of the healthiest ways to petition is to thank. We are called to live in a disposition of trust, expectancy, and celebration.

6. Perhaps true prayer uses words only to enhance stillness. The words of prayer are intended to create space, to open up the possibility, to make available the moment—the now—for the inbreaking of the Holy. When our worship moves into this space, words and silence merge. Then style, method, language, and format become inconsequential, and prayer dissolves into what the mystics so often experienced: a simple "Ah!" before the mystery of it all.

7. The importance lies in the praying, not in the method —and in praying regularly. We pray daily so that our day might be prayer.

8. In us, creation can reflect on its existence and cry out in wonder and in awe. In us the stars of the heavens, the mountains, and the sea praise their God. But they can do so only because in the fullness of our personhood we are empty enough to receive them and return them once again to their Maker in thanksgiving.

9. Prayer, at its deepest, is meant to bring us home to ourselves. It is most fundamentally a state of being, a state we were designed for by a God longing for our love. It is the openness we *are*, directed toward God. It is touching the eternal.

10. The Zen master "sits" for the whole universe and therefore helps bring about its transformation, and so does the person who prays.

Prayer Experiences

PRELIMINARY ADVICE

1. For these experiences it is best to gather in a small group and to allow one person to guide the others through the experience. Since the guiding tends to distract the guide somewhat, it is good to alternate who will do this in order to give everyone a chance to experience the prayer.

2. The environment is important for the prayer experience. Gathering in a circle around a lit candle and introducing the prayer time with soft music is often very helpful.

3. It may be advisable for some to read through the explanations that are given with the recommended steps of the prayer process. This will give the necessary information and free the guide from having to do so. If you are familiar with this form of prayer, just close your eyes and wait for the others, breathing gently, deeply, and slowly.

4. After some moments of introductory music or silence, intended to quiet the mind and heart, the guide begins the actual prayer period, speaking softly and giving ample time for silence during the recommended (pause) periods.

BREATHING GUIDELINES

- Sit comfortably:
    - Hold your back straight but in a relaxed fashion,
    - Keep your feet uncrossed and flat on the floor,
    - Leave your arms uncrossed, and your hands resting in your lap.

- As you move into stillness, become aware of your breathing.

- Breathe gently, deeply, slowly.

[PAUSE]

> As you take these breaths, bow your head forward. This will allow your eyes to move upward behind your eyelids and facilitate slower brain waves (Alpha), which are conducive to the meditative state. This biological fact may be the unconscious reasoning behind the exhortation to "Bow your heads and pray for God's blessing," and also why people often look up, tilting their heads and rolling their eyes up, when they send prayers "heavenward."

- We begin, now, with three deep breaths.
    - Breathe in. Hold it, hold it, hold it. Slowly exhale.
    - Breathe in. Hold it, hold it, hold it. Slowly exhale.
    - Breathe in. Hold it, hold it, hold it. Slowly exhale.

- Now breathe, once again, slowly, gently, and deeply. Become aware of the uptight places in your body. Try to relax your forehead, your facial muscles, your jaw.

> To relax your facial muscles it helps to part your lips slightly and to widen them just a tiny bit into an almost imperceptible smile.

- Relax your neck, your shoulders. Allow your hands to grow heavy in your lap. Relax your knees and your feet, which are firmly grounded on the floor.

- Once again, become aware of your breathing: slowly, gently, deeply.

- Allow everything gently to drift away from you:
  - Your concerns,
  - The stress of the day,
  - Your worries and tensions.

- Become aware of your breathing: slowly, gently, deeply.

[PAUSE]

Experience 1
Finding a Breath-Prayer for Yourself

The point of the breath-prayer, or mantra, is to reduce the number of words in our prayer experience and to move us into silence. When stillness enters your heart, you may let the breath-prayer drift away until distractions break in on you again. Then gently resume the breath-prayer once more.

READING: (John 1:4–5) *"All that came to be had life in him and that life was the light of [humankind], a light that shines in the dark, a light that darkness could not overpower."*

PRAYER: God, source of all that is good, we come to you today to ask for your healing power in our lives. We ask you to surround us with your healing light, to fill our hearts with

your gentle love, and to bring to our minds whatever it is in our lives that needs to be emptied out most urgently so that your Spirit can flow most freely through us. We ask this through Jesus, the Christ.

- Now, as you are breathing gently and quietly:
  - –Allow yourself to scan your present life situation.
  - –Become aware of those issues that seem to draw most of your energy away from you, that worry you the most.
  - –Sift out, if you can, the major concern from all the surface concerns that are there.
  - –Allow God to show you what it is that you need to help you work creatively with this issue.

[LONG PAUSE]

- See now if you can formulate a short breath-prayer (mantra) of around seven syllables that can express your concern and your need and can ask for God's help.

[PAUSE]

> If you are prone to worry and fret, you may want to ask God's Spirit to give you peace: "Spirit of God grant me peace," or "Jesus, let me know your peace."
>
> If you have difficulty doing what needs to be done in any particular situation, you may want to ask God for help to do God's will: "Father [Mother], let your will be done," or "Let your will be done in me."
>
> If you have difficulties with kindness, faithfulness in a relationship, loving, ask God to let God's love empower you: "Spirit of God, love through me," or "Love of Jesus, live in me."
>
> It is important that the breath-prayer come from your heart and not be a formula given to you from someone else. The prayer flows with your breathing and, if it is a "fit," so to speak, it will eventually say itself in you.

- When you have formed your prayer, let it say itself in you, over and over again. Match it, as much as possible, with your breathing, saying it rhythmically and gently.

[LONG PAUSE]

[SOFT MUSIC]

PRAYER: We praise you, O God, and we bless you. Flow through us this day and, from us, into this troubled world and grant us peace.

Gently, now, and when you are ready, go in Christ's peace.

Experience 2
Breathing in the Light[19]

Begin by following the Breathing Guidelines on pages 42–43. The purpose of this prayer is to move us ever more fully into the light of God and into stillness.

READING: (John 8:12) *"I am the light of the world; anyone who follows me will not be walking in the dark, but will have the light of life."*

PRAYER: God, source of life and light, we come to you today to ask for your light. Surround and fill us with your radiance and drive from us everything that is not of you. We ask this in the name of Jesus, the Christ.

1. Now, as you are gently breathing in and breathing out:

–Imagine yourself surrounded by God's presence in the form of light.

–This light surrounds you. It is warm and soothing and gently absorbs all your fears, your anger, your negativity.

–The light richly relaxes you and refreshes you.

–It tells you in a beautifully gentle way—a way beyond words—that God loves you.

REST IN THIS LIGHT.

[PAUSE]

2. Now, become aware that you are breathing in this light. Allow your breathing in and breathing out to remind you of God's Holy Spirit.

[PAUSE]

3. As you are breathing in the light, your heart becomes a glowing center. It warms you deep from within. This glowing center within you expands throughout your body, filling it with light and energy. It warms and relaxes you. It heals whatever is hurting. It soothes you with God's love.

4. Now, gently, let your breathing out become a letting go of all fear and negativity. Let your breathing in be the breathing in of God's Spirit. One replaces the other and you begin to feel very much at peace.

STAY THERE AND REST IN GOD'S PEACE.

[LONG PAUSE]

[SOFT MUSIC]

PRAYER: Spirit of God, I adore you and thank you for your life in me. I praise you and bless you. Teach me with my life to glorify you. I ask this in the name of Jesus, the Christ.

Gently, now, and when you are ready, go in Christ's peace.

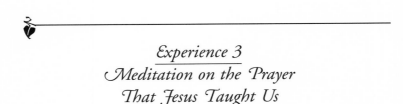

Experience 3
Meditation on the Prayer
That Jesus Taught Us

This prayer experience is intended for private prayer—alone or with a friend.

It is important at all times to place yourself into the presence of God before you start and to follow the Breathing Guidelines on pages 42–43. Any one of the meditative questions suggested here may take a number of sessions. Do not rush the experience, and work with your spiritual director whenever issues surface that need to be worked through in greater detail.

1. *Our Father/Mother who art in heaven.*

a) Become aware of what parenting has meant for you—both as a child and as an adult, if you have any children or parents living. Be with this experience for a while. Allow its joys and/or its sorrows to come into your heart. They are real and need to be honored.

b) The God whom you are addressing is the deepest love

that this image can represent. God is the fulfillment of all your yearning and the contradiction of all your hurtful experiences. God wipes away all tears and cradles you in his/her arms. God cares for your needs and loves you at every moment into life. The love that God has for you is unending and unconditional. Dwell in this love and allow it gently to become real.

c) During the day return to this love experience and allow it to suffuse your every thought and action. It is the ambiance in which you dwell, the foundation on which you rest.

2. *May your name be praised; may your reign be established here on earth even as it is in heaven.*

a) Reread the reflection offered in this section on the call to be about God's reign. Ask yourself: What does this mean to me? What would my life look like if God's reign were primary to it? How do my actions evidence my concern for God's primacy in my life and in my surroundings?

b) Is there a difference between the clear concerns of the institutions I belong to and serve and the concerns for justice proclaimed by the reign of God? Where is the passion of my life? To what do I give my heart?

c) What changes would come about in my life if I were consumed by zeal for God's reign? Do I want to allow this to happen?

3. *Give us this day our daily bread.*

a) What are my needs? Can I admit I have them? Do they point to things or to relationships? What do they teach me about myself?

b) Can I trust God to be with me in my needs, and do I believe God loves me there? Do I love myself there?

c) Would I prefer to rely solely on myself? How much of a control person am I? What do I think of people who seem to have needs I do not have? What does this teach me about myself?

d) Where in life have I learned that I can't go it alone?

4. *And forgive us our sins, as we forgive those who have sinned against us.*

a) *We learn compassion in the dregs of our own passion.* What in my life causes me the greatest pain or hurt? Did I cause this hurt or suffer it? Can I allow God's healing light to surround me in my pain? Can I allow God's healing love to surround and to fill all those caught up in that experience?

b) Is it possible for me to forgive those who have hurt me? (Be specific; avoid generalities.) Do I really want to forgive? If not, can I forgive myself for not wanting to forgive? Can I ask God to be with me in this seeming impasse? Is it possible for me to allow myself to be there with God? Have I ever forgiven too fast, and found out later that I still harbored resentment and anger? If so, I know that in these matters patience with myself is essential.

c) Have I ever done something I thought I would never do? What did I learn from this experience? Can I forgive myself? Do I really believe God can forgive me?

d) What can my sin teach me about compassion?

5. *And lead us not into temptation, but deliver us from evil.*

a) Do I believe in the reality of evil? Do I count on God's protection?

b) Do I understand that asking God to surround me with God's healing Light is a powerful way to guard myself against evil?

c) Do I send forth the Light of Christ that is within me so that I can effect transformation around me and help protect those whom I love, as well as my environment, from the negative forces that surround us?

These meditative questions are meant to evoke thoughtfulness. They are not intended as a questionnaire. They may not yield an immediate answer. They invite us, rather, to dwell in them. Becoming aware that the "Prayer Jesus Taught Us" invites us into a way of being rather than a reciting of a formula will help us to be in these questions and to allow them to help us see with different eyes. It is recommended that one does not work with more than one or two sections of each question at a time, and that one seek the support of a soulmate in the process of interiorization.

PART TWO

The Call to Personal Transformation

*[W]e can change humanity, society, and the world **by our sitting [in prayer] and changing ourselves**. Anyone who enters upon one of the esoteric paths of the great religions is performing the actual work of changing consciousness in our world.*

*The mystics have always been clear on this point. The silent prayer of the men and women who betake themselves into the presence of God is far stronger and far more powerful than any words. Such persons are, as it were, connecting themselves to God's field of force and becoming conductors of energy to others. **We have to learn to become open to this divine source of energy, to which every one of us is linked.***

*God works by means of the order of [God's] creation; creation and redemption are not structured differently. . . . If we press forward into the metastructure of humanity and further still into what we call the divine life in us, we transform the world—not through our own strength but **through the strength of the Divine to which we open ourselves.***[1]

Willigis Jäger

8

Accepting Who We Are

IT IS MY HOPE TO EXPLORE IN THIS SECTION SOME of the essential learnings necessary for the opening-up process mentioned by Jäger in the preceding citation. Perhaps most important among these in our age are the recognition of personal woundedness and the willingness to be healed and to work for healing. In the sophisticated, adult society of our time, it seems surprisingly difficult to broach the subject of healing prayer with any degree of theological seriousness. It is almost as if we *know* that we need help, that we are broken and often broken beyond our control or even *before* our control, but somehow we fight with everything we have against admitting the specificity of this to anyone, least of all to ourselves.

Frequently our denial is exacerbated further by our inability to understand our woundedness. Hence, we tend to pin the blame on someone else—our parents, our teachers, our environment. Yet *we* are the ones who experience "the sting in the flesh," and who, ultimately, do the things we do not want to do, while not doing the things

we want to do. We find it very difficult, therefore, to make sense of our "adulthood"—of the illusion of our "having it all together." As we get older, however, and as we enter ever more deeply into the flow of life, so to speak, and learn to reflect on it, we slowly and often painfully grow to recognize our unity with all of humankind in its brokenness. Mysteriously, and almost in spite of ourselves, we begin to understand what Paul meant in 2 Cor. 12:10, and perhaps we even begin to resonate with his "When I am weak, then I am strong," realizing in our struggle that God's power is "at its best in [our] weakness" (2 Cor. 12:9).

There is a strange paradox here, for this very insight—the recognition of personal sinfulness and subsequent surrender to God's power (experiencing in our very own flesh what Jesus meant by the plea to be forgiven "even as we forgive those who trespass against us")—may hold within it the first actual encounter with God's healing grace. What I am suggesting is that to be able to accept myself as being wounded, as truly in solidarity with broken humanity and in need of forgiveness and healing, *is already grace* and is, in itself in fact, *the first dimension of healing.*

The grace of recognizing sin as being part of me and of assuming responsibility for it happens upon us in a variety of ways. Some call it "bottoming out" or "hitting bottom." Others meet their darkness more gently, but for no one is the experience without struggle. Nor is it a fore-

gone conclusion. I like to refer to it as the gift brought by suffering—a gift, however, that can always be shunned if it is not encountered with thoughtfulness and humility.

One of my most poignant encounters with my own capacity for evil was through a dream I had in 1982 and recounted first in my book *Releasement*, where I used it as an example to illustrate "the unfathomable depth of our own poverty." It happened during my midlife years. I had been involved in a bitter struggle for months with habits of behavior I loathed but seemingly was unable to control. They had been mine from childhood but had come to haunt me now during my transition struggles and had brought me to the point of almost complete intolerance with myself. I felt low, broken, and very keenly aware of my own weakness and need.

> Then one night I had a dream: I was led by my twin sister holding me by the hand (as a wisdom figure would) into a room full of women all of whom were severely deformed. They were identified to me as sisters and reached out to me, smiling, and wishing to embrace. Overcoming what I clearly felt as revulsion, I touched and embraced them. One of them offered me some bitter-tasting [moldy] bread which I ate. Then we left. My guide warned me that eating the bread made me become like them. With this the dream ended. It became clear to me as I reflected on my dream experience during prayer that day that none of the women, including my guide, were strangers or even personalities outside of me. All

were dimensions of myself yearning for reconciliation. The bread I had been offered, the bread I had "broken with them," marked our communion. The deformed women longed for solidarity with *me*. Those broken aspects of myself, hidden sources of my shame, were really gifts to me—oh, happy faults—for they exposed me to my brokenness and liberated me from the flesh-pots of perfectionism and self-righteousness into the desert of need, into the pain of authentic compassion.[2]

Healing begins when, in the face of our own darkness, we recognize our helplessness and surrender our need for control. This experience of embracing our powerlessness permits the demise of ego inflation and the deep-down recognition (neither analyzed, nor rationalized, nor projected outward, nor repressed) of sinfulness—our own and also, equally if not more painful, our family's, our community's, our church's, our country's, our gender's, our race's. We face what is, and we ask for mercy.

Revolutionary Shame

The dream I had many years ago gifted me with an awareness of the depth of grace my life had been and continued to be. It also brought home to me, beyond the shadow of a doubt, that *sin is not outside of me,* to be shunned and denied. It dwells, rather, deep within me and within the human condition to which I belong. There it is waiting to be reconciled and redeemed.

Brennan Manning saw this also and writes about it with uncompromising directness in his book *A Stranger to Self-Hatred:* "Unless we acknowledge that we are sinners, the sick ones and the lost sheep for whom Jesus came, we do not belong to the 'blessed' who know that they are poor and inherit the [reign of God]. . . . Solidarity with human suffering frees the one who receives and liberates the one who gives [care, forgiveness, love] through the conscious awareness *'I am the other.'*"[3]

This awareness is, of course, by no means easily gained, for in many respects we would rather not be associated this way with the other, especially with the other's sin. We have enough guilt to deal with on our own. Solidarity in sin is not something we, therefore, either want or seek. *Yet it is the way it is, and it needs to be recognized as such if healing is to happen.* Strangely, this solidarity, furthermore, is not dependent on having done the deed myself. It goes deeper than that and touches the collective psyche —the human condition to which all of us belong.

Some time ago during a sleepless night in Montreal, I found myself watching an old television documentary depicting the hunt for Martin Bormann, one of Hitler's close associates. The film recounted the last days of the Third Reich and then gave a report of the subsequent, painstaking investigation as to whether Bormann had escaped or was, indeed, among the Nazis who had died or committed suicide during the final days of the war. Much to my surprise, I found myself getting increasingly irri-

tated as I watched. Why, I wondered, was this intense investigation necessary? Bormann, I estimated, would by now be a very old man, and I wondered why one could not simply leave him alone. Where was the justice here, I asked myself. Was this not simply revenge? Then, strangely and quite unexpectedly, I was overcome by a fantasy I will never forget: I saw myself in a concentration camp much like Auschwitz as depicted in films. Surrounded by others equally detained, I found myself forced to watch someone I dearly loved being tortured to death. An unbelievable rage overcame me, and I felt almost sick as I allowed the fantasy to play itself out in me, for suddenly I *knew* that, were this fantasy true, I would hunt the torturers until the end of my days. I *knew* then also, without a shadow of a doubt, that I could kill, and that I would have killed in a situation such as my fantasy depicted. I *knew,* for the first time in my life, what revenge really means. I *knew* hatred, and I *knew* violence during that sleepless night in Montreal. I *knew* with absolute clarity that Auschwitz and Dachau, the Gulags of Siberia, the torture cages in Vietnam, the bombs of Northern Ireland were all within me too. I *knew* what it means to be part of the human condition and what revolutionary shame would ask of me.

The grace of my life is that I was spared the horrors that breed violence and death. Some of my brothers and sisters were not. They became the victims and/or the perpetrators of the violence I was spared, but their story does

not end with them, nor is it limited to them. It is the story of the human condition and, in that sense, it belongs to me and belongs to all of us. *The recognition of this and the commitment to work toward healing is revolutionary shame.* "With us," we say, "and by God's grace, this will end." In a very real sense, we accept the guilt even as we work for its redemption.

Much of what we are struggling with here defies the rational and the legalistic. Guilt, in that realm, belongs to the one who performed the act. For justice to be done, "the punishment must fit the crime." In our courts, we deal death for murder and call it justice. We even believe that capital punishment will allow us to "put the crime behind us and to get back to our 'normal' life." The reason why most of us really cannot do so, and why crime and murder are not prevented by the violence perpetrated through our legal system is that *violence begets violence.* Sin begets sin, and until we realize that and ask for God's gracious mercy, our role in the redemptive plan of God is dangerously compromised.

Paul was serious when he reflected on making up in his own body "all that has still to be undergone by Christ for the sake of his body, the Church" (Col. 1:25). Our exemplar and root archetype here undoubtedly is Christ Jesus, who clearly embraced and now asks us, who are grafted into him, to embrace Isaiah's suffering servant: "Surely you have borne our griefs and carried our sorrows. . . . [Y]ou were wounded for our transgressions, you were

bruised for our iniquities; upon you was the chastisement that made us whole and with your stripes we are healed" (Isa. 53:4–6). As totally innocent, he took on abject sin— he became sin—without uttering a word in his own defense. In the *taking on*, he showed us how redemption in the deepest sense is effected, and he invited us into the process—into the groaning universe waiting for deliverance (Rom. 8:22).

Revolutionary shame stands in the blood-guilt of the race, in the horror of national sin—of genocides, and fire-bombings, and war on others for the sake of national interests. It stands in the cruelty of prejudice against other ethnic groups—against women, the poor, the aged, the wounded in society. Revolutionary shame knows no self-righteousness because it has encountered its own darkness and can only beg for forgiveness and mercy.

A little vignette I used as a case study in my seminary classes a few years back might illustrate the point: A newly ordained priest comes to his first parish assignment, eager and full of enthusiasm. He meets friendly parishioners, of course, but he also meets a great number of active but also very angry women who do not hesitate to make him feel somehow responsible for what they call the oppression against women in the Judeo-Christian tradition and particularly in the Roman Catholic Church. The young man is upset with these encounters. He has never seen himself as someone who does not like women. He feels they should have equal rights within society and

also within the church, and he is chagrined that he is being singled out for these attacks.

He has two choices: One is to defend himself. He can point out to these women that they are attacking the wrong person, that he does not have anything against women and, in fact, likes women as a whole, that he resents being scapegoated. If he makes this choice—and he can certainly be justified in doing so—very little will probably change. The women will continue to be angry. There will most likely be no reconciliation, not even a truce, between him and them. The wounds will persist and perhaps even increase.

His second choice, on the other hand, might rise out of revolutionary shame: He tells his accusers that he senses their pain and is deeply sorry. He assures them of his sadness that women are suffering such discrimination in the world and also in the church. He shares with them that he clearly is very ignorant about the worst of it and feels in many ways inadequate in dealing with it. He asks them to help him learn more about gender discrimination and to continue to sensitize him. He wants, he says, to be about changing whatever he can to make this world and church a better place for all. By this second choice he has opted to stand "within" the sin, to *take on* what is part of his gender and, yes, the wounded part of his clerical state, and to commit himself to conversion. Though perhaps "sinless" in this regard, he knows that he is a brother in the human family and held within its brokenness. And

because he knows this and accepts this, healing can happen through him and can transform his environment.

Knowing that I am wounded means owning that I am part of the story of betrayal that is the sin of the world even if I, for my part, cannot remember a single act of betrayal as such. It means standing in the back of the temple (Luke 18:10) of the whole human race and praying for mercy, because "I am a sinner."

9

Healing and Redemption

THE TOPIC OF SIN AND FORGIVENESS IS ADDRESSED over and over again in our Christian tradition. The Fall, original sin, human depravity, the need for restitution and atonement, redemption through suffering—these are all part of our catechism training, our Sunday homilies, and our religion classes from childhood. They are the key concepts of salvation history. They constitute our faith. And yet I have asked myself of late, Where do we encounter the *healing* here? Where do we *feel* its power? How can we connect it to the real world in which we live?

Because of an act of disobedience and fundamental pride committed by the first human—an act that had universal consequences that were inherited by us through our earthly parents—we find ourselves separated from God and in a state of sinfulness from the moment of our conception. Through the death of Jesus this separation was ended, the gates of heaven were opened, and salvation is, once again, possible for us. Baptism restores grace to us and makes us once again children of God. We all believe these basic truths of

our early catechesis. And yet might one not ask: *Where is the actual experience of this faith in our daily reality and in contemporary society?* Someone said to me not too long ago in a moment of despair: "Baptism wipes away the sin, but I don't feel very healed. And, to top it all off, it's all someone else's fault." It is true that there is clarity and neatness in our catechism explanations and Sunday school classes. It seems to me, however, that in order to be relevant and transformative for contemporary times, the story of our sinfulness and alienation, which calls for exploration today as it has in every other age, needs to be appropriated on a much deeper, existential level. Religion that does not touch the heart dies. Religion that does not effect transformation is not worth believing.

What if we were to see ourselves, as indeed Jesus wanted us to (note the meditation on the prayer that Jesus taught us in Part 1), as originally and unconditionally loved by God? What if we understood alienation from God, from each other, and from the world as the result of *our* massive rejection of this love? What if we saw this rejection as something of which *we are all capable* because of our inherent freedom, as something that was not necessarily just one act but could easily have been and continues to be a whole series of rejections, all of which bear consequences and cry for redemption?

Three perception shifts might follow from these insights: First, alienation might be understood less as a punishment from God for something we really did not

do but inherited from our parents. It might be understood instead as a consequence of freedom abused, for which we are all responsible. Second, we might begin to see *ourselves* as the ones to blame for the rejection that we suffer, rather than envisioning God as having turned from us. No one (except small, innocent children) would remain a blameless victim in this case, suffering from what others did. All of us would assume our share in the brokenness of the human condition into which all of us were born, and to which all of us contribute our part. Third, our understanding of redemption might move from an emphasis on "restitution" to a deepening understanding of what it means to "come home." Redemption would cease to be seen as outside of us and would become instead a unified whole centered in our walking the *way* which Jesus claimed to *be* (John 14:6). It would require personal commitment, a *yes* that arises out of our freedom, ever touched by grace. It would be recognized as our being gathered into the Christ event and as our living out *in our very lives* the story into which we are grafted.

Redemption

Within the above perspective, how would our understanding of healing be altered? How would we come to see the moments ripe for transformation, the sins calling for forgiveness, the existential experiences of brokenness calling for revolutionary shame, the wounds that need

our prayer energy? I suggest that we might consider the ongoing redemptive process as involving a variety of layers. (See the chart on p. 69.) We stand within each one of them, intimately bound up with its healing as, indeed, Jesus was while he was on earth. We truly are his Body in this event of transformation which is our salvation and is the salvation of all things in Christ. As persons of prayer, we gather ourselves, therefore, into the redemptive light of Christ's Spirit and direct our plea for healing and forgiveness into the outermost reaches of human existence. We acknowledge the massive state of disorder in the human condition as a whole, the will to power that is the sin of the world, the arrogance and self-aggrandizement that pit us against each other, the betrayal of our destiny as the children and the beloved of God. We know that this condition of sinfulness touches each of us. We sit in silent prayer, holding ourselves in this recognition, and ask for mercy.

A second layer calling for transformation and healing, though it may take us years of living to recognize this, speaks to the more cultural, the historical, and even the biological aspects of human existence. I am referring here to the conditions of disorder that are the result of intolerance with race, with gender, with sexual orientation, and with anything other than or different from what is perceived to be "the norm." Sins of intolerance have spawned wars and genocides. They have forced starvation on millions, nurtured prejudice, slavery, homophobia,

patriarchism. These, coupled with yet a third layer of brokenness—that of nationalism and the fostering of self-righteousness, greed, and violence to the advantage of some and at the expense of others—create a negative energy field of immense proportions.

We can resist this negativity only if we take it seriously and see it as larger than isolated acts of transgression perpetrated by individuals. What killed Jesus was paradigmatic of the "sin of the world" and was much more than mere evil intent. We would consider it absurd to blame his execution merely on the decree by Pontius Pilate carried out by some Roman soldiers because of the jealousy of some high priests of the temple in Jerusalem. Likewise, what killed Romero, or the four women martyrs, or the six Jesuits in El Salvador was not merely the isolated acts of the cruel, greedy, and power-hungry soldiers serving a dictatorial government. What exterminated Jews in concentration camps, what denies homosexuals access to equal rights, what instituted slavery and planned the potato famine in Ireland, what continues ethnic cleansing in the former Yugoslavia and violence in central Africa, what is responsible for violence, rape, and incest in our homes has deeper roots also. *It is freedom and human destiny betrayed. It is a massive* no *to God's creative energy. It is the acceptance of destructiveness in a blind "I will not serve," that touches the entire universe. It is sin run rampant and sin in which we all share.* Christ entered into this sin and said: "*I will serve.*" In him, therefore, is our redemp-

tion. As persons of prayer we follow his lead and continue the redemptive process.

Our personal effectiveness in this regard can, of course, seem rather small and insignificant when one considers oneself singly sitting in prayer and affirming the reign of God over and over and over again in the face of such massive betrayal. That is why it is important, once again, to stress our membership in Christ's Body. Through Christ's death and resurrection, his lifelong *yes* to God became a cosmic event, for *Christ's* yes *to God was also God's* yes *to Christ.* As believers and as persons of prayer we are inextricably linked to this event and to the Christ in whom all things are and continue to be transformed. Our prayer is, therefore, never isolated. *Redemption is God's work.* It is God's covenant in Christ. It is God's creative moment ever new and ever faithful—an unending love act reaching out and drawing us back to God's heart. Richard McBrien, writing about grace, speaks eloquently to what we are discussing here: "The human community and the entire world in which the human community exists is oriented towards Christ and *is sustained by him. . . .* There is no creation except in view of Christ. There is no Covenant except in view of Christ. There is no human existence, therefore, except in view of Christ and *our New Covenant in Christ.*"[4] Prayer allows us to become transmitters of Christ's Spirit, channels of transformation and healing—nothing more, nothing less. What glory!

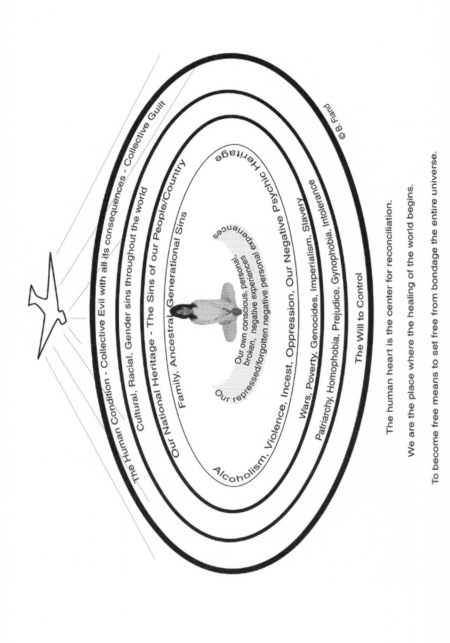

The Human Condition - Collective Evil with all its consequences - Collective Guilt

Cultural, Racial, Gender sins throughout the world

Our National Heritage - The Sins of our People/Country

Family, Ancestral, Generational Sins

Our Negative Psychic Heritage

Our own conscious, personal, broken, negative experiences

Our repressed/forgotten negative personal experiences

Alcoholism, Violence, Incest, Oppression, Our Negative Psychic Heritage

Wars, Poverty, Genocides, Imperialism, Slavery

Patriarchy, Homophobia, Prejudice, Gynophobia, Intolerance

The Will to Control

© B. Fiand

The human heart is the center for reconciliation.

We are the place where the healing of the world begins.

To become free means to set free from bondage the entire universe.

10

Familial and Ancestral Healing

I HOPE THE CHART AT THE END OF THE PRECED-ing chapter may help one visualize the layers for healing that we have been discussing. The most embracive dimension of human brokenness, belonging to the outermost circle, might perhaps best be summarized by the notion of "will to power or control." It flees from the call to surrender, wants to go it alone, and succeeds only in furthering alienation and utter negativity. Cultural, racial, and gender sins narrow the scope just slightly. Together with nationalism in layer 3, they are the primary reasons for most of the evil and the untold suffering inflicted by the human family upon itself in its abuse of freedom and its rejection of the creative love of God.

The next few chapters will address the more individualized familial and ancestral sins that affect all of us through our parents and grandparents. We will discuss also our own repressed or forgotten personal experiences of sin and woundedness and explore our need for healing in these places as well as in our remembered or conscious

70

past. Prayer energy can touch all, and healing and redemption can be effected in even the most hardened areas of sin.

It is today a commonly accepted fact that we are the products not only of our culture, our race, our gender but, most specifically, of our family. We have become aware that ancestral situations of disorder affect us. Alcoholism and other forms of addiction can be in our blood as well as in our environment. Crimes of violence and passion can pervade the atmosphere in which we grow and can influence us from generation to generation. Hardness of heart can spread. Much of this happens, undoubtedly, because of the family and cultural environment that children have to endure with little chance of escape. Although, depending on one's natural disposition or temperament, one can, within limits, use one's freedom in different ways and choose to respond creatively in the face of negative influences, wounds, nevertheless, are created whenever disorder and violence prevail. And wounds need healing. Warring nations foster warring children—thus the violence is continued. There can be no doubt that the children on the West Bank, the children of Northern Ireland, the children of Croatia and Albania, the children of Central Africa are scarred. Their nightmares and fantasies, if not acts of violence themselves, are a sad proof of this.

And then there is the rage of the ages that reverberates through the psyche of oppressed people as a whole, that

flows in the blood of women, of African Americans, of indigenous peoples everywhere. Some members of any one family—perhaps the more sensitive souls—seem to suffer it more acutely than others. We refer to them as emotionally or mentally ill at times. Perhaps they are, instead, the seers, the wise ones, the healthy ones, but also the crucified ones for *experiencing and allowing themselves to feel* the anger against oppression; the hunger for acceptance, for recognition, for care, for love. Our prayer reaches out to them and sends God's light and peace.

The Linn brothers and Sheila Fabricant address the passing on or transmission of generational wounds in their book *Healing the Greatest Hurt*. They are referring specifically to the ancestral influences which I have situated on the fourth layer of our healing chart. In order to get a holistic sense of what we are discussing, however, it will help if we remember here that generations exist in nations, which, in turn, exist in cultures. No layer, therefore, is independent of the others. All interact and influence each other. The authors observe: "Although it is dangerous to trace all psychological problems back to the deceased, the new field of family psychotherapy confirms that it is equally dangerous to ignore the effect of past generations upon present emotional conflicts."[5] Referencing a number of therapists, they conclude that

> [N]ot only marital conflicts but also serious illnesses such as schizophrenia often have their roots in three or more generations of family dynamics which have frus-

trated individuation in a child commanded to mature but kept immature by immature parents.

. . . Because of this "multigenerational structure" in much emotional illness, more and more therapists insist on working with a family unit of at least three generations rather than treating an isolated individual.[6]

The authors cite loyalty networks in families, the sense of betrayal when dysfunction is challenged, and the enabling, rather than the confronting, of disabling behavior as some of the primary reasons for multigenerational woundedness. So often we are afraid of facing the evil in our environment, especially in our family. This kind of loving is easily mistaken for unkindness or for a lack of compassion and is, therefore, avoided. The slogan "America, love it or leave it" symbolizes this avoidance on the national scene. It happens on every layer, however, because of a fear-filled blindness to sin that perpetuates it and serves only to extend its influence. The love that heals, on the other hand, overcomes the fear that blinds us and chooses forgiveness instead.

Forgiveness

Very often in our discussions around the topic of forgiveness we revert to the slogan "forgive and forget." Nothing hinders the healing process more. Perhaps the exhortation "Remember—and pray for the grace to forgive and be forgiven" is more realistic. There is an intimate connec-

tion between forgiveness and healing. The Linn brothers and Sheila Fabricant do not exaggerate when they point out that:

> The reason the "condemnable actions" of our ancestors may continue to affect us "unto the seventh generation" is not because God punishes innocent descendants. Rather, it is because *we tend to repeat whatever we do not forgive.* Whether our parents were overly possessive or neglectful, they and their ancestors who taught them need to be understood, forgiven and vindicated or else our reaction to their mistakes will *need the forgiveness of our children*—or even seven generations of children.[7]

It is true, of course, that forgiveness does not happen at will and needs prayer and grace. Forgiving too readily because that, after all, is what one is "supposed" to do, frequently "backfires," and one can find oneself years later transferring the anger one has not worked through, or the hurt one has not dealt with, onto someone else. In transference we encounter previously unaddressed and now unconscious relational issues in someone generally unconnected with the matter, who for one reason or another triggers the repressed material and releases the emotions. Persistent fear of betrayal or abandonment, for example, which so frequently fosters jealousy and suspicion of even the most loyal of friends, may have its origins in childhood trauma repressed or denied. It is as if the human heart blocks off even the possibility of fidelity and acceptance, though it yearns for these qualities

almost insatiably. When someone enters our life who speaks to these yearnings, our unaddressed hurts run interference with the relationship. We can easily find ourselves seeing in the present what was denied existence in the past and accusing where no blame is justified.

In order to minimize what can be both embarrassing and painful situations caused by transference in a non-therapeutic setting, it is helpful to allow oneself to feel the pain of injustice and betrayal, to experience the anger of abuse. Children may find it close to impossible to do this because it is in their highly controlled living situations that they experience injustice and abuse in the first place, but even for adults it is not easy. It helps to remember, therefore, that emotions are just what they are. They are there for a reason and can only help the healing process if they are acknowledged and worked through. Denying one's feelings for fear of their inappropriateness or for the sake of what can only be pseudo-forgiveness will merely postpone genuine healing. It can easily lead to repression and to injustice toward others in the long run. The prayerful person is called, instead, to develop what might best be called a contemplative attitude toward feelings: recognizing them, acknowledging them, and letting them be what they are. This does not mean that one needs to act them out. One simply holds them in consciousness and in prayer and chooses to channel them into appropriate action when necessary.

Forgiveness is not easy. It is clearly a gift. It is a grace

for which we must earnestly wait and pray, even if the waiting can be excruciating at times. For a while we may find ourselves having to forgive ourselves for not being able to forgive, for not wanting to forgive, or for not wanting even to pray for the grace to want to forgive. Theodore Dobson is right when he observes that "Forgiveness is necessarily a process, and one that happens according to its own schedule. We cannot force our hearts to do that which they are not yet ready to do."

Often, he says, "we need to wait for the right time and circumstances to forgive a big hurt."[8] It is important to admit this both to ourselves and to the one asking our forgiveness. Gentle honesty is very important here. Being able to own that we are still too confused or angry, that perhaps a bit of distance both in time and space is necessary before the equilibrium in a relationship can be established once again, is important for our own integrity as well as for the honesty required of love. But this is very difficult in a culture where propriety demands apologies and the acceptance of them, where feelings are underrated, and few know how to express them appropriately.

> To forgive people means to restore them to their rightful and honored place in our hearts. It means to let go of any demand for repayment of hurts suffered. It means to be willing to treat them with kindness, respect, and heartfelt courtesy. It is the free act of people who are in touch with their true selves. None of us can do this alone, especially when we remember Jesus' insistence

that we forgive *every* hurt and offense . . . ; so, finally, to forgive means to pray for the grace of forgiveness from God, Who has first forgiven us.[9]

The reflections of Part 1 come to mind here: "All prayer needs to be prayer for forgiveness as well as for the grace to forgive, and the latter is predicated on the recognition of the former." The awareness of our own brokenness and sinfulness is essential if we are to prevent any self-righteousness from creeping into our forgiveness of others. As Dobson insists, when we forgive, we state that our relationship with the person who has offended us is "more important than the hurt we feel." In so doing, "we acknowledge that we ourselves have hurt others just as badly or worse, and in the strength that can only come from Jesus we let go of our bitterness while He heals the hurt, and our true selves are set free."[10]

In an exquisite reflection entitled *Touching Peace*, Thich Nhat Hanh offers the following exercise to further the compassion so necessary for forgiveness and healing.[11] As is appropriate to the Eastern way, he first helps us to become aware of our breathing. Then he suggests quite simply that in "breathing in," each of us see himself or herself as a five-year-old child, and in "breathing out," we smile at this child. Again, "breathing in," we see our father or our mother, or whoever has hurt us and needs our forgiveness and reconciliation, as a five-year-old boy or girl; "breathing out," we smile at this five-year-old boy or girl who was our father, our mother, etc. The intention

here is to allow this breathing prayer to become a type of visual mantra repeated over and over again.

We are rooted in each other, Hanh tells us. Without each other we are like "hungry ghosts," hurting and longing to be connected to the human family to which we belong. We are the continuation of our parents who transmitted themselves to us. They really had nothing else to give but themselves and their past. If they were unable to heal their past, they too have remained unhealed and are looking to us for reconciliation. We are what we have received and cultivated. To reconcile with our parents or ancestors is to reconcile ultimately with ourselves. *"Breathing in, I see myself as a five-year-old child,"* recalls my innocence to me and evokes compassion. It bridges the gulf of brokenness that is my life. *"Breathing out, I smile at this five-year-old child,"* and gentle myself, embracing the one person I may find it most difficult to forgive. Similarly, seeing my parents as five-year-olds reminds me that they are victims too of the vicissitudes of life, and I am helped to embrace their vulnerability and woundedness.

Not being a parent myself, I was blessed with a powerful opportunity to learn from the parents who participated in my classes on "The Experience of Prayer." Quite often the pain and sorrow were evident on their faces when we discussed familial healing. It is difficult enough to accept the need to work through the childhood

wounds of one's own past. But then to be invited to face the pain inflicted (however unintentionally) on one's children in turn and to have to pray for the grace to forgive oneself is often excruciating.

The matter is made even more complex by the fact that the material that calls for healing can often be quite elusive. One may not remember or be aware of the hurt inflicted, and, even when one remembers it, it can appear deceptively insignificant. A personal experience shared with me by a friend who participated in an Experience of Prayer class I offered not too long ago illustrates this painfully well:

Once during my summer vacation I stayed with my sister and her two little girls, then two and three years old, when she was going through a major crisis in her marriage. Normally a very attentive and good mother, she needed a lot of space for herself during that time. We were talking one evening when the little two-year-old flung open the door, ran to my sister, and grabbed her vehemently for some sign of affection and love. My sister could not give it to her at that moment, and so she sent her away.

I saw the tiny figure in her pajamas withdraw toward the balcony and the door close. I went after her, and there she was, hunched in a corner of the wall, her tiny fists clenched and her face distorted with rage, without crying. I knelt down beside her, and had hardly done so, when she thrust herself into my arms, trembling and sobbing, clinging for sheer life.

I felt as if her little body, which I was holding tightly, went right into me. Nothing less could console her.

We stayed like this for a long time while I was caressing her. Many thoughts and feelings went through me during that time. I knew that for once I was able to protect this fierce and passionate little girl from drowning in her own rage and despair. For once I could prevent darkness from having its full impact on her, from taking hold of her inner space to poison it with bitterness. She fell asleep in my arms and I took her to her mother. It was in her mother's arms that she woke up some time later with a big smile on her tear-stained face.

A great hurt for a little heart! It could have easily gone unnoticed but for a sympathetic aunt who soothed the pain. Was there nevertheless a scar? My friend tells me that the little one, now eighteen, *goes her independent way, trying out love to its limits for all it has to give. She "plays it cool" on the outside, but disappointments and pain are already working toward a later recognition that a fear of clinging and of surrender to a loved one is not the ultimate answer.*

One cannot help wondering about the suffering of children inflicted on them by suffering parents—unintentionally and eluding clarity, yet devastating nevertheless and ever in need of healing. I want to believe that most of us "do the best we can with what we have," but

often it still falls short, and inevitably wounds are inflicted that need the forgiveness of those who once were vulnerable and in our charge. This requires profound prayer and deep repentance.

Repentance

In *Releasement* I identified repentance as "a *matter of love consummated:* a form of surrender, where sorrow at and recognition of one's own limitation are mingled with abandon and surrender to the self *and* to the One who is even deeper than the innermost self and in whose mercy one trusts." Just like prayer, repentance is primarily a disposition. "One does not perform acts of repentance, one repents. One is *in* repentance."[12] The healing required for our family and ancestors calls for just that. Repentance is the prayer that flows from sorrow, and often quite wordlessly it "rises like incense" and gently effects transformation.

A mother who, upon the advice of her infant daughter's physician, had decided early on to put the child into a hospital facility since she was developmentally disabled, found herself in later years greatly distraught and guilt-ridden. She could not forgive herself for what she perceived to be her selfishness, and her guilt seriously affected her relationship with her daughter who, a young woman by then, was living in a group home and work-

ing. Mother and daughter never spoke about their feelings toward each other, although they were together every weekend. An unaddressed distance pervaded their togetherness like an impenetrable wall.

Years passed, and as the mother was getting older, she took to doing exercises with her daughter, both for her own health and in order to help her daughter's general physical bearing and well-being. One weekend the mother, who had just returned from a healing retreat where she had learned about body prayer, invited her daughter to join her in the gentle movements that quite spontaneously follow chosen religious music and involve the entire being in worship. She closed her eyes as, with her whole body, she listened to and followed the sacred melody, expecting her daughter to imitate her. Both mother and daughter were lost in prayer, moving slowly about the room when suddenly they found themselves facing each other. Their unexpected presence to one another startled them. It was not only surprising, but also intense and deeply moving. Tears welled up in their eyes and, of one accord, they embraced. No words needed to be spoken. Both were healed.

The intensity of the prayer of repentance is not in the words spoken but in the acceptance of personal woundedness and the abandonment that comes with the utter recognition of powerlessness. One yields to the One who alone can heal and then lets go. Contrary to the belief that surrender speaks of weakness and defeat, there is

unfathomable energy in this, and our personal healing sends forth a radiance that is far beyond the singular event. It affects everything around us. Just as the wounds of our past touch our lives today (Thich Nhat Hanh's "transmissions"), so the healing of today affects the wounds of the past. Our ancestors touch our lives, even as we touch theirs, in an ever-deeper circle of healing and homecoming. The Linn brothers and Sheila Fabricant say it well: "[I]n prayer we are touching not only a memory in a living person but also a deceased person [or persons] who through Jesus receives love and then becomes in turn a loving intercessor. . . . [W]hen the Spirit heals us, the Spirit is healing wounds that go back generations and touch multitudes."[13] Quoting William Johnston's observations in *The Mirror Mind,* they summarize all the layers for healing we have been discussing and conclude:

> [T]here takes place a healing of something more than my little ego with its memory of a mere forty, fifty or sixty years. There is more to it than this. There is a healing of the archetypes, of the collective unconscious, of the wounds I have inherited from my ancestors. There is healing of the cosmic dimension of the psyche; there is healing of the basic human condition which we call original sin.[14]

But healing prayer moves even deeper and calls for ever greater intimacy. It touches all of us in a profoundly personal way as well: "The hurts and pains that have been

lurking in the psyche from early childhood, from the moment of birth, from the time in the womb, from the moment of conception—all of these are floating to the surface and are being healed by the love of the indwelling Spirit in whose presence one quietly sits."[15] The following chapter will invite us to touch these insights in our own individual stories and to assume responsibility for the healing that is calling us to an ever deeper personal transformation.

11

Homecoming

IN THE STRUGGLE TO COME TO TERMS WITH AND
work toward the healing of much of what we have discussed concerning sin, negative ancestral and familial influences, and the general atmosphere of alienation that
pervades the human condition, it may be helpful to delve
briefly into the field of Jungian thought in order to understand the distinction between what Carl Jung identifies as
the collective and the personal unconscious, and to see
their spheres of influence as different, though by no means
disconnected, from our conscious choices. There is a certain clarity provided by Jung to spirituality which has
recently been maligned by some as being too "New Age."
I have little patience with this kind of criticism. It seems to
me that openness to, and dialogue with, other disciplines
as we investigate the mystery of human existence can only
help the human family and will, therefore, enhance honest
theological discourse rather than hinder it.

Simply put, the unconscious is that area of the human
personality which is beyond our immediate awareness.

According to Jung, it is divided into the *personal uncon-*
scious and the *collective unconscious*. The former, quite
simply, holds the forgotten and repressed experiences of
one's life—one's past. These experiences are not subject to
voluntary recall but may emerge through dream images
or sudden associations triggered by conscious experiences. The personal unconscious, as well as our conscious
memories, holds, among other things, the wounds of our
life—our own personal sins and betrayals as well as the
hurts inflicted on us by others. They contain most of the
material of the last two layers of our diagram and will
need further elucidation later on in this chapter.

We share the collective unconscious with the whole
human race. It carries the human story and all potential
modes and models of interpretation and of meaningful
response to the world that the human family has developed, for better or for worse, through the ages and now
holds in common. These shared, preformed patterns of
behavior and meaning are referred to as archetypes. They
await our use of them in conscious acts; they break in on
us and invite our response often when we least expect
it—synchronistically at times, always drawing us deeper.
Archetypes are the result of thousands of years of human
interactions and learning. They are, as Jung sees them,
propensities in humans to respond symbolically to similar situations in similar ways. They can be universal, but
at times they are also culturally conditioned. Among reli-

gious archetypes, the death/resurrection (re-birth) motif of our faith can be seen as universal. Quite apart from the story of the historical Jesus, it has existed in what might be described as the "human religious instinct" from time immemorial, and therefore finds its place as well in numerous non-Christian traditions throughout the world. We respond to the painful ending situations of our life and to the numerous moments of transformation these invite in terms of this archetype. Baptism uses the death/resurrection motif sacramentally. We might best understand it as a universally understood mode of giving significance to and of interpreting the depth reality of change and conversion.[16]

The cross, on the other hand, is an example of a cultural archetype. It belongs to and is deeply rooted in the Christian culture. It does not have the same significance elsewhere, especially as it touches both glory and ignominy. To "bear one's cross," to "be crucified," to "be sent crosses" are ways that Christians use to interpret their suffering. These ways of embracing pain do not speak to other religions, which may even be repelled by them, though they clearly struggle with suffering and utilize different ways to symbolize their experience.

With respect to the topic of healing to which we want to apply the above considerations, personal weaknesses, propensities to harm ourselves and others, sins and transgressions belong, as I mentioned already, to the conscious

dimension of our personality as well as to the personal unconscious (where Jung refers to them as the "personal shadow"). They point to the "I," to our unique life experience, even when they have been forgotten, denied, or repressed. Their effects on us or, through us, on others belong to our personalized task of healing and "homecoming." We have either suffered from transgressions or have ourselves transgressed the law, whether it be the outer law of our society or religion, or the inner law of the heart. We have desires and tendencies to step beyond the boundaries of the good or what is socially acceptable. We need to face our sin and our habits of sin and pray for healing and forgiveness. (See Part 1, chapter 2, with reference to: "Forgive us our sins, as we forgive those who have sinned against us.")

When, on the other hand, Jesus admonishes us to pray that we might be *delivered from evil*, I believe he is referring to the collective phenomenon of darkness, which is much broader and, although it flows through our individual psyches and influences all of us, finds its home in the collective psyche of the human condition. Evil is more than a personal sin, even though personal sin contributes to it and may arise because of it. Evil, as Esther Harding would have us see it, is "daemonic energy rising from the depths of the unconscious in [among others] power driven [humans]. . . . [G]ood and evil as principles, or powers, spring from the collective unconscious." These principles or powers manifest themselves in

the form of compulsions, of temptations to evil deeds, or perhaps as impulses to good ones. At times we see them as good and evil forces, or as spirits, possessing demons. . . . At such times they may indeed possess us, so that we act and feel compulsively, regardless of our conscious wish and intent.[17]

Much of the material in our earlier reflections concerning our need for healing stemming from our connectedness to the human condition, our race, culture, gender, and even our national heritage, fits more readily into the area of the "collective shadow." As we discussed already (see chapter 8, "Accepting Who We Are"), we carry collective darkness even if we did not personally commit the sin of our race, of our gender, or of our nation. The "blood guilt" I and many other Germans of my age had to struggle through because of the atrocities of the Nazi regime, even though we were children during that time, belongs to this category. Because we carry the darkness, however, we can also work for its redemption, and therein lies our vocation and our responsibility.

It may be easier to understand the depth dimension of this responsibility and our connectedness to the human condition if we regard the influences from our unconscious as positive or negative energy—energy from which, if negative, we need to be delivered or freed. The more unconscious this energy is, the more harmful it can be. We see here the will to power, the rage of the ages, the spirit of prejudice, of revenge, of racial superiority, of cul-

tural or national self-righteousness. Jung insists that individuation (wholeness, "homecoming") requires first and foremost a bringing to consciousness.

For some of us this task is much more formidable than for others, and we need a good dose of compassion all around. For as much as we need to *bring to consciousness,* we can also *resist* it. We can be very afraid, and we may fight against and persecute the prophets and the "saints" who call us to the task. We may even kill them because we do not want to be reminded of our connection to, and our own part in, the darkness. As much as we may declare our hunger for wholeness, we can often quite unconsciously work against healing and sabotage ourselves.

Paths Toward Healing

Dreams are in-built messages from the unconscious that open up avenues of encounter between ourselves and our repressed or denied darkness (the collective or the personal shadow). The example given in the first chapter of this part, "Accepting Who We Are," speaks to this encounter. It would seem that the meeting point between psychology and prayer, between theory and conversion, between insight and grace, is the attentive heart. One recognizes in the dream the presence of something more profound, holier, than mere psychic ruminations or diverse brainwave activity. One delves deeper, therefore,

in order to allow the meaning and conversion opportunity of the dream experience to reveal itself.

In *Where Two or Three Are Gathered,* I discussed other ways of touching our unconscious darkness.[18] Among these, the intensity of our shock at another's misdeeds, the fierce denial of our own brokenness, the condemnation of others, and the pointing to sin (always outside of ourselves, of course) are perhaps the clearest indications of shadow repression and denial. Quite often it is not so much the recognition of darkness in itself that hints at personal repressed material, but rather the *intensity* of our reaction to it when it appears.

We all can surmise that the same signs of shadow repression can occur on the national and international front, between cultures and races, the rich and the poor, believer and unbeliever, men and women. It is called *projection,* and it is responsible for much of the self-righteousness that inhibits rapprochement. National, racial, gender, cultural shadows belong to the collective unconscious. Our need for self-aggrandizement, to keep up appearances, to "love or leave" our country can blind us mightily. Each of us must pray for light and redemption here, for much injustice can be perpetrated through self-righteous projection.

I remember my prayer during the Gulf War was a plea for mercy on us all, as the enemy's atrocities were loudly proclaimed around this country, while slogans about

Saddam Hussein being another Adolf Hitler were bandied about, and fingers were pointed with great indignation—all for the sake of oil. What would have happened, I asked myself, if the Middle East export had been bananas? Would liberation of the oppressed have then been such a priority for us? The collective shadow can often elude us. When we glimpse it, the only thing we can do is explore its ramifications in our own behavior and pray that God's healing light will surround and transform all of us held in the throes of collective evil.

Our own personal shadow, on the other hand, demands a more concentrated and different effort and responsibility. According to Jung's theory, it develops during our years of greatest vulnerability—our early childhood, when our socialization is our parents' primary preoccupation, while the expression and exploration of our newly discovered instincts and drives are ours. In balancing out our need to please—a survival instinct ensuring that we receive the affection and attention that are indispensable to us at this age—and our desire and urge to express ourselves and our drives and feelings, the latter can get shortchanged. Socialization demands certain appropriate conduct, which, in turn, demands the control of cravings and inappropriate behavior. Expressed parental displeasure or even punishment can give the impression that our parents' love for us depends on our compliance to their demands. Our vulnerability cannot withstand the withdrawal of their love, while our imma-

turity does not always lend itself to the desired "control." Hence we adapt our behavior by way of repressing those aspects of our budding personality that evoke displeasure (our shadow side). Ultimately, we learn to present an appropriate personality (Jung's "persona"), and we eventually grow into it so completely that we identify ourselves with it. With repression, the shadow moves into the unconscious, and our newly acquired "persona" deludes us into seeing ourselves with a socially acceptable identity.

The shadow, however, does not disappear. It is part of our personality, kept at bay in the darkness of our personal unconscious by our fear of rejection and our inability to face the deprivation of love. Our hatred of it when we see it in others testifies to the difficulty it will have in surfacing and claiming its place in consciousness. What healing asks for, however, is awareness, not denial. The energy required in the repression of our shadow side is wasted energy that needs to be liberated. The aspects of our personality that have been denied through the years need to be owned. Their vitality needs to be recognized, and their power harnessed for transformation. In this lies our homecoming. We need to claim our shadow rather than have it claim us and bind us to endless blindness and projection. Coming home to oneself means learning to stand in the truth of one's past and there to accept the unconditional Love that has cradled us into life and continues to hold us in existence. Only prayer can help us do this.

It is clear that in our personal struggle toward individ-

uation and wholeness, the distinctions between collective and individual darkness are not easily drawn. We all partake of both. The former flows through us and can easily contribute to the sins we commit and then deny. The latter adds to the power of the former by strengthening its stranglehold on the human family. The will to power that afflicts the human race can, for example, enhance my desire for control and thus further the actual subjugation of others to my whim. My acts of oppression, in turn, increase the negative energy of our collective condition in a never-ending vicious circle that can find redemption only through *recognition* and the *prayer for healing*.

12

Bearing the Suffering of Others

A FEW YEARS AGO, PAT, A VERY DEAR FRIEND OF MINE, was diagnosed with inoperable stomach cancer and given only a few months to live. During the weeks that followed her diagnosis and until her death a group of us took turns visiting and praying with her. One day while I was at her bedside together with another friend of mine, the latter became violently ill. She left the sick room without telling me about her condition and sat down in the living room of Pat's apartment with stomach pains so severe that she was thinking of calling an ambulance and going to the hospital emergency for help. When I found her, doubled over and white as a ghost, I suggested that we get her help. We left the apartment, and I assisted her toward the parking lot when all of a sudden she straightened up and smiled with relief and astonishment. The pain had left her.

It seems that, while being close to Pat, she had *picked up her pain*. Proximity to Pat's suffering had momentarily enabled her to touch into and bear her friend's death

agony. Although picking up the feelings of others and
praying for them was not a new experience for her,
enduring with someone the pain of the last stages of
stomach cancer was, and, to her sadness, she had found
herself helpless in the face of it.

Books are full of explanations concerning para-psycho-
logical phenomena—why and how certain persons can
pick up the sufferings of others, whether the sufferings
are physical or spiritual; what hidden potential we all possess and why we ought to develop it.[19] This book will not
attempt an explanation of these mysteries. It has occurred
to me, however, that the previous chapter's discussion of
the collective unconscious and of the interwovenness of
the human condition at least opens the door to an awareness and acceptance of our deep connectedness on all levels and to our consequent responsibility for one another.

Ours is the age of individualism and even isolationism.
"Picking up" the pain of another in one's very embodi-
ment seems foreign to most of us. The all-too-frequent
atomization in our interactions with one another shuns
intimacy. It leaves no room for such an experience, and
we readily dismiss it as bogus. Yet I believe that we can
miss a valuable opportunity for prayer and for healing
this way. My friend, who, as I mentioned, is not unfa-
miliar with touching into both the physical and the spiritual pain of others, is nevertheless more often than not
stunned when it happens to her once again. Because of
the very clear boundaries we imagine around us, it seems

extremely unusual and foreign to most of us to connect into another's field of affect and feelings. Yet I wonder whether it is not really a more natural way of being—a way from which, in this mechanized world, we have been separated; a way we are desperately in need of today. It is my sense that all of us are called to deeper vision and can develop this art *if we allow ourselves to be vulnerable enough to permit access to the mystery that pervades human relationship and permeates, in fact, all of nature.*

Of late it has come home to me that, whereas the human psyche as such may be bound at least in some respects to the matter and environment in which it finds itself by reason of our incarnation, there is a dimension of the soul that dwells in the eternal and transcends space and time, that touches the other at depth levels beyond scientific elucidation. Soul can meet soul, and the two can merge without destroying individuality or personal authenticity. A great amount of healing energy can be released in such an encounter. It is my sense that some persons have a clearer intuition of this than others, and, although few have a detailed explanation of what exactly is happening to them, they use it diligently for the good of their neighbor.

Soul Contact

My purpose in writing about what I have come to see as "soul contact" is to bring it into the sphere of meaningful

discussion and to invite all of us to take our experiences around this topic seriously. It seems to me that, at the end of the twentieth century and the beginning of a new millennium, the time is ripe for this; that somehow we are being invited beyond the cerebral and intellectual approaches to the Holy to which many of our religions have for so long limited themselves. We are being invited, I believe, to see that we are greater than what we have been told we were and have come to accept about ourselves; that we extend beyond space and time and can connect with one another and with the entire universe in powerful and healing ways far beyond our present, very limited perspective.

Some among us are already aware of this and are working effectively for the wholeness of the human condition and for all of creation, but others are afraid of it. I had a student in my prayer course some years ago who quite unwillingly found herself entering my soul-space every time she sat in my class and listened to me lecture. She literally "saw" whatever was going on in me beyond the subject matter we were engaged in and was quite horrified at her involuntary "invasion" of my space. During the quiet of our prayer experiences, she found herself connecting with the pain and even the woundedness of others in the room and had difficulty concentrating on herself. When she told me about it, I tried to encourage her to use her gift rather than to deny it or run away from it; to pray into whatever she was seeing and to commit it

to the love of God. Clearly, this kind of "connecting" has its built-in difficulties. One needs to work with it and develop boundaries with the help of a disciplined prayer life and good spiritual direction. But *it is gift*, nevertheless. Running away from it, castigating oneself for it, or rejecting it as abnormal can only lead to frustration and diminishment. It helps no one.

Many involved in the growing ministry of "healing memories" may experience visual or other physical sensations that depict the area in need of healing. These could include present or past moments of pain or sin; they could be ancestral events of hurt and abuse; they could be birth or even pre-birth experiences. Others may perhaps not *see* in images but may simply experience intellectual intuitions that can either be direct or symbolic concerning another's need for healing. My own sense about a young man with whom I was sharing a long retreat experience many years ago would fit into this latter category. As I saw him struggle through the long days of silence, he seemed to me like a young and vibrant stallion wanting to be tamed. His intense sexual struggles and failed attempts at celibate chastity, which he shared with me at the end of the retreat, proved my intuition true. His director, interestingly enough, had seen what I had but through a different medium: The night before the retreat began, and before he had ever laid eyes on the young man, he had had a dream about him in a stallion's body.

We could dismiss these seemingly unusual experiences

and symbolic messages as silly or dangerous because we are afraid of them. We could claim that they inappropriately lead us to unkind judgments of others that we have no right to make, since "we do not have the facts." We could, however, also see them as signals telling us that we are bonded with our brothers and sisters on deeper levels than we dare to dream of, and that we are here *being called to pray for them.*

I surrounded my young friend with light during those long silent days of retreat. We never spoke, but he knew I cared, simply, I believe, by the exchange of energy between us. At the end of our thirty days he felt the need to share his story with me because our souls had touched and wanted to stay connected.

The Ministry of Light

Soul contact can be profoundly powerful and deeply intimate. Our inner depths are as wide as the love we allow to flow through them. We carry each other into wholeness. Depth contact with another's wounds, and even another's most blatant sins, speaks to our most sacred call: to pray for healing. I remember one morning in an airport restaurant watching a man rudely belittle the woman who was serving him. I felt my anger rise, and I wanted to lash out at him, to return his rudeness in kind. Instead, my friend, who had also witnessed the behavior, sug-

gested we surround both with the light of Christ and pray for healing.

It may seem difficult to see intimacy in this example. Yet, as we have discussed already, touching another's sin ever returns us to ourselves and to our own need for forgiveness. Even though we may not like what we witness, we do not judge. We meet ourselves and the entire human family in the other and beg for mercy. *We* pray, and *God* heals.

The how and the when of this healing are rarely very clear, and often they do not happen the way we would prefer. What we need to remember at those times, over and over again, is that the power to heal is from beyond. Our call is to trust. Soul contact and the healing that accompanies it have little to do with "being in the know." They speak to a deeper wisdom that concerns itself solely with *holding oneself and others in the light and surrendering to God.*

Thoughts and Questions for Meditation

1. What is your response to the observation that we are "broken *before* our control?" How does this insight play itself out in your life?

2. To be able to accept myself as wounded, as truly in solidarity with broken humanity and in need of forgiveness and healing, is already grace and is, in itself in fact, the first dimension of healing. Does your experience affirm this?

3. The grace of recognizing sin as part of me and of assuming responsibility for it is a gift frequently brought by suffering—a gift, however, that can always be shunned if it is not encountered with thoughtfulness and humility. How do you respond to this statement?

4. What is your reaction to the phenomenon of "revolutionary shame," and how do you see it connected to the Christ event that still is ongoing? How is the "suffering servant" theme of Isaiah relevant in present-day spirituality? In your life?

5. There seems to be a dichotomy between our general understanding of redemption and our experience of healing. What are your thoughts on this? What does the switch from

redemption as "restitution" to redemption as "homecoming" do for you, personally or theologically?

6. What are your thoughts on the "layers" calling for redemption? We stand within each one of them, intimately bound up with its unique healing as, indeed, Jesus was while he was on earth. We truly are his Body in this event of transformation that is our salvation and is the salvation of all things in Christ.

7. Through Christ's death and resurrection, his lifelong *yes* to God became a cosmic event, for Christ's *yes* to God was also God's *yes* to Christ. As believers and as persons of prayer, we are inextricably linked to this event and to the Christ in whom all things are and continue to be transformed. What responsibility does such a statement evoke in you?

8. "The new field of family therapy confirms that it is . . . dangerous to ignore the effect of past generations upon present emotional conflicts." What is your reaction to such insights?

9. What are your thoughts on our call to forgive, but our seeming difficulty in doing so and subsequent guilt feelings? Can you let emotions be just emotions and develop a contemplative attitude toward them? Can you wait on God for the grace of forgiveness?

10. We are the continuation of our parents, who transmitted themselves to us. They had nothing else to give but themselves and their past. If they were unable to heal their past, they too have remained unhealed and are looking to us for reconciliation. Can you accept this?

11. Reflect on your own life and try to detect the helpful

hints from your unconscious in your own healing process. Are dreams significant to you? Have you had experiences of association, where a present event triggers a past forgotten or repressed experience? Do your excessive emotional reactions to the behavior of others point you to personal issues not dealt with? The meeting point between psychology and prayer, between theory and conversion, between insight and grace, is the attentive heart.

12. What is your reaction to the theory that we, at times, bear the suffering of others in our very incarnation? Are you familiar with this experience? "Soul can meet soul and can merge without destroying individuality or personal authenticity. A great amount of healing energy can be released in such an encounter." What might this mean? Do you have any personal response to this citation?

13. We are being invited to see that we are greater than what we have been told we are and have come to accept about ourselves; that we extend beyond space and time and can connect with one another and with the entire universe in powerful and healing ways beyond our present and very limited perspective. How comfortable are you with these thoughts?

14. Soul contact can be profoundly powerful and deeply intimate. Our inner depths are as wide as the love we allow to flow through them. We carry each other into wholeness. Depth contact with another's wounds, and even another's most blatant sins, speaks to our most sacred call: to pray for healing. We meet ourselves and the entire human family in the other, and we beg for mercy. We pray, and God heals. Do these observations ring true in your experience?

Prayer Experiences

Begin by following the Breathing Guidelines on pp. 42–43.

Experience 1
Healing the Inner Child[20]

READING: (Isa. 42:6, 7, 16) *"I, Yahweh, have called you to serve the cause of right; I have taken you by the hand and formed you; I have appointed you as covenant of the people and light of the nations, to open the eyes of the blind, to free captives from prison, and those who live in darkness from the dungeon.*

. . . I will make the blind walk along the road and lead them along paths. I will turn darkness into light before them. . . ."

PRAYER: Spirit of God, light and energy of our life, we praise you and thank you for your presence here among us and within us. We ask you to strengthen and protect us with your healing light. Permeate our very being with your love and compassion. Hold us safe in your peace and drive from us whatever is not of you. We ask this in the name of Jesus, the Christ.

[SLIGHT PAUSE, THEN MOVE INTO GUIDED MEDITATION, PAUSING FREQUENTLY]

- You are finding yourself on a long country road that stretches far out into the distance toward the ocean.
- Way down the road—quite far away—you see someone walking toward you.
- You strain your eyes to see, but have to wait until both of you are nearer to each other.
- As the person comes closer, you notice that it is a child, a very small, young child.
- And as you get closer to each other, to your astonishment, you recognize the child as yourself.
- You come even closer. What does the child say, do? What do you do?

[LONG PAUSE]

- You start walking together along the road and come to the beach.
- It is a beautiful beach—full of white sand.
- You sit down with your feet in the water.
- The water is warm. Both of you lie down in the sand and look at the blue sky above you.
- The breeze is gentle. Sea gulls glide by.
- The waves begin to break over you both as you reach out and hold hands.
- You begin to sense that this is a special ocean. This is the ocean of God's love. It is endless.
- Feel the waves breaking over your whole body, one after another. The water is warm and healing. Its waves surround and enter your body. They soothe you and connect you to each other.
- They gently carry away all anxieties and fears, sad memories and disappointments.

- They fill you with deep peace and joy as they tell you of God's love and tenderness. You feel very peaceful.
- Rest for a long time in this peaceful place and let God heal you and embrace you both.

[SOFT MUSIC]

PRAYER: Oh God of our life, we praise you and thank you now and forever. Amen.

Gently, now, and when you are ready, go in Christ's peace.

Experience 2
Healing of Memories

Our intention is to place ourselves into God's presence, ask for God's light, for the presence of the Spirit, for a forgiving heart. Then, starting with today, and perhaps restricting yourself to a one-year period (or whatever time frame seems appropriate —varying for each of us because of our different histories), ask God to bring to your mind an event that needs healing.

The event can be something that you have suffered at the hands of someone else, or something you have caused someone else to suffer.

Do not force the memory when it surfaces. Be very gentle with it. Do not rationalize or argue with it, or figure out who is to blame, or relive it.

Simply look at it; become aware of the persons involved, including yourself. Gently lift them to God and ask for God's healing light to surround all of you and restore you to peace.

Then move on to the next memory. Do not dwell on any of the memories. Simply allow them to surface, lift them up for healing, and let the next memory surface.

READING: (Micah 7:8) *"Though I have fallen, I shall rise; though I live in darkness, Yahweh is my light."*

PRAYER: Spirit of God, Source of compassion and love, we praise you and thank you for your presence in our midst. We ask you to surround us with your healing and protecting light, to permeate us with your love and forgiveness. Bring into our consciousness any of the hurts in our immediate past that are in particular need of healing. Help us to face the pain and then to release it into your healing light. Be with us in our dying to anger, to hurt, to sin, to insecurity, and to self-doubt. Help us experience the resurrection into your peace and joy. We ask all of this through Jesus, our strength and our life.

- Now, move gently into the releasing of your memories and raise them to God for healing.

[LONG PERIOD OF SILENCE]

PRAYER: O God of compassion and forgiveness, we praise you and thank you for your healing energy which you have poured into our hearts, into our past, into our memories. We ask you to hold us in peace and forgiveness and to drive from us all that is not from you, your love and compassion. We ask this in the name of Jesus, the Christ. Amen.

[SOFT MUSIC]

Gently, now, when you are ready, go in Christ's peace.

PART THREE

Expanding Our Horizons

Spirituality concerns an ancient and primal search for meaning that is as old as humanity itself and . . . belongs—as an inherent energy—to the evolutionary unfolding of creation itself. . . .

[H]umanity today yearns for a bigger picture than our currently subsumed perceptions which entangle us in webs of religious minimalism. . . .

We are witnessing a movement of our time motivated or driven by a creative evolutionary force over which we humans have little or no control. We are being carried along by a new search for meaning, which . . . is not drawing us away from the world but plunging us more profoundly into it, not alienating us from the divine but re-connecting us with the God who co-creates at the heart of creation. . . .

No one discipline, no matter how sanctioned by time, will enable us to comprehend this new upsurge; it requires a multi-disciplinary analysis . . . [for] we find ourselves drawn into considerations and engagements that push the horizons on understanding beyond every 'here-and now' reality.[1]

—Diarmuid Ó Murchú

13

Paradigm Shift

EMBRACING THE NEW IS NEVER EASY. EXPANDING one's horizons does not usually happen automatically, and yearning for the "bigger picture" happens most often only after years of suffering in contexts that no longer fit and therefore constrain and hamper every movement. Perhaps no other story illustrates more clearly the difficulties and the pain involved in transforming consciousness and gaining a larger perspective than does the story of Job.[2] Although many of us see him primarily as one of Scripture's preeminent examples of holy endurance and patient suffering, Job's experience at its deepest level is really about a needed paradigm shift in religious self-understanding, about a change of vision.

The religious context to which Job was accustomed, in which he and his culture lived and were comfortable, was that of a God who rewarded goodness and just behavior and punished evil. Now, since Job was a just man par excellence, the model for all, upright and beloved, it followed that according to the context within which he

operated (his culture's frame of consciousness) God's benevolence toward him was expected. When Job starts to suffer, however, the rules are changed, the worldview is threatened, something has gone astray.

We have here, clearly, a major crisis, a turning point that is resisted mightily by everyone involved in the story because a different view is simply not fathomable. Job's friends conclude with loud protestations that he must have sinned, and they urge him to repent. They are vexed when he insists on his righteousness and challenges God to explain what has happened and to justify this apparent injustice. All are caught up in, locked into, their particular level of religious consciousness that apparently and for some inexplicable reason no longer holds up, but from which they seem to have no way of extricating themselves.

It takes, so the story goes, a major, somewhat mysterious and even strange response from God to clarify matters (or perhaps to defend their obscurity) and to make the point, among others, that God is not bound by our image of God, by our expectations, by our world- or our God-view, by our human context. (Using the terms of contemporary physics, we might say that God is not bound by the frequencies on which humans take in and respond to reality.) Job's difficulty is therefore, above all, contextual. The old had to give way to a new and much deeper vision. That kind of change is never easy and is usually wrought with incredible pain.

Job experienced what we would today call a major cri-

sis of consciousness in his own life and, paradigmatically, in his culture's religious self-understanding. In Part 1 we have already discussed the paradigm shift that is needed in our time—the one that is calling us into depth prayer out of the hunger that is gnawing at our hearts. In many respects our age is experiencing Job-like confusion and desolation. Job's friends today, with all their explanations and solutions for the crisis of our time, are legion. The fact that a sometimes painful transformation of consciousness is an *essential prerequisite* for recognizing the paradigm shift to which we are being called, however, may still not be adequately recognized and may, therefore, call all of us to still deeper exploration.

It is quite true, I believe, that our times are propelled forward, as Ó Murchú says, "by a creative evolutionary force over which we humans have little control." Numerous books, nevertheless, (including his own) are struggling with its meaning and attempting to understand its whence and wherefore in order to help the process along and to enable us to become creative transformers in what otherwise could look hopelessly discouraging.[3] What may help us gain some equanimity in all this is the realization that human consciousness—both individual and collective—passes through numerous levels of openness as it journeys toward integrity. Its ultimate goal is the mystical level, the level of union with the divine and with all of creation. Depth integrity, "the deep Self," as Desmond Murphy calls it, "is the very essence of

what it is to be human." It can be found, he claims, at our very core[4] and signifies clearly whence we came and where our destiny lies.

Our journey home, however, is not easy. We struggle toward it in our individual maturation processes, as well as nationally, culturally, and even as a human species. (Our reflections in Part 2 on the various phases calling for healing prayer addressed this struggle directly.) The paradigm shift that we are experiencing in our time, and the turmoil that comes with this shift—often most clearly recognized, as Job would teach us, in individual as well as group resistance to it and in the endless use of "tradition" to justify atrophy—can perhaps best be explained in terms of an ontological crisis* that always accompanies profound transformations in levels of consciousness.

The suffering experienced during such ontological turning points is intense (Job-like), because what one has known and what one is familiar with are collapsing, and the new shows itself only very slowly and cannot be rushed. There is, therefore, great uncertainty and fear during a time of crisis, and the temptation to hold on to what was, or to close up and refuse to grow, is often overwhelming. The agony, however, is only increased through resistance. The "creative evolutionary power" will ultimately not be prevailed against, although human resistance can cause much grief.

---

*Identified as at the very core of our being, as of our very nature.

The Collapse of the
Cartesian-Newtonian Paradigm

What Diarmuid Ó Murchú, Desmond Murphy, and others see as the crisis point of our time—providing us with uncertainties, suffering, but also untold opportunity for growth—can perhaps best be identified in the concrete as the demise of the Newtonian-Cartesian model of a mechanical universe. Isaac Newton and René Descartes saw the world as machine-like, governed entirely by mechanistic laws. For them, nature was determined. It was predictable, controllable, and knowable in terms of mathematical principles. Objectivity implied certainty and could be attained by detached reason. Objectivity, in fact, determined the truth and was seen as essential in our search for meaning. Not only was nature understood mechanically, but humans, following Newton's and Descartes' perspective, approached themselves and human interactions and, in many respects, even their relationship to God that way as well.

The mechanistic paradigm ruled what today we call the "modern era." It gave us most of our contemporary "progress." It was an era of success and technological advances. What we are beginning to discover during this time of crisis, however, is that, whereas it spoke eloquently about external reality, the modern era had few if any answers for the soul. Today our hunger for "more" is, therefore, drawing us beyond mechanistic or logical responses and moving us into depth questions.

Surprisingly, both science and spirituality are finding themselves dissatisfied with the mechanistic approach to the world. We hear talk today of the postindustrial, post-mechanistic, postmodern era in almost every discipline of note. It seems ever clearer that all of us are, as Ó Murchú points out, "being carried along by a new search for meaning." Nor are spirituality and the world separated in this search any longer. They seem rather, for the first time in millennia, mutually supportive. Science today can actually be found on the side of prayer, even as many of our traditionalist models for approaching ultimate reality are collapsing, and chaos seems to prevail everywhere.

In this last part of the book we will attempt to explore the interdisciplinary approach to which contemporary science—ever since the Heisenberg/Bohr encounter with paradox and their subsequent rejection of a purely mechanical universe[5]— invites all those questing for depth meaning. For us to expand our horizons, it will be necessary to become comfortable with the discoveries and insights of contemporary science and to relate them to our own deep intuitions and age-old wisdoms. Even as the science of the "modern era" influenced the self-understanding and thought patterns of the religious consciousness of its time, so contemporary science affects the contemporary religious psyche. It behooves us to understand and appreciate its insights, to grow deeper into the horizons they open up for us. Fritjof Capra is right: "Modern physics has had a profound influence on

almost all aspects of human society. . . . It extends to the realm of thought and culture where it has led to a deep revision of [our] conception of the universe and [our] relation to it." Many of our basic concepts (including, and perhaps especially, our religious concepts) have, therefore, been in need of revision. This heralds a "radical transformation of our whole world-view."[6]

It is clear that the scope of this reflection will not permit a full-scale investigation into this topic. Others have done so already and expertly.[7] Ours will, therefore, be a modest attempt, restricting itself merely to a few select insights of modern science that seem to yield particular fruit for anyone seeking a deeper understanding of prayer and its healing power today.

> It is probably true quite generally that in the history of human thinking the most fruitful developments frequently take place at those points where two different lines of thought meet. These lines may have their roots in quite different parts of human culture, in different times or different cultural environments or different religious traditions: hence if they actually meet, that is, if they are at least so much related to each other that a real interaction can take place, then one may hope that new and interesting developments may follow.[8]

14

Cosmic At-onement

A Theological Reflection

The New Age is heralded with the call:
"Open, open the door! Let darkness perish,
And lustre, borne of sorrow and pain,
Shine forth in you."[9]

—Rabindranath Tagore

It is my intuition that among contemporary theologians few have allowed for this shining forth to happen as authentically as has Karl Rahner. A scholar who was firmly rooted in the tradition of Catholic Christianity and Thomas Aquinas, he was, nevertheless, wide open to the possibilities of the new and was very capable of expressing them. Using his considerable skills both as thinker and as theologian, he often provided a bridge that could span what for lesser minds appeared to be an impassable divide.

Rahner's thoughts concerning the nature of the human soul and our profound interconnectedness with the cos-

mos seem to me a case in point and of particular interest to those seeking deeper insight into prayer and its transformative role in the universe. Though his reflections may appear quite revolutionary from a traditionalist perspective, they are clearly among the more revisionary contributions theology has offered in this time of change and of dialogue between science and religion.

An interesting study by Marie Murphy entitled *New Images of the Last Things: Karl Rahner on Death and Life after Death* explains his position simply: In order to make sense of the soul's existence after death, "Rahner proposes a new understanding of the unity of the body and the soul which he calls the *all-cosmic dimension.*" Holding on to the Thomistic-Aristotelian position that the soul is the form of the body, Rahner accepts that, therefore, soul cannot be without body. "While in death the soul ends its present relationship with a particular body," however, it nevertheless "continues a relationship with the world and the universe." Rahner, Murphy explains, proposes a different existence for the soul after death. Quoting his reflections in *On the Theology of Death,* she points out that the person (soul) who has left the body in death moves into "some deeper, all embracing openness in which her [his] cosmic relationship to the universe is more fully realized."[10]

It is clear that Rahner's reflections on this topic attempt to transcend the dualistic distinctions of traditional philosophy (although he holds on to some of its

categories) and to invite us into a deeper appreciation of matter (body). Murphy explains this as follows:

> In time and space, human beings express themselves through their physical bodies during life. Our bodies show who we are, and what we feel and think. But our physical bodies are also limited by time and space. . . .
>
> In death human beings are freed from the physical limits of the body and enter into a new relationship with the world. Rahner notes that we should not limit our understanding of "world" to those things which we experience through the senses. According to Rahner what we call world extends beyond that which is immediately observable and what we call our body does not "stop where our skin stops . . . in some sense we are an open system."[11]

It is my contention that *what Rahner anticipates for human life after death and presents in his theology in order to expand our sense of cosmic at-oneness, the person of prayer experiences in some fashion already while here on earth. It is, furthermore, the same phenomenon that the quantum physicist declares as revelatory of actual reality:* "In the all-cosmic dimension," Rahner holds, "the person becomes open to the universe and united to the basic unity of the world. . . . There is in the world and in the universe a ground of unity in which all things communicate."[12]

Although critics may claim that Rahner does not go far enough, that by continuing to hold on to the duality of body and soul in the living human being he persists in the

dualistic tradition, I suggest that Rahner paved the way for the holistic possibilities we can now envision. He pioneered and, consciously or not, showed even in his writings of the sixties an extraordinary affinity with contemporary scientific theory. From a theological and a Christian perspective, it is clear that the "ground of unity" Rahner is referring to is the creative, incarnational, and redemptive love of the Triune God expressed in Christ as the "heart of the world." It is God sharing God's self and drawing the world into oneness with God. Contemporary science does not use these theological interpretations, but nevertheless confirms Rahner's basic intuitions, which insist on the profound reality and sacredness of an ultimately unified and deeply relational universe.

Scientific Reflections

It is my sense that only the mystics can match in insight the paradox and wonder that science today opens up for us and, however unintentionally, offers for our spiritual sustenance. David Bohm's observation that "*the whole can be found in each part*" is a case in point.[13] Most of us learned it differently, did we not? We learned that the whole is the sum of its parts—that, therefore, the part should be seen as a segment of the whole, as less than the whole. We learned this in geometry class, and we applied it unwittingly to every other aspect of reality including

religion, our membership in the church and in the wider community. Our worldview was, consciously or not, based on it. We saw ourselves as part of a larger entity—sometimes an important part, sometimes not so important, but always as smaller, less significant than the whole. Statements such as "I'm only a cog in the wheel," or "What does my contribution matter? No one will miss me," can therefore be seen as "spiritual fallout" from our geometry classes and the worldview based on them.

It is true that, as articulated in Euclidian theory and measured by ordinary sense experience, the whole is made up of the sum of its parts. The question that must be asked, however, is whether any worldview or personal self-esteem should be based on this; whether our perceptions about ourselves and our relations to each other and even to God—whatever these may be—should be influenced by this, for within a different and more contemporary perspective one can also say that the whole is larger than the sum of its parts and, what is stranger still, that each of its parts can be shown to contain the whole.*

*We learn this from holographic experiments: "A hologram is produced when a single laser light is split into two separate beams. The first beam is bounced off the object to be photographed. Then the second beam is allowed to collide with the reflected light of the first. When this happens they create an interference pattern which is then recorded on a piece of film" (Michael Talbot, *The Holographic Universe* [New York: Harper Perennial, 1991] 14). The picture on the film appears as concentric circles interfering with each other. But if another laser beam is shined through the film, a three-dimensional

It is here, I suggest, where, as Ó Murchú would say, we find ourselves drawn into considerations that push our horizons beyond our original perceptions and the framework of meaning that arises from them. Contemporary science can be amazingly helpful to those of us who seek after depth—to the soul hungry for the bigger picture and willing to go looking for meaning and questing for revelation beyond the boundaries of religious minimalism that quite often are enslaved by the contexts and worldviews of bygone times.

The internalization of holography's discovery that the part contains the whole has significant applications for the person of prayer. We cited already William Johnston's observation that the Zen master "sits" for the universe, as does the person of prayer. Perhaps we can see more readily now that this is true precisely because *we contain the universe within our deepest selves* and are, as Rahner insists, *one with it.* Quite often prayer is understood too simplistically in terms of the Newtonian cause-and-effect sequence. It is believed (although it is rarely presented so simplistically) that an individual, as an external agent, brings about change through prayer, influences behavior,

---

picture of the original object appears. Should the film then be cut into pieces and these illuminated, or should only a small part of the film be focused on and illuminated, each part will present the three-dimensional picture to view. *Each part of the hologram, even the smallest, contains the whole picture three-dimensionally,* though as the parts get smaller, the picture becomes less clear.

or affects positively undesirable conditions. We influence God; God, in turn, influences the circumstances we pray about. The whole business is not too different from the bouncing-off effect of billiard balls, and, sadly, much of what we understand as the prayer of petition falls into this category.

But if the whole is in the part, *no one I pray for is separate from me, nor is the cosmos whose tranformation I am about, nor is the God to whom I pray.* The reflections of the previous section addressing our connectedness to our culture, our race, our gender, and, in fact, to the entire human condition find a deeper meaning here; for interconnectedness—at-onement—is the fabric of reality as a whole. We cannot stand apart from one another and still be authentically ourselves. Hildegard of Bingen realized this hundreds of years ago: "Everything that is in the heavens, on the earth, and under the earth is penetrated with connectedness, penetrated with relatedness."[14]

Aboriginal peoples also see our cosmic interwovenness and often can teach the Western theologian profound lessons here. In the now-classic movie *I Heard the Owl Call My Name* (based on a book by the same title), Jim Wallace, the Indian guide for the newly arrived vicar to a remote Indian village in northern British Columbia, answers a question concerning the size of his village as follows: "My village is so big it never gets rained on, because the rain is my village too, and the wind, and the sea. All the history of my tribe and all its legends is my

village too. And me, I am the village, and the village is me." He pauses, then looks at the vicar and shakes his head. "You don't get it, do you?" he says. Depth prayer and its effects, like depth existence, are cosmic in nature, because *we* are cosmic. For Rahner, our cosmic connection is highlighted most particularly after death. Through prayer, however, we can touch who we truly are already in the here and in the now; we enter the realm of eternity, transcend space and time, and experience the All.

William Johnston speaks to this well: "One thing becomes increasingly clear," he says in *Silent Music*,

> that the universe is so unified that every movement or action, however slight, has its repercussions throughout the whole. And [we are] part of this network. . . . Receiving influence from every corner of the mysterious universe, [we] likewise influence it; and [our] actions are like the proverbial pebble thrown into the pond and causing endless ripples.

Johnston believes that "next to God the most influential person in the cosmos is the mystic."[15]

It is clear that a dualistic perspective on the world will find these observations difficult, if not impossible, to integrate. Dualism is built on a framework of over-againstness that posits the observer as separate from and, in fact, in opposition to the observed. It maintains that for true objectivity, distance is required; it sees the "merely" subjective as akin to reveling in one's own fantasies and posits

detached reason, rather than one-sided, personal opinion, as essential in attaining the truth. Today, however, the very discipline that gave us objectivity, certainty, and predictability urges us to overcome them and offers us a different paradigm with concepts much more likely to be real.

David Bohm suggests a total rejection of dualism when he postulates that "the ultimate nature of physical reality is not a collection of separate objects" that can be encountered with detached indifference, "but rather . . . an *undivided whole* that is in perpetual dynamic flux." In this whole, matter and mind are interconnected. They ought not to be understood as "separate substances. Rather they are different aspects of one whole and unbroken movement," and their interaction opens up reality neither as subjective nor as objective but as *omnijective*—interlaced and interwoven, with mind and matter inextricably linked, and each part of reality containing "information about the whole. . . . [I]n some sense every part of the universe 'contains' the entire universe."[16]

The Befriending of the Disciplines

The mystics sensed these scientific postulates from the beginning and in their very flesh long before scientists and their various disciplines were ready to acknowledge and ultimately to accept the encounter with what Lincoln Barnett ultimately called that "final featureless unity of

space–time, mass–energy, matter–spirit—[that] ultimate, undiversified, and eternal ground beyond which there appears to be nowhere to progress."[17] Mystics lived in the experience of divine–human harmony, of cosmic at-one-ment, but had none of the tools, either linguistic or philosophical, to articulate their insights. They moved in a world context and interpretation alien to them.

Today this is no longer so, and we are the beneficiaries. Even the simple wonder at a star-filled sky that has been for so many of us from time immemorial an unfathomable experience of the holy holds within it the lessons of connectedness and can today open us up to even greater relationship and depth, as science and the mystical partner and help each other into insight and adoration.

William Keepin offers the following meditation:

Imagine yourself gazing upward at the night sky on a clear night, and consider what is actually taking place. You are able to discern structures and perceive events that span vast stretches of space and time, all of which are, in some sense, contained in the movements of light in the tiny space encompassed by your eyeball. The photons entering your pupil come from stars that are millions of light-years apart, and some of these photons embarked on their journey billions of years ago to reach their final destination, your retina. In some sense, then, your eyeball contains the entire cosmos, including its enormous expanse of space and immense history in time—although, of course, the details are not highly

defined. Optical and radio telescopes have much larger apertures, or "holographic plates," and consequently they are able to glean much greater detail and precision than the unaided eye. But the principle is clear, and it is extraordinary to contemplate.[18]

The prayer that enters into this wonder pulls us ever more deeply into our center even as it flows through us into the cosmic expanse.

As Rahner would have us see, Christians touch here the mystery of the cosmic Christ—that powerful mystery of God's creative love, incarnate in and through space and time, that unites us with all of creation, that heals and makes whole and draws us inexorably back into the divine. Cosmic prayer leads us to a recognized at-onement with everything and especially with those we love. Cosmic prayer is love energy channeled and directed toward ever deeper transformation, thanksgiving, and healing. "Here," William Johnston assures us, "is a knowledge of identity, of empathy, of indwelling. And when it gets really deep we become part of others to such an extent that what happens to them happens to us—their joy becomes our joy, their sorrow becomes our sorrow."[19] Our energies intermingle, and our prayer becomes one hymn of praise and thanksgiving. Through cosmic love all is unified in our hearts.

> *All things are yours . . .*
> *and you are Christ's,*
> *and Christ is God's.*
>
> (1 Cor. 3:21–23)

15

Thought Is Energy

There was a famous monastery which had fallen on very hard times. Formerly its many buildings were filled with young monks and its big church resounded with the singing of the chant, but now it was deserted. People no longer came there to be nourished by prayer. A handful of old monks shuffled through the cloisters and praised their God with heavy hearts.

On the edge of the monastery woods an old rabbi had built a little hut. He would come there from time to time to fast and pray. No one ever spoke with him, but whenever he appeared, the word would be passed from monk to monk: "The rabbi walks in the woods." And, for as long as he was there, the monks would feel sustained by his prayerful presence.

One day the abbot decided to visit the rabbi and to open his heart to him. So after the morning Eucharist, he set out through the woods. As he approached the hut, the abbot saw the rabbi standing in the doorway, his arms outstretched in welcome. It was as though he had been waiting there for some time. The two embraced like long-lost brothers. Then

they stepped back and just stood there, smiling at one another with smiles their faces could hardly contain.

After a while the rabbi motioned the abbot to enter. In the middle of the room was a wooden table with the Scriptures open on it. They sat there for a moment, in the presence of the book. Then the rabbi began to cry. The abbot could not contain himself. He covered his face with his hands and began to cry too. For the first time in his life, he cried his heart out. The two men sat there like two lost children, filling the hut with their sobs and wetting the wood of the table with their tears.

After the tears had ceased to flow and all was quiet again, the rabbi lifted his head. "You and your brothers are serving God with heavy hearts," he said. "You have come to ask a teaching of me. I will give you a teaching, but you can only repeat it once. After that, no one must ever say it aloud again."

The rabbi looked straight at the abbot and said, "The Messiah is among you."

For a while, all was silent. Then the rabbi said, "Now you must go."

The abbot left without a word and without ever looking back.

The next morning, the abbot called his monks together in the chapter room. He told them that he had received a teaching from "the rabbi who walks in the woods" and that this teaching was never again to be spoken aloud. Then he looked at each of his brothers and said, "The rabbi said that one of us is the Messiah."

The monks were startled by this saying. "What could it mean?" they asked themselves. "Is Brother John the Messiah? Or Father Matthew? Or Brother Thomas? Am I the Messiah? What could this mean?" They were all deeply puzzled by the rabbi's teaching. But no one ever mentioned it again.

As time went by, the monks began to treat one another with a very special reverence. There was a gentle, wholehearted, human quality about them now which was hard to describe but easy to notice. They lived with one another as men who had finally found something. But they prayed the Scriptures together as men who were always looking for something. Occasional visitors found themselves deeply moved by the life of these monks. Before long, people were coming from far and wide to be nourished by the prayer life of the monks and young men were asking, once again, to become part of the community.

In those days, the rabbi no longer walked the woods. His hut had fallen into ruins. But, somehow or other, the old monks who had taken his teaching to heart still felt sustained by his prayerful presence.[20]

Many of us are familiar with this story. It speaks to us of conversion and of grace. It also speaks to us, however, of the power of thought and of the energy that can be transmitted, both positively and negatively, by the way we think of ourselves and of each other. When the monks moved from discouragement and despair and began to *wonder* once again, space and time were transformed. The decrepit buildings of the old monastery could no longer

contain them even though they were physically living within. Energy went out from them. It literally broke through the previous negative and death-dealing boundaries and attracted new life. The *vision* of the rabbi and *their subsequent thoughtfulness* brought about a *Presence* that transformed them and could not be contained.

This story is extraordinary not only because it symbolizes so profoundly the power of grace and Christification, but also because at this stage in our history it affords us the opportunity to reflect on God operating *in and through nature*—a nature reencountered through the discoveries of modern-day research and offering us potential for transcendence undreamed of.

In contemporary physics, Heisenberg's "Uncertainty Principle" suggests that, in the subatomic realm, reality gives itself to us according to our expectations, that *our thought literally helps bring about what is.* In the case of Heisenberg's discoveries, subatomic particles as well as light appeared either in the form of particles or in the form of waves, depending on how one observed or measured them. They revealed themselves as thoroughly *relational*, representing *probabilities of interconnectedness.* Heisenberg found that "neither the electron nor any other atomic 'object' has any intrinsic properties independent of its environment,"[21] that there is a basic interrelationship and unity of mutual implication between observer and observed. Although his discovery shattered

all notions of detached objectivity and, for some time, threw science into major confusion, many scientists and scholars today are beginning to ask themselves whether Heisenberg's discovery may not be paradigmatic of all of reality; whether observation affects data; whether thought influences its environment; whether change can come about because of my belief; whether, even with us, negative thought or positive thought can lower or raise persons to our expectations. For Barbara Ann Brennan, both physicist and healer, the answer is *yes*. She sees us clearly and holistically as part of the cosmic organism. To contemporary research, "The whole universe appears as a dynamic web of inseparable energy patterns," she claims. It is "a dynamic inseparable whole which *always includes the observer in an essential way.*" [22]

Francis Dorff's monastery parable exposes to us this inseparable whole. It illustrates the power of belief and the energy and positive transformation generated by wonder. Researcher and author Larry Dossey, M.D., warns that negative relationality can affect the environment as well. Speaking about the power of "medical hexing," he warns doctors against overeagerness in offering negative prognoses based on personal opinions. Telling a patient "You have only six months to live" can easily hasten death. He maintains that comments such as "This is the worst case of this disease I have ever seen," or "You're a walking time bomb," can be lethal. [23] We *are* the inter-

connection of energies. Thought is energy and affects our surroundings as well as ourselves for good or ill.

Transcending Time and Space

Nor is this interconnection restricted to the framework of either time or space. The considerable research of Karl Pribram into the holographic nature of both human brain activity and of the universe as a whole leads scientists today to the conclusion that linear reality is at best a secondary construct—a way in which *we* structure our surroundings so that we can function logically within them. It would seem that on a deeper level of awareness we are all capable of learning to transcend space and time and of encountering, as well as influencing, events both simultaneously and everywhere.[24] Parapsychological experiences—telepathic or psychokinetic, as well as Carl Jung's "meaningful coincidences" or synchronistic events—are examples of this. The latter may not be as "coincidental" as we would like to think. They are non-sequential, simultaneous, a-causal in and of themselves and show our connection with a deeper order. David Bohm calls it the "implicate" order. (Might not Rahner's transcendental experience be a theological parallel?) In this order the apparent separateness of consciousness and reality does not exist,[25] past and present melt away, and the mystical present becomes our home. Meditation and the willingness to engage paradox and move beyond the

logical, as some prayer practices today encourage, can be extremely helpful in having us expand our energies in this direction.

Our reflections in the preceding chapter on the need to overcome dualism in our appreciation of reality's inter-connectedness come to mind once again. We move even deeper when we reflect on the time-space transcendence of all relationality and on the power of intentionality (consciousness, awareness) in effecting transformation. What, therefore, might we appropriate here concerning our call to prayer and concerning the possible change for better or for ill that can be effected by our relationship to our surroundings? If contemporary science is to be taken seriously and our environment gives itself to us according to our expectations, then prayer and a healing and recon-ciling attitude become indispensable. If prayer as depth thought or meditation can, furthermore, transcend "the limits of the linear mind and allow the connectedness of all things to become an experiential reality,"[26] then its effects are not time-bound, and both past and future can be reached and can even be transformed in the *now*.

Dossey confirms this conclusion. God is neither a giant "communications satellite" somewhere up there, nor is human prayer localized and dependent on this kind of God. "Although there is compelling evidence that prayer works, there is no experimental evidence whatever that prayers *go* anywhere," observes Dossey. The inter-connection between God and us transcends spatial and

temporal categories, as may the interconnection between those who pray and those for whom they pray. Dossey notes that

> actual experiments in prayer and distant intentionality confirm this point of view. In these studies, space and time are completely overcome, because there apparently is no 'travel time' for the mental intention, and the strength of these effects don't [*sic*] deteriorate or diminish with increasing spatial separation. Moreover, in some studies, mental intention seems unconfined to the present moment.[27]

Dossey's studies point unequivocally to "the *non-local* quality of consciousness." The mind cannot be confined to the here and the now.

My sense is that the heart cannot be confined either. Perhaps one of the easier ways, therefore, to approach this seeming paradox of trans-temporality is through the experience of depth love. There is in the here-and-now of deep love an element of the eternal, a sense of touching and knowing deeply out of the unknown past and into the future even as one is rooted in the moment. Love knows existential presence—a nearness to the distant; a touching that combines the earthy and ethereal and dissolves the sometimes necessary spatial separation into a unity that defies the ache and melts into the other. Love for God and our depth love for one another are not different here. The essence of love is one. As the creative

energy of the divine, it flows through us undivided and finds its deepest expression in communion.

Healing prayer is rooted in the trans-spatiality and trans-temporality of love. Because of this, one can conceivably move back into one's ancestry or previous personal states of existence and can effect reconciliation and forgiveness: one can be simultaneously in the now and in the eternal. One can touch what appears as past and draw it into wholeness. The unforgivable can be forgiven; the unthinkable, transformed. These possibilities may seem upsetting to those who have not as yet experienced them, or to those so bound by linear concepts of time and cause-effect notions of intercessory prayer that touching in the now what has been or what is not yet seems magical and unreal. However, our previous reflections—concerning the healing of memories, of the family tree; concerning the experience of blood guilt or revolutionary shame and of embracing the human condition in all its brokenness and glory; concerning reconciliation with those who have died—all find their place here and gain a deeper more holistic meaning. And as I have already suggested, so do psychic experiences, telepathy, clairvoyance, the paranormal ("normal" here meaning according to the constructs of linear time and space), the mystical. The popular wisdom of farewell expressions such as "I will be with you," or "I will never be far away," or "I'll take you with me wherever I go," make sense within this context as well. The growing practice of kything prayer (see

Prayer Experience I at the end of this section), during which one intentionally either sends life-giving or supportive energy to someone or draws that energy from others, whether they are living or dead, is a clear example of the transcendence of space as well as of time and of the powerful energy transmitted through thought—an energy, by the way, that, like love which is its source, is not diminished by transmission.

Bede Griffiths, O.S.B., had it right when, commenting on our times, he observed that "we find ourselves divided between conscious and unconscious, psychological and physical, mind and matter. At the deepest level of consciousness, division disappears. All is one."[28] Our prayer is often inhibited by the dualisms listed by Griffiths, because the categories we take for granted are those of the mechanistic, Cartesian-Newtonian worldview that has governed our way of seeing for so long that we can barely fathom other forms of perception, although mystics have told us about them from time immemorial.

A touching story illustrates the necessity of severing our ties to dualism and embracing the new worldview (and the new prayer-view) being offered in our time. It happened during Richard G. Young's freshman year in college, when he had pretty well dismissed intercessory prayer as either unenlightened or superstitious. He was taking a music theory class with a professor who every morning started his lecture by asking for prayer requests

from his students for which he would then softly pray each in turn.

One day, a girl in the class began to cry as she related that her mother had just been diagnosed with an inoperable brain tumor and was not expected to live through the weekend. When Sarah finished telling the story of her mother's terrible pain, Dr. Tapsfield fixed the entire class with an intense stare I had never seen before. In a voice shaky but stern he said, "If there is anyone who does not believe that God not only **can** *but* **will** *heal this woman today, I want you to leave the room now and wait in the hall. Someone will come out and get you in a few minutes."*

No one moved. I thought about leaving but changed my mind. I wasn't ready to make a public statement concerning the questionable efficacy of prayer. Dr. Tapsfield took one more look around the class, lowered his head and prayed very simply. **"Dear God, I want to thank you for healing Sarah's mother of her tumor in this very hour. May your name be glorified. In the power and name of Jesus Christ, Amen."**

After an absence of two weeks, during which we all feared the worst, Sarah returned to class to report that her mother was still alive and totally symptom-free. A stunned silence swept through the room, punctuated only occasionally by a whispered "Amen," or "Praise the Lord." Sarah went on to say that the neurologist had run several tests and there was

no sign of a tumor in her mother's brain! Dr. Tapsfield [who himself was suffering from a progressive nerve disease that partially paralyzed him] *didn't say a word, but I saw the hint of a smile steal across his nerve-damaged face as several of us wiped tears from our eyes. That was the day I decided to pray for **him**. He died a year later. No easy answers.*[29]

Thought is energy and thought creates. The thoughtful and faith-filled prayer of Jesus was creative energy, indeed! It transformed and transcended space and time. So can ours. Dr. Tapsfield prayed as Jesus prayed. He took responsibility only for the present. It was gift (as the etymology of the word indicates) and assured him of the holy ground he was finding himself on in the presence of God. His response was, therefore, not supplication but gratitude. His God was the "I AM"—a God, not of the past, nor of the future, but of the *now.* Where time and distance are gathered into presence, God's power and ours become one, for separation ceases where presence is experienced.

The person of depth prayer knows this. If God is "I AM," then any articulation about what *is* becomes a statement of praise. A friend of mine pointed out to me not long ago that negativity, therefore, should have no room in our self-appraisal, and that fear of the future is useless. When I say "*I am* afraid, worried, not faithful,

not able, etc.," I am denying Presence, acknowledging lack, and, thus, betraying the power in which I am always held. I am separating myself from the goodness that at every moment builds creation because it affirms it and holds it in the divine "I AM." If thought is energy, and thought creates, then negative thought, doubt, and fear create negativity. When I begin with a thought of lack, I attract more lack. Supplication arises out of a position of lack. As I pointed out already in Part 1, when we reflected on the prayer that Jesus taught us, we really do not have to ask God for anything. All our needs are already met and are just waiting for this recognition. The future is held in the *now*, in the "I AM" that is God.

Jesus began all his prayers with thanksgiving ("I thank you, Father/Mother . . .") because he recognized in the very core of his being that God was present and, with God, all that was needed was present also. He recognized God's power because he felt it within himself. Dr. Tapsfield prayed out of the same recognition. When we live in the embrace of God, all fear is eliminated, as is our need to control our environment and manipulate others or the future. Prayer voids distance and identifies us as one with each other and with the divine. That is why supplication makes way for thanksgiving. When we thank God, we *see* what is already there and our needs are taken care of.

The utter trust required for the healing brought about

by praise and gratitude comes from the spirit of poverty that Jesus identified as essential for recognizing and entering the reign of God. Prayer and poverty, then, go together. Poverty is releasement—the letting go of control. When we truly learn to trust God's presence in every moment of our lives, we no longer need to control our outcomes. We are set free, as it were. We can let go and find peace. We accept the harmony and the oneness of it all.

16

Prayer Resonance

Scientific Theory

PERHAPS NO OTHER SCIENTIFIC HYPOTHESIS SPEAKS more eloquently about the possibilities for transformation and, by extension, the power of prayer than does biology's theory of morphogenetic fields and morphic resonance. Rupert Sheldrake, a biologist who is also interested in spirituality and relationality and has written extensively on this topic,[30] proposes in his work *A New Science of Life* that "all systems are regulated not only by known energy and material factors but also by invisible organizing fields." These fields, he suggests, serve as blueprints affecting both form and behavior. They cannot be said to have energy in the normal sense of understanding "energy," since *their influence is felt without diminishment across both time and space*, something "energy" cannot do. Their effect, in other words, "is just as strong at a distance as it is at close range."[31]

According to Sheldrake's hypothesis: "Whenever one

member of a species learns a new behavior, the causative field for the species is changed, however slightly. If the behavior is repeated for long enough," and especially if it is imitated by an increasing number of members of that species, "its 'morphic resonance' affects the entire species. Sheldrake called this invisible matrix a 'morphogenetic field,' from *morph*, 'form,' and *genesis,* 'coming into being.'"[32] Because morphic resonance is not deterred by spatial or temporal barriers, past events can affect other events everywhere.

The influence is best understood as being brought about by way of "collective memory." Members of a species, rather than "having" this memory inside them, "tune into it" via morphic resonance. This "tuning-in" builds up the memory until the behavior becomes habitual for the species. Sheldrake maintains that there is no evidence that either human behavior or natural processes are "governed by eternal laws" or a transcendent "mathematical mind."[33] The universe in all its facets, instead of being seen as a machine, is really better understood as a self-differentiating and developing organism whose creativity images itself forth. According to Sheldrake, therefore, inherent memory (rather than eternal laws) is the regulating force. In addition, he maintains that the more an initially original behavior or event is repeated, the deeper it is ingrained into the memory of the group in which it happens, until it becomes habitual and looks as if it has been that way from the beginning. He identifies

morphic resonance as "the influence of like upon like through space and time. Similar patterns of activity or vibration pick up what's happened to similar patterns before."[34] The activity becomes easier as it is repeated.

Morphic resonance applies throughout the universe and can influence human learning and transformation as readily as it does other, less sophisticated organisms. Thus, what happens in the lab with crystallization that becomes easier the more often it is repeated, or with rats whose learning capacity for certain tricks improves as the number of rats being taught the trick around the world increases (because the species as a whole takes in the memory), can also happen with humans. Theoretically, if a crossword puzzle is solved successfully one night by a large number of people in Sydney, Australia, and is then printed in the Melbourne paper the next night, Melbournians should find it easier to solve the puzzle because of the morphic resonance sent their way from Sydney. Likewise, thoughts—whether correct or not—conceived by an individual and then accepted over a span of time by more and more people eventually become common assumptions, habitual ways of seeing, which everyone accepts as indicative of reality.

Perhaps nothing illustrates Sheldrake's hypothesis better than the now famous "Hundredth Monkey" experiment on Koshima Island, Japan:

The Japanese monkey Macaca Fuscata has been observed

in the wild for a period of over forty years. In 1952, on the island of Koshima, scientists were providing monkeys with sweet potatoes dropped in the sand. The monkeys liked the taste of the raw sweet potatoes, but they found the dirt unpleasant. An eighteen-month-old female named Imo found she could solve the problem by washing the potatoes in a nearby stream. She taught this trick to her mother. Her playmates also learned this new way and they taught their mothers, too.

This cultural innovation was gradually picked up by various monkeys before the eyes of the scientists. Between 1952 and 1958, all the young monkeys learned to wash the sandy sweet potatoes to make them more palatable. Only adults who imitated their children learned this social improvement. Other adults kept eating the dirty sweet potatoes.

Then something startling took place. In the autumn of 1958, a certain number of Koshima monkeys were washing sweet potatoes—the exact number is not known.

Let us suppose that when the sun rose one morning, there were ninety-nine monkeys on Koshima island who had learned to wash their sweet potatoes. Let us further suppose that later that morning, the hundredth monkey learned to wash potatoes. And then it happened. By that evening almost everyone in the tribe was washing sweet potatoes before eating them. The added energy of this hundredth monkey somehow created an ideological breakthrough.

But notice. A most surprising thing observed by these scientists was that the habit of washing sweet potatoes then

jumped over the sea! Colonies of monkeys on other islands and the mainland troop of monkeys at Takasakiyama began washing their sweet potatoes as well.

Thus, it would seem that when a certain critical number achieves an awareness, this new awareness may be communicated from mind to mind regardless of space and time. Although the exact number may vary, The "Hundredth Monkey Phenomenon" means that when only a limited number of individuals know of a "new way," it may remain the consciousness property of these people. But there is a point at which if only one more person tunes in to a new awareness, a field is strengthened so that this awareness is picked up by almost everyone.[35]

Theological Reflections

The implications for human behavior and human transformation are staggering. Our behavior, be it positive or negative, can deeply influence and transform the behavior of others. Morphic resonance needs to be reckoned with, therefore, as we study the increasing violence in our cities, the greed of the consumer society, the increase of sexual promiscuity and licentiousness, and the influence of television. Morphic resonance also gives persons who pray encouragement beyond the cause-effect ideology of our mechanistic worldview. If William Johnston is correct in asserting that meditation transforms not only the spirit but also the body—that a deep state of rest and

peace pervades the person who meditates—then the theory of morphic resonance might give us hope indeed for our inner cities and places of violence. "Meditation is not just an occupation taken on night and morning for several hours each day," Johnston reminds us; "it is a whole way of life or, more correctly, a way of being. Once one gets into it, it tends to take over, to change and to transform."[36] Morphic resonance assures us that this transformation is societal. Indeed, it is cosmic.

Every organism, Sheldrake tells us, has within its morphogenetic field an attractor (entelechy) drawing it toward its full potential. For him, the attractor is science's version of "soul." He maintains, however, that "the morphic fields of organisms underlie not only their form but also their behavior,"[37] which, given the power of morphic resonance, is transformable and deeply responsive to the togetherness and intimacy of the species. And it is here, it seems to me, that our interest in prayer as changing and healing power must take note and make the appropriate application.

Sheldrake sees the universe and, indeed, human life as well as an interplay between *creativity*—visible in the "ongoing flux of things that's always bringing about surprises"— and *habit*—represented by the morphic fields[38] discussed above. Creativity emerges out of possibilities rather than preordination and, in the process of being responded to by the various individuals of the species, it

eventually affects the whole. As Terence McKenna, friend and colleague of Sheldrake, would put it, the world is not an engine but ought to be seen as a kaleidoscope of open-ended activity—out of chaos, through creativity, into imagination, back to creativity, toward a deeper and deeper destiny, drawn on by the inner attractor into ever-greater fulfillment. What appears random really moves toward unimaginable beauty. Chaos is the birthplace of order.[39]

The above discussion is undoubtedly novel to many and may also seem confusing to those of us used to, and comfortable in, the mechanistic paradigm of our tradition. We do not, however, need to understand the intricacies of these theories in order to grasp the possibilities they offer for spirituality and healing. Barbara Brennan states it well when she concludes her reflections on Western science's contributions to the transformation of healing paradigms with the observation that

> [T]he universe is an inseparable whole; a vast web of interacting interweaving probabilities. . . . I suggest that since we are inseparable parts of the whole, we can enter into a holistic state of being, become the whole, and tap into the creative powers of the universe to instantaneously heal anyone anywhere. . . .
>
> Becoming a healer means to move toward [the] universal creative power which we experience as love by re-identifying self with and becoming universal; becoming

one with God. One stepping stone to this wholeness is to let go of our limited self-definitions based on our Newtonian past of separated parts.[40]

Brennan suggests meditation to bring about the needed transformation of consciousness that enables us to see what our Celtic ancestors[41] would call "our ancient belonging" to all things, our intimate togetherness and connectedness with the universe.

Once again, it becomes clear that relationality is primary for anyone who is serious about prayer and about healing today. In the preceding chapter when we discussed the nonlocal quality of consciousness in the light of the holographic nature of the universe as well as of the human mind, we touched on the scientific foundations for ancestral healing. They make our attempts at embracing the past and bringing about the reconciliation of what in a linear time sequence would be beyond reach credible and understandable. Sheldrake's theory of morphic resonance expands these foundations even further. It opens our present and our very personal here-and-now behavior to the future. It bestows transformative power to everything we do. Our ordinary gestures and dispositions, our personal attitudes and opinions, which in a mechanistic paradigm would easily be ignored as inconsequential, take on real significance and call us to profound responsibility. The morphogenetic field of my entire species is affected by my behavior. My actions, even if seen by no one, nevertheless are transformative of the whole. If I

want the world to change, the transformation can literally start with me. If I want peace, my peaceful heart is essential. My vow of nonviolence and the disposition that flows from it affect my environment. My desire for justice calls me first and foremost to just relationships, which in turn further justice everywhere.

Because the culture in which we live encourages atomization, isolationism, and disconnectedness, we can easily doubt the efficacy of our actions. An interesting experiment was conducted after the Koshima discovery to test our positive or negative influence on the environment around us and to see whether little Imo's behavior together with her mother monkey and her playmates could find a human parallel. Clearly, the belief in our interconnectedness on a deeper level of consciousness, which allows us to send "prayer resonance" or healing power to one another, was on the experimenters' mind as they gathered in a large U.S. city for prayer. They singled out an area noted for its high crime rate. Twenty-eight persons met in this area for six nights in a row and meditated there for one hour. During the time they prayed, computerized police statistics indicated a drop in crime of 29 percent below the crime rate in the rest of the city. When the experiment was repeated several weeks later the results were similar.[42] Years later, computer measurements were taken again, this time in Los Angeles during the Olympic games as well as during the papal visit, when almost all television networks were carrying these

events—healthy and wholesome programming. The crime rate there also dropped significantly. Personal modeling of behavior as well as morphic resonance identify our power for good as well as for ill. We cannot afford to ignore them.

Among scientists, the medical profession is perhaps most deeply interested in the power of prayer and its effects on healing. Studies dealing with trans-spatial prayer "resonance" have involved both humans and non-human "targets" and have demonstrated clearly our interconnectedness with all things. They have shown, also, that love, empathy, and compassion serve quite literally as a form of "go-between," an affective connection that unites and bonds the person who prays with the one being prayed for. One might wonder why anyone would expect anything else. God, after all, is love, and love's presence, therefore, seems of primary importance in all "prayer resonance." Within the human condition, furthermore, we know that prayer is primarily soul-activity, and love, so Celtic wisdom teaches us, "is the nature of the soul. The soul needs love as urgently as the body needs air."[43] Soul work, therefore, unleashes love. It unleashes new possibilities in all those with whom it is concerned and thus opens up the passages for healing.

Among the most famous and also most interesting prayer studies is no doubt that of Randolph Byrd, staff cardiologist at the University of California San Francisco School of Medicine. Although it dealt specifically with

intercessory prayer rather than meditation and personal transformation and their effects on others via morphic resonance, the "prayer resonance" factor obviously still applies here. In 1988 *Byrd randomized 393 patients in the coronary care unit at San Francisco General Hospital to either a group receiving intercessory prayer or a control group. Intercessory prayer was offered by groups outside the hospital; they were not instructed how often to pray, but only to pray as they saw fit. In this double-blind study, in which neither the patients, the physicians, nor the nurses knew who was receiving prayer, the prayed-for patients did better on several counts. There were fewer deaths in the prayer group (though this factor was not statistically significant); they were less likely to require endotracheal intubation and ventilator support; they required fewer potent drugs including diuretics and antibiotics; they experienced a lower incidence of pulmonary edema; and they required cardiopulmonary resuscitation less often.*[44] Larry Dossey, who recounts this experience in his article "The Return of Prayer," admits that a great many variables make the interpretation of studies with humans such as this one somewhat difficult and the results unclear. Nevertheless, we can get at least a general sense that "prayer resonance" is both physically and spiritually effective.

Prayer opens us up and allows for conversion, for healing, for change. Its efficacy, far from being magical, is rooted in the transformative power of creation itself, in its interconnectedness and relationality, in the vibrations

that pass through everything that is—out into the remotest corners of the universe. Willigis Jäger sums up well what we have been exploring here in his chapter on "Science and Mysticism" in *Search for the Meaning of Life:*

> Both Zen and Christian contemplation are about opening up in all directions. It's as if we build up consciousness and, indeed, it is something like an accumulation of consciousness. When many people open up in the same direction, a powerful force develops. Then there can be what is called a leap of consciousness: other men and women are influenced by us without ever coming into physical contact with us. Why shouldn't the Divine work on us in this way—as a metastructure of our world? It is by means of these fields, one imagines, that what we Christians call grace comes into effective play.[45]

17

Transformation of Space

YEARS AGO, ON A BLUSTERY WINTER EVENING IN MONTREAL, during a time of major and painful change in my life, I happened upon the Anglican Bookstore in the center of the city and went in to browse. I was a poor graduate student at the time and had little money to spare, but I had been drawn into the store by a book I had seen displayed in the window: *And I Look for the Resurrection*. It was a thin, hard-covered work by Kay M. Baxter. I struggled with the price for a while and then bought it. I could not resist the title. Years have passed and my library has undergone numerous "prunings." This book, however, has never left me. I still am fascinated by its title.

What does it mean for a person of prayer to *look for the resurrection*? What does it mean to discover its truth, and then to live in it? In her introduction, Kay Baxter suggests the following:

> Good Friday has no meaning if it is regarded simply as a recalling of the defeat and death of a good man. It is of

155

value to us only if we can, from its observance, gather strength to meet the stern demands of a resurrection faith—a *faith*, not a certainty—a faith that death is the inevitable prelude to any new life whatsoever. Death comes to us in many guises and not always all at once. . . . But it comes—and only on the other side of death is the fullness of new life possible. Some of us believe this to be the truth about human existence, and it is because the Christian church helps us to hold and penetrate and face up to this belief that we are Christians and dare to say that we believe in the Resurrection. We must try to understand what conduct such a belief demands from us in contemporary life.[46]

At the beginning of this book I suggested that our depth probings into prayer would demand a "shift at our core." That prayer, instead of being a *task,* is really a *way of being.* That it is a "dwelling in" rather than an "approaching," a celebrating of the Light by which we are surrounded, a continuous *yes* to life, to love—a perpetual affirmation and surrender. I proposed that when Jesus taught us how to pray, he taught us what our fundamental "way of being" ought to be. He taught us the attitude, the disposition that would make our life a prayer. He taught us about a hunger, a passionate longing for God's reign. It is my belief that he taught us about the *resurrection.*

There are a number of ways in which one can reflect on the resurrection and allow it to penetrate one's life. Of

significance to the concerns of this book, however, are the stories about the women's Easter morning visits to the tomb as they are depicted both in Luke and in Mark. It is of interest to note that Luke's women are challenged almost immediately by the heavenly visitors who question their searching "for the Living One among the dead" (Luke 24:5). I am always grateful that this search was quickly ended. Its symbolic significance to those of us wishing to take the resurrection into our prayer seems to point to an attitude that has difficulty believing in God's transformative power and, therefore, *petitions* rather than *thanks.* The emphasis in this account is on the concerns the women felt about fulfilling their works of mercy. The angels urge them to remember what Jesus had told them not only about his necessary death, but also about his resurrection. They urge a transformation of attitude, a movement toward a faith that expects life and responds with joy. *To believe in the resurrection means to be filled with gratitude that God's power is so revealed and to enter into its "resonance" even in the face of apparent death.* When one authentically believes, one *acts* according to one's faith. That is why one's prayer can move mountains. "Father [Mother] I thank you for having heard me," Jesus prayed before he commanded Lazarus to come forth (John 11:41). He *expected* life and transformed space and time with his praise.

Mark's account does not emphasize the search for Jesus "among the dead." Instead it opens up a task for the

women: ministry to his disciples. "Turn those who are frightened into resurrection people," I hear the angelic being tell the women. The tomb is empty. The place of ignominy, of disgrace and infamy no longer holds any power over them and over anyone who is of the Christ. "Go now," the angel tells them, "and tell his disciples and Peter, 'He is going ahead of you into Galilee'" (Mark 16:7). The tomb on Easter Sunday is of significance only *because it is empty*, and "the Living One can be found only when we experience that he 'is ahead of us,' that he opens a future for us."[47]

It seems to me that a person praying into the meaning of the resurrection for contemporary life needs first and foremost to keep in mind that the women at the tomb had witnessed execution and death. They were no strangers to cruelty and absurdity, to injustice and the abuse of power. They had laid its victim into the tomb. The proclaimers of the resurrection, therefore, were not nostalgic dreamers, nor can we be who live into its truth. The experience of the women on Easter morning was truly "on the other side of death," a death that had manifested the dregs of ugliness and barbarity and had climaxed the will to power in all its grotesqueness. The empty tomb, then, precisely *because it was empty*, heralded glory. It spoke to them, as it speaks to us who search for its depth today, of the "open space" that allows us to proclaim hope "in the face of dehumanization and oppression."

The significance of the empty tomb is that it calls all of us who proclaim its hope to become transformers of space—the space, namely, of oppression and of the abuse of power. The empty tomb stands for the vindication of the crucified ones, the nonpersons, the victimized of our time. It calls us, with everything we have and are about, to stand in the face of violence and of killing and to proclaim with our very lives a different world. In the resurrection event of the Christ, our prayer and our lives are merged, and we are held without compromise to justice—a justice whose symbolism climaxes in the proclamation: "He is going ahead of you into Galilee."

The essence of this Easter announcement, which can easily escape anyone who romanticizes the event into a simple victory party, is put clearly by Elisabeth Schüssler Fiorenza:

> Jesus' struggle did not end with execution and death. The tomb is empty! But the Living One is not going "away," not leaving us to struggle on our own while he is "ascending to the Father" to live in heavenly glory.
>
> The empty tomb does not signify absence but presence: it announces the Resurrected One's presence on the road ahead, in a particular space of struggle and recognition such as Galilee. The Resurrected One is present in the "little ones," in the struggle for survival of those impoverished, hungry, imprisoned, tortured and killed, in the wretched of the earth. The empty tomb proclaims the Living One's presence in the [reign of

those] gathered in Jesus' name, in the faces of our [ancestors] who have struggled for survival and dignity. Jesus is going ahead—not going away: so the women in the Gospels, and we with them, are told.[48]

And here it is that radical honesty is required of us, and Kay Baxter's observation that if as Christians we dare to say we believe in the resurrection, "we must try to understand what conduct such a belief demands from us in contemporary life," comes back to challenge us. For the resurrection is a clarion call to commit our lives to God's reign. What Jesus had begun in Galilee, he challenges his living Body to continue throughout the world. As Christian women and men of prayer we are transformers of space or we are not Christian at all.

It is too easy to "spiritualize" suffering. We seem to have done so for ages. The death of Jesus, for too long now, has been interpreted not as execution—as an encounter with brutality and horror—but as divinely decreed "atonement," as a willingly accepted immolation worthy of imitation because it would bring us eternal glory in the end. Its violence and dehumanization were sacralized—hailed as obedient self-sacrifice. In the process, we unwittingly turned God into a vengeful tyrant and Jesus into a blind victim. The spirituality that arose from such a stance bordered on masochism: God sends suffering to those God loves. If we endure the misery now, just as Jesus did in his time, heaven will be our reward.

But the resurrection stories tell it differently. The place of humiliation and death is empty. God does not will God's children to suffer injustice. The Risen One and the liberation he had stood for before his execution have been vindicated. Christ is now going ahead of us. He is bidding us follow because his work has to be continued. What he had been born to proclaim, to work for, and what he was killed for must be completed. God is not finished with Christ's work yet.

Liberating the oppressed, setting free those who are downtrodden, standing with them against oppressive systems, and radically challenging our own conduct, our institutions and policies on behalf of justice—that is what walking the road to Galilee is all about. That is what believing in the resurrection means. That is what Christianity and discipleship point to and what a Christian's prayer resonance is oriented toward: for the ultimate Christification of the universe.

Broadening our horizons in contemporary times means embracing the vision of the Resurrected One, using all the discoveries and consequent resources of our age to work for justice, to "make all things new." It means being consumed with transformative energy.

There is no room in the Christian's life for political or economic expediency, for convenient silence and compromise where the oppressed are concerned. This is undoubtedly easier said than done in a world where Christian institutions seem to be able to survive only by

following the same rules of success that others espouse. But what voice have the destitute and marginalized of our society, if it is not ours? And what right have we to call ourselves followers of Jesus—*Christ*-ians—if we will not stand by them even if it means our disadvantage?

If our prayer life is to broaden the horizons of love beyond what this world has up to now seen as possible, and if we are to be authentic witnesses to the reign of God, we have no other option. The resurrection provides the perspective that opens our eyes. Without it, our faith is in vain.

Thoughts and Questions for Meditation

1. What are your thoughts around Ó Murchú's statement: "Humanity today yearns for a bigger picture than our currently subsumed perceptions which entangle us in webs of religious minimalism"?

2. Do you see a bigger picture offered in the chapters of this part? If so, does this picture excite you or disturb you? Why?

3. How do you relate to the story of Job and the suggestion that God is not bound by our image of God? Does religion sometimes act as if God were bound? If you think so, can you give examples?

4. "The paradigm shift that we are experiencing in our time, and the turmoil that comes with this shift [are] often most clearly recognized in individual as well as group resistance to it and in the endless use of 'tradition' to justify atrophy." What is your reaction to this observation?

5. "The person (soul) who has left the body in death moves into 'some deeper, all-embracing openness in which her

[his] cosmic relationship to the universe is more fully realized.'" How comfortable are you with this suggestion? What does it mean to you?

6. How do you relate to the theological implications of David Bohm's observation that "the whole is in the part"? How does it affect your self-image, your relationship with the community and with God? Does a statement like this "push your horizons"? How does it affect your prayer? Can science help mysticism and vice versa?

7. How does the story of the monks who were rejuvenated by the message that the Messiah was in their midst illustrate the fact that "thought is energy"?

8. How relevant is Heisenberg's Uncertainty Principle to human interaction?

9. "If prayer as depth thought or meditation can transcend 'the limits of the linear mind and allow the connectedness of all things to become an experiential reality,' then its effects are not time-bound, and both past and future can be reached and can even be transformed in the now." What is your reaction to this statement? Do you have experience here?

10. What are your feelings about Dr. Tapsfield's kind of prayer? How do you react to the observation that all prayer ought to be thanksgiving?

11. What are your thoughts about morphic resonance and the power as well as the responsibility it gives us? How does accepting this theory influence your reaction to the observa-

tions regarding our call to "walk the road to Galilee," offered in the last chapter?

12. "My actions, even if seen by no one, nevertheless are transformative of the whole. If I want the world to change, the transformation literally can start with me." How has the theory of morphic resonance added to your understanding of this statement?

13. If prayer is primarily a way of being, a fundamental disposition, how are prayer and walking the road to Galilee related?

14. How does meditating on the empty tomb broaden your horizons, expand your view of God and of your role in the world? Why does a Christian have no choice but to be about justice?

Prayer Experiences

Begin each exercise by following the Breathing Guidelines on pp. 42–43.

Experience 1
Kything [49]

READING: (John 12:46) *"I, the light, have come into the world, so that whoever believes in me need not stay in the dark anymore."*

PRAYER: Spirit of God, light and energy of our life, we ask you today for your strength, your light, your goodness. Help us to find these in each other, to strengthen one another and be strengthened. Surround us with your healing and protecting energy and drive from us whatever is not of you. We ask this in the name of Jesus, the Christ.

[SLIGHT PAUSE, THEN MOVE INTO GUIDED MEDITATION. PAUSE FREQUENTLY.]

- Now, as you are gently breathing in the love of God which surrounds you with light and warmth, ask God to

surface in you your greatest need—those dimensions of your brokenness that you tend to avoid, those emotions you find hardest to channel and to use creatively.

- Be with this need for a while. Do not judge yourself. (Breathe in the gentle love of God.)
- Look at this greatest need, dwell in awareness of it, and know the loving gaze of Jesus who is beside you.

[LONG PAUSE]

Now, turn to Jesus and ask him to show you someone whose energy might help you to heal this need. The person may be a friend, a spiritual director, someone who has died. She or he may be a saint, the Mother of God, maybe even Jesus, himself.

[LONG PAUSE]

- Gently let your center—your innermost self—find itself within the person with whom you are kything.
- Do whatever is most comfortable to your imagination:
  —standing or sitting beside the person,
  —holding hands in exchange of energy,
  —being held or hugged,
  —finding yourself simply inside the person—within his or her heart,
  —standing with your partner in the light of God's energy,
  —inviting your partner's spirit into yours.

[LONG PAUSE]

- Now invite the giftedness or energy you need to flow

through your partner into you. Be open, and welcome the gift.

[LONG PAUSE]

• Gently thank God for the gift that comes to you through the loving communion with other persons. Ask God to bless and pour forth gifts upon them, to energize them in turn.

[SOFT MUSIC]

PRAYER: We praise you and thank you, loving God, for your presence here with us in and through others. Bless us all with your gentle goodness and help us to celebrate your breakthrough in our lives. We ask this in the name of Jesus, the Christ.

Now gently, and as you are ready, go in the peace of Christ.

Experience 2
Prayer Resonance: Healing a Hurting World[50]

READING: (1 Thess. 5:4–11) *"But it is not as if you live in the dark, my brothers and sisters, for that Day to overtake you like a thief. No, you are all daughters and sons of light and sons and daughters of the day: we do not belong to the night or to darkness, so we should not go on sleeping . . . but stay wide awake. . . . [W]e belong to the day. . . . [L]et us put on faith and love . . . and the hope of salvation. . . . [G]ive encouragement to each other, and keep strengthening one another, as you do already."*

PRAYER: Spirit of God, our life and our love, we give you thanks and praise for your presence in our lives, in our midst, in the depth of our being. We trust in your healing power flowing in and through us. Fill us with your compassion both for ourselves and for each other. Drive from us whatever is alien to you. Hold us in your peace. We ask this in the name of Jesus, the Christ.

[SLIGHT PAUSE, THEN MOVE INTO GUIDED MEDITATION, PAUSING FREQUENTLY.]

- Imagine yourself, once again, surrounded by the beautiful light of God's presence, warming you and radiating into every part of your being. Feel the love and compassion of God moving through you and holding you.

- Now gently allow yourself to see images of your fellow human beings who are in need of love and compassion: They are hurting, sick, starving, dying on battlefields, of AIDS, on skid row, abused. Allow these images to emerge in you. They are possible because of our interconnectedness in Christ's Body, in the universe.

- Allow the pain these images cause you to wash over you.

- Be also aware of the suffering of the planet, of trees, and animals, and water. Be especially aware of the abused creatures of this earth.

- Take the pain into your breathing. As you breathe in, let God's healing love fill you and all of creation inside you with peace. As you breathe out, release the pain into God's healing light which absorbs and transforms everything.

- Know that in this breathing in and out, all is taken into

the soothing presence of God's love. Know that in you, redemption is ongoing and creation is renewed.

• Trust your own capacity for pain and God's willingness to use you as a healing agent. Allow God's light to absorb all and bring you peace.

[LONG PAUSE]

[SOFT MUSIC]

PRAYER: O God, we know that you love us. Love through us the whole world. Widen our hearts so that we might bear with compassion our at-oneness with our brothers and sisters and with all of creation. Help us to see as you see. Teach us forgiveness for ourselves and for each other and deliver us from evil. To you be glory and praise in Christ Jesus, our brother.

Gently, now, and when you are ready, go in Christ's peace.

Notes

Part One: Our Hunger for God

1. Sebastian Moore, *The Fire and the Rose Are One* (London: Darton, Longman & Todd, 1980), 144.

2. Barbara Fiand, *Embraced by Compassion* (New York: Crossroad, 1993), 112.

3. *Thich Nhat Hanh: Touching Peace*, 90-minute video presentation, produced by Legacy Media, Inc., Berkeley, California.

4. Margaret Laurence, *The Stone Angel* (Toronto: McClelland & Stewart-Bantam, 1978), 261.

5. *The Way of the Pilgrim*, trans. Helen Bacovcin (Garden City, N.Y.: Image Books, 1978), 13. "Lord Jesus Christ (Son of the living God), have mercy on me."

6. Taken from Barbara Fiand, *Wrestling with God* (New York: Crossroad, 1996), 42, 43. Adapted there from a tape recording of Sufi mystical poetry, read by Coleman Barks, "I Want Burning," from *Ecstatic World of Rumi, Hafiz, and Lalla,* Sounds True Recordings, Boulder, Colorado, tape number A197.

7. Among the many authors, I would recommend any books by William Johnston; Thich Nhat Hanh; Matthew Linn, Dennis Linn, and Sheila Fabricant; Eddie Ensley (*Prayer That Heals Our Emotions*); Barbara Metz and John Burchil (*The Enneagram and*

Prayer). These books are, for the most part, easy to read and easy to follow. Tapes that are especially helpful: "The Meditation Audio Series" by Fr. Emery Tang, O.F.M., and Sr. Joan Marie Sasse, O.S.B.

8. Karl Rahner, *The Practice of Faith* (New York: Crossroad, 1983), 63.

9. Ibid., 78 (emphasis mine).

10. Stephen Mitchell, *The Enlightened Heart* (New York: Harper & Row, 1989), 87.

11. Ibid., 89.

12. Barbara Fiand, *Releasement: Spirituality for Ministry* (New York: Crossroad, 1987). This book deals with the attitude of letting go and letting be, Eckhart's *Gelassenheit,* which is essential for authentic God-relatedness.

13. In this discussion of human consciousness, borrowed from reflections by Meister Eckhart, there is no intention to insist on anthropocentric triumphalism or domination vis-à-vis the rest of creation. The emphasis is rather on the necessary emptying out required to encounter creation reverently. The peculiar kind of reflective consciousness with which humans on this globe are gifted makes gratitude and praise, receptivity and releasement their calling. I am not foreclosing the existence of other beings who have similar or superior forms of consciousness. In a universe of this magnitude, that is certainly possible. I am merely stressing our role in the creative plan of God.

14. Fiand, *Embraced by Compassion,* 40, 41.

15. *Meister Eckehart, Deutsche Predigten und Traktate,* ed. Joseph Quint (Munich: Carl Hanser Verlag, 1978), 159.

16. Thomas Merton, "On Prayer," unpublished sermon given in Darjeeling, India, November 1968, cited here from Richard J. Hauser, S.J., *In His Spirit: A Guide to Today's Spirituality* (New York: Paulist Press, 1982), 50.

17. William Johnston, *Silent Music: The Science of Meditation* (New York: Harper & Row, 1979), 90, 91 (emphasis mine).

18. Diarmuid Ó Murchú, *Reclaiming Spirituality* (New York: Crossroad, 1998), 42 (emphasis mine).

19. This experience was adapted from Eddie Ensley, *Prayer That Heals Our Emotions* (Columbus, Ga.: Contemplative Books, 1986), 55, 56.

Part Two: The Call to Personal Transformation

1. Willigis Jäger, *Search for the Meaning of Life* (Liguori, Mo.: Triumph Books, 1995), 27 (emphasis mine).

2. Fiand, *Releasement,* 29.

3. Brennan Manning, T.O.R., *A Stranger to Self-Hatred* (Denville, N.J.: Dimension Books, 1982), 119, 120 (emphasis mine).

4. Richard P. McBrien, *Catholicism* (Minneapolis: Winston Press, 1980), 1:159 (emphasis mine).

5. Matthew Linn, Dennis Linn, and Sheila Fabricant, *Healing the Greatest Hurt* (New York: Paulist Press, 1985), 77.

6. Ibid.

7. Ibid., 79 (emphasis mine).

8. Theodore E. Dobson, *How to Pray for Spiritual Growth* (New York: Paulist Press, 1982), 96, 97.

9. Ibid., p. 96.

10. Ibid.

11. *Thich Nhat Hanh: Touching Peace.*

12. Fiand, *Releasement,* 17, 18.

13. Linn et al., *Healing,* 93, 94.

14. Ibid.

15. Ibid. The authors are among many who have written elo-

quently about the healing of childhood trauma and shame. I will, therefore, not develop this theme any further. In my own writings, chapter 3 of *Embraced by Compassion* addresses the birth trauma briefly; *Living the Vision* (New York: Crossroad, 1991), 100, touches on the wounds of narcissistic deprivation. The talks and workshops by John Bradshaw are very helpful here.

16. For the theological interpretation of this archetypal phenomenon, see Fiand, *Embraced by Compassion,* 57, 59.

17. M. Esther Harding, *The 'I' and the 'Not-I'* (Princeton, N.J.: Princeton University Press, 1973), 200.

18. Barbara Fiand, *Where Two or Three Are Gathered* (New York: Crossroad, 1992), 40, 41, 42.

19. The writings and tapes of Caroline Myss are very helpful here. Kenneth McAll's *Healing the Family Tree* (London: Sheldon Press, 1987) and the works of the Linn brothers and Sheila Fabricant are also recommended.

20. This prayer experience is adapted in part from Ensley, *Prayer That Heals Our Emotions,* 57.

Part Three: Expanding Our Horizons

1. Ó Murchú, *Reclaiming Spirituality,* vii, ix, 12, 13.

2. I owe my reflections here to Camilla Burns's public lecture on Job given at Loyola University Chicago, on November 6, 1998.

3. Among the many books written on this topic, I find Ó Murchú's *Quantum Theology* (New York: Crossroad, 1997) and *Reclaiming Spirituality* (1998) among the easiest to read. Desmond Murphy's *A Return to Spirit after the Mythic Church* (New York: Crossroad, 1997) is excellent as well. The latter draws heavily on the works of Ken Wilber, all of whose books seem appropriate for this topic. A work that is very readable for anyone interested in depth

prayer is Frank X. Tuoti's *The Dawn of the Mystical Age* (New York: Crossroad, 1997).

4. Murphy, *A Return to Spirit,* 36.

5. See Fritjof Capra, *The Turning Point: Science, Society and the Rising Culture* (New York: Simon & Schuster, 1982), 76, 77, 78.

6. Fritjof Capra, *The Tao of Physics* (New York: Bantam Books, 1975), 3.

7. See especially Ó Murchú, *Quantum Theology.*

8. Werner Heisenberg, cited by Capra, *Tao of Physics,* xi.

9. Cited in Tuoti, *Dawn of the Mystical Age,* 4.

10. Marie Murphy, *New Images of Last Things* (New York: Paulist Press, 1988), 14.

11. Ibid., 14, 15.

12. Ibid., 15.

13. William Keepin, "Lifework of David Bohm: River of Truth," in *Re-Vision: A Journal of Consciousness and Transformation* 16/1 (Summer 1993): 34.

14. Hildegard of Bingen, cited here by Ó Murchú, *Reclaiming Spirituality,* 85.

15. Johnston, *Silent Music,* 132, 133.

16. Keepin, "Lifework," 34.

17. Lincoln Barnett, cited here by Aniela Jaffé, *The Myth of Meaning,* trans. R. F. C. Hull (New York: Penguin Books, 1975), 34, 35.

18. Keepin, "Lifework," 34.

19. Johnston, *Silent Music,* 136, 137.

20. The author of this story is Francis Dorff. Over the years, it has been cited in a number of works: I cited it first in *Living the Vision,* 140–41. It was cited also by M. Scott Peck in the prologue of *The Different Drum* (New York: Simon & Schuster, 1988), 13–15; and by Mary Wolff-Salin, in *The Shadow Side of Community*

and the Growth of the Self (New York: Crossroad, 1988), 82–83. She claims to have "heard" the story from Joan Chittister, O.S.B., *Living the Rule Today: A Series of Conferences on the Rule of Benedict* (Erie, Penn.: Benet Press, 1982), 98–99.

21. Capra, *Turning Point,* 79.

22. Barbara Ann Brennan, *Hands of Light: A Guide to Healing Through the Human Energy Field* (New York: Bantam Books, 1988), 25 (emphasis mine).

23. Richard G. Young, "Be Careful What You Pray for, An Interview with Larry Dossey, M.D.," *Pathways for Spiritual Living* 7/1 (Spring 1998): 14.

24. Brennan, *Hands of Light,* 25, 26.

25. Talbot, *Holographic Universe,* 79–81.

26. Ibid., 26.

27. Young, "Be Careful," 14.

28. Bede Griffiths, O.S.B., cited here by Tuoti, *Dawn of the Mystical Age,* 30.

29. Richard G. Young, "Speaking of Prayer," *Pathways for Spiritual Living* 7/1 (Spring 1998): 39.

30. See, among other books, Rupert Sheldrake, *A New Science of Life: The Hypothesis of Morphic Resonance* (Rochester, Vt.: Park Street Press, 1995); *The Presence of the Past: Morphic Resonance and the Habits of Nature* (Rochester, Vt.: Park Street Press, 1995); and *Natural Grace,* which Sheldrake coauthored with Matthew Fox (New York: Doubleday, 1996).

31. Sheldrake's theory is explained here by Brennan, *Hands of Light,* 27.

32. Ibid.

33. Sheldrake and Fox, *Natural Grace,* 164.

34. Ibid.

35. Ken Keyes, Jr., *The Hundredth Monkey* (New York: Bantam

Books, 1980). This book is not copyrighted. According to the book's preface, you are asked to reproduce it in whole or in part, to distribute it without charge as widely as possible. The above version comes from one of these copies.

36. Johnston, *Silent Music,* 109.

37. Sheldrake and Fox, *Natural Grace,* 81.

38. Ibid., 38.

39. Remarks made by Terence McKenna in *Metamorphosis: A Trialogue on Chaos and the World Soul,* a video tape, presenting Rupert Sheldrake, Terence McKenna, and Ralph Abraham, Mystic Fire Video, Inc., P.O. Box 422, Prince Street Station, New York, N.Y. 10012.

40. Brennan, *Hands of Light,* 28.

41. John O'Donohue, *Anam Cara: A Book of Celtic Wisdom* (New York: Harper Collins, 1997), 24.

42. Information obtained from Lynn Sparrow, *Meditation Made Easy,* audio tapes from Association for Research and Enlightenment Inc., P.O. Box 595, 67th Street and Atlantic Ave., Virginia Beach, VA 23451.

43. O'Donohue, *Anam Cara,* 9.

44. Larry Dossey, M.D., "The Return of Prayer," in *Pathways for Spiritual Living* 7/1 (Spring 1998): 21.

45. Jäger, *Search for the Meaning of Life,* 27.

46. Kay M. Baxter, *And I Look for the Resurrection* (Nashville: Abingdon Press, 1968), 13.

47. Elisabeth Schüssler Fiorenza, *Jesus: Miriam's Child, Sophia's Prophet* (New York: Continuum, 1994), 123. My reflections throughout this chapter dealing with the symbolism of the empty tomb and the resurrection event are heavily indebted to the scholarship of Elisabeth Schüssler Fiorenza in this book, especially pp. 119–28.

48. Ibid., 125, 126.

49. This prayer experience draws from the suggestions offered by Barbara Metz, S.N.DdeN., and John Burchill, O.P., in *The Enneagram and Prayer* (Denville, N.J.: Dimension Books, 1987), 107–10.

50. This prayer experience is adapted in part from Ensley, *Prayer That Heals Our Emotions*, 103.

UNITED NATIONS PUBLICATIONS OF RELATED INTEREST

THE FOLLOWING UN PUBLICATIONS MAY BE OBTAINED FROM THE ADDRESSES
INDICATED BELOW, OR AT YOUR LOCAL DISTRIBUTOR:

An Agenda for Development
BY BOUTROS BOUTROS-GHALI,
SECRETARY-GENERAL OF THE UNITED NATIONS
E.95.I.16   92-1-100556-6   132PP.

Building Peace and Development, 1994
ANNUAL REPORT OF THE WORK OF THE ORGANIZATION
BY BOUTROS BOUTROS-GHALI,
SECRETARY-GENERAL OF THE UNITED NATIONS
E.95.I.3   92-1-100541-8   299PP.

*New Dimensions of Arms Regulations and
Disarmament in the Post–Cold War Era*
BY BOUTROS BOUTROS-GHALI,
SECRETARY-GENERAL OF THE UNITED NATIONS
E.93.IX.8   92-1-142192-6   53PP. $9.95

Basic Facts About the United Nations
E.93.I.2   92-1-100499-3   290PP. $5.00

Demographic Yearbook, Vol.44
B.94.XIII.1   92-1-051083-6   1992   823PP. $125.00

*Disarmament—New Realities: Disarmament,
Peace-Building and Global Security*
E.93.IX.14   92-1-142199-3   397PP. $35.00

United Nations Disarmament Yearbook, Vol.18
E.94.IX.1   92-1-142204-3 1993   419PP. $50.00

Statistical Yearbook, 39th Edition
B.94.XVII.1 H   92-1-061159-4   1992/93   1,174PP. $110.00

Women: Challenges to the Year 2000
E.91.I.21   92-1-100458-6   96PP. $12.95

World Economic and Social Survey 1994
E.94.II.C.1   92-1-109128-4   308PP. $55.00

*World Investment Report 1994—Transnational Corporations,
Employment and the Work Place*
E.94.II.A.14   92-1-104435-9   446PP. $45.00

Yearbook of the United Nations, Vol. 46
E.93.I.1   0-7923-2583-4   1992   1277PP. $150.00

* * *

THE UNITED NATIONS BLUE BOOKS SERIES

The United Nations and Apartheid, 1948-1994
E.95.I.7   92-1-100546-9   565PP. $29.95

The United Nations and Cambodia, 1991-1995
E.95.I.9   92-1-100548-5   360PP. $29.95

FORTHCOMING:
The United Nations and the Nuclear Non-Proliferation Treaty
The United Nations and El Salvador, 1990-1995
The United Nations and Mozambique, 1992-1995

UNITED NATIONS PUBLICATIONS
2 UNITED NATIONS PLAZA, ROOM DC2-853
NEW YORK, NY 10017
UNITED STATES OF AMERICA

UNITED NATIONS PUBLICATIONS
SALES OFFICE AND BOOKSHOP
CH-1211 GENEVA 10
SWITZERLAND